# THE FOUNDING FISH

# THE
# FOUNDING FISH

## JOHN McPHEE

FARRAR, STRAUS AND GIROUX

NEW YORK

FARRAR, STRAUS AND GIROUX
18 West 18th Street, New York 10011

Printed in the United States of America
Published in 2002 by Farrar, Straus and Giroux
First paperback edition, 2003

*Shad dart by Yolanda Whitman*

Some parts of this book first appeared, in slightly different form,
in *The New Yorker*.

The Library of Congress has cataloged the hardcover edition as follows:
McPhee, John A.
    The founding fish / John McPhee.
      p.   cm.
    ISBN-13: 978-0-374-10444-3
    ISBN-10: 0-374-10444-1
    1. American shad.   2. Shad fishing—North America—History.   I. Title.

QL638.C64   M4   2002
597'.45—dc21

                                                          2002025012

Paperback ISBN-13: 978-0-374-52883-6
Paperback ISBN-10: 0-374-52883-7

*Designed by Gretchen Achilles*

www.fsgbooks.com

11  13  15  17  19  20  18  16  14  12

For GEORGE HACKL, of the Roebling Flats, of Chicken
Island and the New York Eddy, of Portofino and
Trans-Keld, of High Lee, Middle Lee, Deep Lee, and,
sine qua non, The Patch

For RONNIE and ALAN LIEB, without whom not much

For JIM MERRITT, the master

# CONTENTS

# THE FOUNDING FISH

THE FOUNTAINHEAD

# ONE

# THEY'RE IN THE RIVER

I hadn't been a shad fisherman all my days, only seven years, on the May evening when this story begins—in a johnboat, flat and square, anchored in heavy current by the bridge in Lambertville, on the wall of the eddy below the fourth pier. I say Lambertville (New Jersey) because that's where we launch, but the Delaware River is more than a thousand feet wide there, and, counting westward, the fourth of the five stone bridge piers is close to New Hope, Pennsylvania. Yet it rises from the channel where the river is deepest.

American shad are schooling ocean fish, and when they come in to make their run up the river they follow the deep channels. In the estuary toward the end of winter, they mill around in tremendous numbers, waiting for the temperature in the cold river current to rise. When it warms past forty Fahrenheit, they begin their migration, in pulses, pods—males (for the most part) first. Soon, a single sentence moves northward with them—in e-mails, on telephones, down hallways, up streets—sending amps and volts through the likes of me. The phone rings, and someone says, "They're in the river."

No two shad fishermen agree on much of anything, but I would say that if a female takes your lure you know it from the first moments, or think you do, and you're not often wrong. If you have a male on, you may be at first uncertain, but then he displays his character and you know it's a buck shad. The roe shad is often twice the size of the buck shad. She may weigh five to six pounds, while he weighs two or three. Shad don't exactly strike. First there's a fixed moment—a second or two in which you feel what appears to be a snag (and might be); then the bottom of the river seems to move, as if you are tied to a working trampoline; and you start thinking five, six pounds, big fillets in the broiler, the grained savor of lemoned roe; but now this little buck shad—two and a half pounds—takes off across the river, flies into the air, and struts around on his tail. He leaps again. He leaps once more and does a complete somersault. He can't be said to be cocky, of course, but he suggests cockiness and pretension. He's all show and no roe. She doesn't move. Her size and weight are not at first especially employed. Yet here is the message she sends up the line: If this isn't bedrock you'd be better off if it were; if you're in a hurry, get out your scissors. She stays low, and holds; and soon you are sure about the weight and the sex. Now, straight across the river and away, deep, she strips line, your reel drag clicking. She turns and moves back, an arcuate run. You're supposed to keep things taut but often she'll do it for you. When, rising, she rolls near the surface, she looks even larger than she is. She, too, can leap, can do a front flip, but she obviously knows that her shrewdest position is broadside to full current. It's as difficult to move her as it would be to reel in a boat sideways.

Like salmon, shad return to their natal rivers and eat nothing on the spawning run. Like salmon swimming two thousand miles up the Yukon River, migrating shad exist on their own fat. So why do shad and salmon respond to lures? Up and down the river, almost everybody has an answer to that fundamental question, but no one—bartender or biologist—really knows. A plurality will tell you that the fish are expressing irritation. Flutter something colorful in their faces and shad will either ignore it completely or snap at it like pit bulls. More precisely, they'll swing their heads, as swordfish do, to bat an irritant aside. They don't swallow, since they're not eating. Essentially never does a hook reach the gills, or even much inside the mouth. You hook them in the mouth's outer rim—in the premaxillary and maxillary bones and sometimes in the ethmoid region at the tip of the snout, all of which are segments of the large open scoop that plows through plankton at sea.

Below the Lambertville–New Hope bridge that evening, I was using a shad dart of my own making. A small metallic cone, it trailed bucktail tied on in a vise. Its body was chartreuse. Its base was dark green. It was coated with clear gloss. Extending with the bucktail from the tip of the cone, its No. 2 hook was black and chemically sharpened. Because the hook shaft includes a right angle and the eye emerges from the side of the cone, a shad dart is hydrodynamically hapless. It flips and flops and buzzes around like a fly that needs killing. If it snags, you're likely to lose it. Snags happen often. Held in the water column by the driving current, my dart was out about seventy feet.

Three of us were in the boat, close and tandem. I was in the middle, fishing over the shoulder of the skipper, Ed Cervone. Fishing over my shoulder was Ed's son, Edmund Cervone. Each of them had caught several shad, varying in sex, notable in size. I had caught two roe shad. The sun was setting. It was seven-thirty. Quitting time was upon us, but the rod in my hand was suddenly pulled by a great deal more than the current. The Cervones reeled in their darts and stowed their rods. They would wait and watch, as people do when someone else in a boat has a fish on the line.

It felt heavy. It maintained for some time a severe tug without much lateral movement. "Female," I said. "Six pounds." Cervone the Elder, who has a doctorate in psychology, seemed unimpressed—seemed to be suggesting, through a light shrug, that he knew bullshit by its cover. He knew he wasn't fishing with Buddy Grucela. He knew he wasn't fishing with Erwin Dietz or Gerald Hartzel—living figures in the Cooperstown of shad. He knew that in my seven years as a shad fisherman I had risen steadily into a zone of terminal mediocrity. And he was well equipped to empathize. Ours was one of twelve boats below and around the western bridge piers. Nearly all the others had been doing well, too. When that fish of mine came on the line toward the end of the day, a guy in the boat next to us looked over and said, "It doesn't get any better than this, does it?" At that moment, thirty feet of line came off the reel against the drag. I thought the line would snap.

Dietz and Hartzel are waders, bank fishermen, and you'd usually encounter them far upriver—at least three hundred miles above the sea buoy—where the Delaware is narrow, is punctuated with riffles and rapids, and has cut a deep gorge in the Pocono-Catskill plateau. The night air, cooler than the water, makes a thick early mist there. If you wanted to fish near a monumental figure like Dietz, and possibly be there ahead of him, you had to be on the river before dawn. As the light came up, it revealed a dark silhouette in the drifting vapors, standing on a rock catching fish. He always knew how many. "How many is that?" "Eleven." I could fish near him until the sun was high, doing everything he did, and catch nothing, or one or two. Nearing retirement, he was a mason then, in New York City construction. He lived in Queens. Somewhere in my fishing diaries I wrote: "He recovers his dart and casts anew faster than anyone I've ever seen. He brings fish in rapidly, and swiftly releases them. Then his dart is in the air. He is very sensitive on the jig, his rod tip high, his twitch minimal. While I am fishless, Dietz's rod is electric with excitement. Two. Three. Four. He works fish. I watch. And watch. He loses a dart to a snag. Cool. He is idle. Out of it. I am casting—two, three, four. The numbers refer to casts but not to shad. At last he finishes tying on a new dart, and he flings it into the river. It swings through the current, and his rod is bent by another fish. How . . . Does . . . He . . . Do . . . It? After he casts, he holds his rod at a forty-five-degree angle. His wrist flicks almost imperceptibly at a consistent rate of about once a second. He says he can feel the shad bump the dart in the center of the current, bump it again, and then go for it. His line and his lures are identical with mine. I imitate him as precisely as I can. He hooks fish, I hook water."

As Gerald Hartzel stepped into the upper river at five-thirty of a June morning—after driving more than three hours—his shad net would be holstered on his back so that its hoop rose above his head like a circular antenna. He reached for it often. He used a five-and-a-half-foot rod with four-pound line and an ultra-light reel. He had a long wooden staff that floated on a tether beside him. He was slim. Six feet. Polaroid glasses. On his brown hat were two fishing licenses. Sewn on both his hat and his vest was the orange-and-green emblem of the Delaware River Shad Fishermen's Association. He cast with a short direct punch from eye level, as if he were throwing a dart not so much at a fish as at a tavern wall. As one such morning began, he caught a shad, and then another, but not rapidly, and he seemed puzzled. Then, arms up, he began to hold the rod high before him, as if he were reaching for a shelf; and, in quick succession, he flipped up the tip, up again, up once more—fish on the line. Rooted in fast water, apparently tireless, he caught shad after shad after shad, always with his arms extended high. His darts were very small. Across the morning, they were in the water an amazing percentage of the total time. He was efficient in the rhythm of his casts. Page 1, line 1: If your dart is not in the water you are not catching fish. Jigging—twitching—the line, he gave complete attention to each moment of every swing, his eyes swinging, too, like a long-ball hitter's. After fishing downstream from him, I quit when he did. In four and a half hours, I had caught six shad, including one roe that I kept. In the four and a half hours, he had landed twenty-one shad. Wearily rubbing a shoulder, he said, "Did you see what I had to do?"

Hartzel had been shad fishing more than thirty years. He spoke of fifty-shad days. Since page 1, line 2 of this enterprise is "Position counts"—that is, a person in the right place can bring fish in steadily while a neighboring line is scoreless—I said as he was leaving that I thought I would fish awhile just where he had fished. "Good idea," he said. "Be careful. This is a treacherous river. Start in that little eddy behind the rock there, and then move out a little." With my arms above my head, twitching, I started in the eddy behind the rock there, and soon edged out closer to the channel. I fished for two hours just where he had fished. I caught nothing. I felt no hits. My fishing diary from that day says, "When I played basketball, I was very much less effective when I went to the right. When I dribbled, I sometimes had to glance at the ball. I had no reverse pivot. I didn't roll. I sucked. And if I didn't know it before, I know now that there are Larry Birds in the river. Joe DiMaggios. Ben Hogans. Reds Grange." The annual run was about over, and as I was leaving the river another fisherman asked me how I'd done for the year. "About fifty," I said. He said, "That's quite a season." By that standard, Gerald Hartzel has a new season every time he leaves home. The diary continues: "There is more to the association of Delaware River shad fishermen than a bunch of people whose success uniformly depends on the presence and mood of the fish. If it's the last thing I do on this earth, I'm going to have a fifty-shad day. It's that or live forever."

The great Buddy Grucela, whose domain of the American shad runs from Easton to Portland, Pennsylvania, was a bank fisherman when he was young and often had fifty-shad days. He is the author of "The Original Guide to Better Shad Fishing on the Delaware River" (Grucela, Easton, 1980), of which I have six copies, one of them covered with shad blood and puffy from river and rain. It's on a shelf between C. Boyd Pfeiffer's "Shad Fishing" (Crown, New York, 1975) and Henry B. Bigelow and William C. Schroeder's "Fishes of the Gulf of Maine" (United States Government Printing Office, Washington, D.C., 1953). When Grucela was thirty-five, he was more or less forced to get a boat, because shad fishermen had become so numerous that he needed to get out onto the water to find a position that counted. In a manner of speaking, he had to accept a cut in pay ("I caught more shad from shore than ever from the boat"), and, while he wasn't exactly hemmed in by other floating fishermen, they were pretty close. His favorite anchorage was two hundred yards upriver from the tributary Martins Creek. A lot of people followed him there. One morning, he had a buck shad on his line running upstream, running downstream, leaping, tail-walking. It jumped into another guy's boat.

Grucela: "I knew the guy. He'd been catching nothing for three days. He wouldn't give me the shad. He said he needed it to prove to his wife he was shad fishing. Some guys can fish in a hatchery and catch nothing. He was one of those guys."

Buddy Grucela did not require another experience like that one to cause him to arrive at the river routinely before dawn. "The shad aren't stirred up yet," he explains. "The more they're stirred up, the spookier they get. At daybreak, it's just you and the geese, man."

If, say, three hundred thousand shad come up the Delaware River, three hundred thousand shad come to Buddy Grucela. Or something near it. Shad are long-term spawners, doing it nightly for many nights, and they seem to prefer to be well above Trenton. Easton to Portland is twenty miles of river. A claim could be made that those twenty miles relate to the American shad as the Doaktown pools of the Miramichi relate to the Atlantic salmon. To the Delaware River Shad Fishermen's Association—a conservation group that tries to keep the river healthy—Easton to Portland is, by and large, where the dues payers are in April. Halfway up the reach is Foul Rift, a quarter mile of haystacks and standing waves, the preëminent rapid among the several hundred in the Delaware. A few miles south—close to Martins Creek, Pennsylvania—is a ledge of white water that slants downstream from right bank to left, its base the base of Buddy Grucela.

He grew up in Martins Creek, to which his grandfather (originally named Grutzela) had emigrated from Poland to work in the cement plant. Buddy's father worked in the cement plant, and so, eventually, did Buddy. When he was a kid, he saw big silver fish in the river in spring and had no idea what they were. In his twenties, he was catching so many shad he carried them home on a tree limb. After the cement plant closed, in the nineteen-sixties, he worked in a mill that was generous with vacations. He took them when the shad appeared, and, as long as the run lasted, spent all day every day on the water. Later, working as a traffic director on a Delaware River bridge, he was rebuked for fishing on the job.

No piece of tackle is more effective for a fisherman than his own daily data: weather, water temperature, water volume, lure, line weight, line density, and many an etcetera. Just the act of recording such things imprints them in cumulative memory, and you move forward learning where to be and what to do when. Grucela's sense of the run and the river is so refined in this respect that he envisions in his season a single apex day. Not that he wouldn't go out on the Ides of March or give it a try on the Fourth of July. At the latitude of Martins Creek, though, if his season were somehow restricted to just one day the day would be the twenty-fourth of April. Year upon year, it has been his best day. In the off season, just thinking of April 24th will cause him to smile like a winning coach, and say, "When you're fishing, nothing beats catching fish."

On the twenty-fourth of April, above Easton, the roes are in the river—April 24th and a week or two on either side. "The roe run comes in two parts—the early roe run and the late roe run. Then you get a late buck run—real small and too young, precocious bucks." Shad are not always swimming near the bottom of the water column, as some shad fishermen inflexibly believe. Grucela starts low, then removes weight incrementally until he finds the level of the fish. All that notwithstanding, he will state summarily, "The secret of shad fishing is depth." And he adds, "That's why they kill them with downriggers." Grucela spurns downriggers—devices that pinch your line far below your hull and keep the dart at depth. He prefers to do the fishing himself. "I just throw my dart and let it rattle in the current."

He uses two rods, a dart on one line, a flutter spoon on the other—no droppers, no doubling up (two lures on one line). A flutter spoon has the slim shape of the leaf of a white willow. He pays it out behind his boat and leaves it in the water, fluttering. The dart he casts repeatedly, retrieving it after its swing through the current. A machinist custom-made his dart mold. If Buddy Grucela were a golfer, he would not be attracted to an iridium driver. His gear is conventional, starting with six-pound line. He keeps a small split shot within twelve inches of the dart, so minor debris will collect on the shot and not on the hook. When the river is full of aments, also known as catkins (flower clusters of willow, birch, or alder), the split shot catches the catkins.

Record American shad have been caught in the Delaware River (eleven pounds, one ounce) and the Connecticut River (eleven pounds, four ounces). Buddy Grucela is certain that he had one heavier than that. After the dart stopped in mid-swing, and the moment of stasis was over, this fish, close to the surface, went straight up the river. Grucela watched it go, wondering what would happen next. This happened next: "He swam right by me like a shark. He was going upstream and he saw me. He looked me in the eye. Then he came right at the boat like a torpedo. He's coming right at me, and I'm reeling fast. He went under the boat, right under me. He bent the rod tip under the boat. He broke the rod off. All I had in my hand was the reel and the handle. That fish—I'm telling you—was a record shad." It was also, beyond doubt, a female. Shad fishermen can't seem to help virilizing gender when they tell stories about big, powerful animals.

Grucela owns a piece of undeveloped, parklike riverfront land, tight between the water and Pennsylvania 611. Under a red granite tombstone there is Redgie, his Doberman of fifteen years. Redgie died watching television with Buddy Grucela. Toward the end of shad season, a bright-red tulip blooms beside the headstone, on which are carved two fish, one bearing the date of Redgie's birth and the other the date of his death. Etched above the fish is a dog bone bearing Redgie's name. In the Redgie years, after Grucela hooked a shad, Redgie watched the action until the fish was beginning to lie on its side. Then Redgie went after it. He went into the river like a bird dog and retrieved Grucela's shad. One day, a carp pulled Redgie under.

Gradually, I got some of my line back that evening by the bridge pier in Lambertville, but only to watch it go out again. After twenty minutes, I had not moved the fish two feet upcurrent. It didn't come out of the water. It didn't even come up in the water. It acted like a shad. It went to the right. It went to the left. It lingered in reaches broadside to the current. The fish was so strong it just would not come toward me, and it felt very heavy. I was using one of my Daiwa SS 700 lightweight reels, with no backing. They don't carry much line. I was using six-pound test. Now thirty minutes had passed. The fish went downriver in another long run against the drag. Ed Cervone's pebbly chatter was turning quizzical, his mind an open pamphlet. He was thinking, What is the problem here—the fish or the fisherman? Edmund Cervone, behind me, said nothing. Edmund was an instinctive, natural, absolute river fisherman. On various outings, fish had come to his line while avoiding his father's and mine. You learned things from Edmund. You learned, for example, that small darts catch shad. The smaller the dart the more shad. Edmund was a college student, however, and could not afford much time on the river. His father and I, being teachers, were not similarly burdened. Many a day we had sat in the boat catching nothing but each other's words, and pondering the psyche of the planet's largest herring. We were sharing the river with half a million shad, whose interest in us was inverse to our interest in them.

Ed Cervone is the sort of person who, when he is fishing, might as well be chained among the shadows in a cave. No nuance of depth or color is too subtle to prevent his frequent adjustments of style. Chartreuse? Orange and black? Red and white? Gold? Low? Medium? High? He changes his dart, returns it to the water, and speaks: "In a field that is filled with ignorance, everyone is an expert." In the education of secondary-school students with dyslexia and many other learning disadvantages, Ed is a highly reputed practitioner of a variety of effective techniques, many of which he devised. He is a pioneer in his field. But not in this one. His doctorate may be in psychology, but these ocean fish are too much for him. Groping for reason, he essays, "What they do today they will not do tomorrow." For that one, I'd give him credit for a ton of insight. "You and I know as much as they do," he offers. "Or as little." Among other things, the fish are apparently aware of what Ed is thinking: "I was fishing two days ago. People covered themselves with shad—except for me. I can't get desperate because it is transmitted through the line into the water and the fish know it."

You can learn a lot about shad just from their appearance. Their bodies predict what they can do. Nowhere is this as emphatic as in the deeply forked tail—the caudal fin—which is tall, and, as seen from the side, narrow. It is not as tall, narrow, and deeply forked as a tuna's tail, but it's getting there. It has the high aspect ratio (span versus width) associated with extreme high speed. The dorsal fin, like a sail rising up from the shad's back, is centered—midway from nose to tail. Dorsal fins in various fishes can be forward, or aft, or anywhere along the back. The centered ones speak of an ability to swim steadily, sustaining high speed. The range of the American shad is from northern Florida to the Labrador Sea, and within the range a typical individual will swim two thousand miles in a year. They return to their home rivers after four or five years. One look at that forked tail and you know that the fish is active in the middle of the water column and not sitting around on the bottom like a bullhead catfish, whose tail is so rounded it looks like a coin. A trout has a rounded tail as well, and, as a swimmer, is one notch up from a catfish.

I am indebted for these descriptions primarily to Willy Bemis, an anatomist of fishes, who is a professor of ichthyology at the University of Massachusetts.

A shad in clear water, seen from above, is very dark greenish-blue, with an almost metallic lustre. Its flashing sides are silver, its belly white. The body is deep, meaning that in outline it more closely resembles a zeppelin than a snake. The body is laterally compressed, meaning that in cross-section it is not fat. The largest shad I've ever caught weighed a little over six pounds and was two feet long, a not uncommon size. The scales are deciduous, diaphanous, and the size of dimes. In their treelike rings and other markings a practiced eye can discern the age of the fish and whether it has spawned before. Chemical analysis of a scale will reveal—among other things—what river the fish was born in. A deciduous scale is loose and comes off easily. A fish with the mobility and flank speed of a shad needs a loose-fitting scale in order not to be constrained. The fins, taken altogether, are like the stabilizing feathers of an arrow. The spines of the pectoral fins are right-angled levers. The pectoral fins are steering mechanisms, anti-roll devices, and brakes; and when they are not in use they are faired into the body, like retractable landing gear. A shad is supremely streamlined—a concept that came into hydrodynamics in the nineteenth century and was also known as "fish-body form." Under broad, shieldlike, adipose eyelids, the eyeballs are faired into the head. You can predict from a shad's large eyes the effects on its behavior of vision and light.

When the fish had been on my line forty minutes, dusk had begun to gather. Forty minutes was twice as long as any shad had been on my line anywhere before. The bridge above, with its open-grate steel roadway, was humming with tires—cars in rhythm like breaking surf. On the bridge walkway were prams, strollers, couples on their way to dinner. In the festival ambience of New Hope and Lambertville, babies never sleep. People stopped to lean over and watch. They shouted encouragement. They hung around to see the fish. No fish. Just a taut line, a rod tip high, an occasional plunge or lateral dash, a stripping run downriver. This was a scene from the nineteenth century below the old green bridge over the wide river between the two steepled towns, with narrow streets among riverine houses. Downriver past rapids was a stone tower—Bowman's Tower—rising from the top of a hill. And just above the bridge, off Lewis Island, Lambertville, a crew rowing a small boat was hauling a nine-hundred-foot seine in a great circle in the river, making—as the Lewis family has since 1888—a commercial catch of shad. I had essentially no time to look around, however. Past my rod and line, I was getting an increasingly concentrated, Warholian look at a small swatch of New Hope—sightseeing pontoon boats shutting down for the night, the many-windowed wall of the Club Zadar, the mansard roof and high-rising fly of the Bucks County Playhouse. Other shad boats were weighing anchor and departing. The boat next to us was about to leave, but its three occupants changed their minds and decided to stay and watch. More people collected on the bridge above. Because I'd been dealing with this fish for three-quarters of an hour, Ed Cervone—not for the first time—referred to me as "the Old Man" and to the river as "the Sea." He would be saying that again, and again, as the sky turned a deeper gray, and then black.

It's a bad idea to horse a shad. That is, if you become impatient or for any other reason try to shorten the story by muscling the fish into submission, you'll almost surely lose the fish. In the words of Buddy Grucela, "Shad have paper-thin mouths and under no circumstances will they allow themselves to be railroaded." The maxillary and premaxillary bones, which constitute a large percentage of that big open mouth, run down its sides like a drooping dihedral mustache, and are very hard at the leading edge. A hook often wraps around that leading edge, penetrating the insubstantial membrane that lies behind. The hook is like a coat hanger swinging from a bar. The longer the shad is on the line, the greater the opening the hook will make in that thin membrane. Suddenly, the fish is gone. A fisherman doing everything right loses many shad. It's a basic component of shad fishing. Not all shad are hooked in just that way, but most seem to be, and when they are netted—or the tension on the line otherwise drops—there's usually no need to detach the shad dart; it just falls out of the mouth. The lower extremities of the premaxillary bones widen out like strips of durable plastic. If the hook lodges there, your chances of netting the fish are considerably larger. Of course, while the fish is in the water you've got no idea where the hook is and your only rational strategy is finesse.

More time went by. I'd had the fish on the line for an hour, and then an hour and a half. The guys in the boat next to us—now the only other boat—finally pulled anchor and left, mentioning something about their wives. There were people on the bridge who had been watching earlier, and had gone off to dinner, and now had come back from dinner and were watching again. One of them shouted, "Are you still catching that same fish?" I nodded without looking up. In the darkness, I was staring instead at the black vertical rod against the disco lights of Club Zadar, which had grown ever brighter with the fall of night and were flashing colors on the river. While the fish moved and sounded, and came up a little, and then sounded again, it almost hypnotized me as I concentrated on the swaying rod against the whirling colors. Gingerly, I worked it to the left and the right, trying to move its head to one side and then to the other side, to confuse it, and try to get in charge of it psychologically. But I'll tell you, I never got in charge of that fish psychologically. At nine-thirty, completing two hours on the other end of the line, it made the reel scream as it took off downriver like a tarpon.

Tarpon? Well, hardly. But the Delaware is a river of prodigious fisheries, and for the past hour we had been doubting, speculating, wondering. What species could this fish be? It had been on the line more than five times as long any of us had ever required to bring in a shad. We now decided that it was not a shad. It felt like a shad in strong current, but the passage of so much time made us think elsewhere. The Delaware is the premier wild-rainbow-trout river in the eastern half of the United States. Ed Cervone and I had watched a shad fisherman catching a rainbow only ten miles north. The big native rainbows, though, were two hundred miles up the river. Besides, no rainbow could ever qualify to be this fish. Once, after I threw a shad dart into the current far upriver, the dart swung into a fish that felt like a shad with a bad cold. It moved around like a shad, but it just felt, by comparison, weak. It turned out to be a fat native wild rainbow, a beautiful fish, not much under two pounds.

There were numerous alternative possibilities. Edmund mentioned the muskellunge. If an alligator had the swimming skills of a barracuda, that would be a muskellunge. Muskies are lone ambush hunters, as much as six feet long, and are not uncommon in the Delaware. With two hours behind us, Ed Cervone dismissed the notion. "They give up," he said. "They roll over."

A walleye? Never. "A walleye would be fatigued in five minutes."

A striped bass? Never. "A striped bass would be fatigued in ten minutes. Stripers fight very, very strongly—savagely. However, after a certain point they fade. They exhaust themselves. They use up their oxygen. Once you control the first few rushes it's awfully hard to revive them. They give up. They roll over."

A carp?

Edmund: "Whatever it is, if we catch it we're going to eat it."

Ed: "A carp wouldn't fight like that."

Me: "Oh, yes it would."

I remembered shad fishing one evening at the Trenton power plant when a guy had a carp on four-pound test. Carp can be three feet long, and his was not far off it. He struggled more than an hour. The power plant is on Duck Island, below the Trenton fall line, and the tide was coming in. The best shad fishing from Trenton downriver is said to be on the incoming tide. Duck Island is as far as you can drive along the river down Lamberton Road in Trenton. Then you put on your waders and walk at least half a mile around a high chain-link fence to an artificial bay at the edge of the river—a square bay, where the power plant discharges its cooling water. The water is warm, and fish collect there. More than two dozen fishermen were present that Monday evening, some in boats, some closely spaced along the shore, fishing in the effluent pond, the warm, man-made eddy. A kid caught a big roe shad while I watched. The same kid had a shad on his line every ten or fifteen minutes. I caught nothing. I was going too low—amateurishly using a quarter-ounce dart. It was sinking fast, and travelling under the shad, which were at the surface, where the warmth was. The kid was using a small green dart. I had nothing but the big darts. As dusk came, the shad were breaking water, hitting lures, working up a frenzy. But I could not hook one even while rods all around me were bending. The man with the carp at long last landed it. He used my net. The carp probably weighed twenty-five pounds. I was discouraged, walking back to the car. I was discouraged by my own failure and discouraged by the scene I had just left: a bay of right angles raked with lures and fed with hot water that brought in the fish.

Edmund: "Maybe it's a catfish."

Ed: "That is a distinct possibility."

While fishing for stripers, Ed had caught a "huge blue cat" in Trenton. The biggest catfish I'd ever seen—far larger than any I'd seen in the bayous of the Atchafalaya—came out of Lake Carnegie, in Princeton. Eventually, we agreed all around that the fish on my line was probably a big channel cat—a catfish with a head at least the size of a basketball. Two hours, fifteen minutes. By now, that's what it felt like.

When Edmund mentioned a sturgeon.

Ed: "Yes! Yes!"

Me: "A *sturgeon*?"

Ed: "A spawning fish that goes up the river and has tremendous energy."

Me: "I know what a sturgeon is."

Ed: "That's it. Completely possible. They never give up. Eventually, you have to go in and wrestle them. You don't land them, you capture them. I saw one by the 202 bridge a few years ago."

Looking up the river in daylight from New Hope, you can see the 202 bridge.

For that matter, a man I once talked to had seen a six-foot sturgeon in New Hope. Eventually, we agreed all around that the fish on my line was a sturgeon.

When a shad is foul-hooked—caught in the tail, or another fin, or any part of the body other than the mouth—the shad loses its grip on reality, sprints away in total rage, and thrashes the river on erratic vectors. It is very difficult to hold on to a foul-hooked shad. This fish, of course, could be a foul-hooked shad.

Among the spectators on the bridge, a cop appeared. He shouted, "Does one of you guys down there own a green Jeep?"

Ed Cervone shouted back, "Yes, Officer, I do."

"Well," the cop continued, with the slightest pause. "Your wife called. She wants you home. She thinks you're dead."

Laughter on the bridge—9:50 P.M.

It was not true that Marian Cervone was concerned about her husband. By her own account, the man is too unpredictable to worry about. She wasn't worried about Edmund, either. It was my wife, Yolanda Whitman, whose mind had been crossed by the ultimate possibility. This was a few years before the sudden bloom of cellular phones. I had no way to tell her why I was late, and deliberately breaking off that fish never crossed my mind.

Yolanda seems to remember the evening with total recall. For one thing, it was my turn to cook. "By nine o'clock, I was just plain mad," she has said for the record. "You were dithering too long. I was waiting for my dinner. You were taking your sweet time, failing in your responsibilities."

Yes.

"At some point after that, I shifted from mad to concern. You had fallen out of the boat. Gone through the rapids."

The rapids, not far from the bridge, cross a diabase ledge and are tumultuous in spring.

"It was pitch black. Cold. I imagined you with hypothermia in the river. So I called Marian. I told her I was worried because your absence was 'out of character.' "

Marian must have marvelled that someone could seriously use a phrase like that about a husband. Marian said she would call back if she learned anything. After hanging up, she called the Lambertville police. She said her husband and son and a friend were out in a boat and had not returned "way beyond the time" she expected them. Would the police check the boat-launch parking lot and see if a green Jeep was there? The woman on the other end of the line said the police surely would.

A while later, the police called Marian, and Marian called Yolanda, who continues the narrative: "While I waited, a tear or two actually squeezed out. I had let myself wander into the impossible. Perhaps I was madder at Ed than at you—who knows? After Marian called back, I was again spitting mad. She said, 'They're still fishing.' "

Two hours, thirty minutes. At last the fish had come up enough in the river so that the people on the bridge caught glimpses of it as, now and again, it canted—silver flashing—and changed direction. We heard them go "Ooh!" We heard them shout, "Wow, what a huge fish!" When we, in the boat, finally got a glimpse of it, we thought it enormous, too. Toward the end, I kept pressing it, tightened the drag even more, a risky, foolish thing to do. I just hoped it would not make a sudden run. If it did so, at least I had turned off the anti-reverse button, and the reel could spin free. Buddy Grucela, page 22.

The fish was close now. When it saw the boat, it dived. After it came up, and saw the boat again, it took off for the bottom of the river, slowly to rise once more. At some point in the last five minutes, Edmund tried for it with the boat net and missed. I finally worked it up to the side of the boat. It was still swimming, unspent. It did not roll over. It never gave up. On the second try, Edmund got it into the net, and the dart dropped out of its mouth. He brought into the boat a four-and-three-quarter-pound roe shad.

I still have the dart—secured with monofilament to a small piece of cedar shingle. It was only the second dart I had ever retired. On a bookshelf, I propped it up beside a dart of the same weight and colors, with which, on an upriver day the spring before, I had caught seventeen shad without changing or losing the lure. The chemically sharpened hook was a novelty I had succumbed to in a catalogue. That shipment of hooks was uneven, to say the least. Some of them were so weak they were bent out straight by the force of tugging shad. But not this one. Despite two hours and thirty-five minutes in the shad's mouth, the curve of the black steel looked as it had when I made the dart and festooned it with buck-tail in a vise. At home, I studied the fish with a magnifying glass. It had not been hooked on the top of the head or in any other place on the outside. It was not foul-hooked. It was hooked in the roof of the mouth, very near the front, slightly off the midline, to the right. I saw a narrow hole there, and I put a toothpick in it, which did not come through to the outside. The connection of hook and shad had been something like a trailer hitch.

Mindful of the species' paper jaw and its legendary fragility, I would one day lay a shad on a dissecting table at the University of Massachusetts and show Willy Bemis just where my fish had been hooked.

"How would you describe that, Willy?"

"It's the ethmoid cartilage of the braincase. It's the part of the braincase that everyone would understand as, regionally, the nose. One solid cartilaginous structure forms the braincase during early development. This is the anterior tip of it. The brain is back in the center of the head. Most of the braincase is protected by bone, which would make it a very tough place for a hook to latch on to. But once you've got a hook past the bone and into that little piece of cartilage, it doesn't come out. If a hook goes through that, it's going to hook on to the fish in a very serious way. There's no way that fish is ever going to throw that hook."

The monofilament line felt sandpapery. When I took it off the reel, it contracted instantly into coils from a hundred and fifty-five minutes of twisting. A thick mass of bunched contracted circles hopelessly intertwined, it looked like something an owl dropped.

I sent the reel to the Daiwa Corporation, in California, for an assessment. They wanted $54.40 to fix it, because the shad had bent the pinion gear, the shad had bent the drive gear, the shad had damaged the oscillating system and gone a long way toward wearing out the drag system. The reel required two new gears, a new pawl, a new worm shaft, and three new drag washers.

I still have some of the scales. They report the shad's age as three. For a female that young to be on the spawning run is more than uncommon. It's rare. The scales record strong growth in the river in the first summer, as the egg turned into a larva, and the larva into a juvenile. They record normal growth in the ocean in each of the following years. Then they show the shad coming back into the river—two years earlier than most females do.

Soon after that evening in Lambertville, I told this story to Richard St. Pierre, of the U.S. Fish and Wildlife Service. Headquartered in Harrisburg, on the Susquehanna River, he is a shad specialist, who has worked as a shad consultant on the Hudson River, the Columbia River, and the Yangtze. He said that it must have been a letdown for me to learn that the fish was not a striped bass or a sturgeon or a muskellunge "but just a shad."

It was not in any sense a letdown, I told him. I'm a shad fisherman. I was fishing for American shad.

# A SELECTIVE ADVANTAGE

The Connecticut River is rich in shad but not in places to cast for them. The fall line is above Hartford, at Enfield, where a rock ledge and the rubbled remains of a dam give pause to the annual spawning run, attracting boats in large numbers, and a density of wading fishermen to the right bank of the river. The fish slide by in thousands, and then go on to find eighteen easy miles before the thousands catch up with earlier thousands, which in turn have caught up with earlier thousands in Holyoke, Massachusetts. Holyoke Dam is thirty feet high and was built in 1849. The bucks stop there. And then the roes. Thomas Chalmers may have been slow to figure this out, but in 1871, secretively, he addressed himself to the river below the dam with a fly rod and a dry fly. In the twenty-first century, fishing for shad with a dry fly is regarded as an eccentric and essentially pointless stunt. On his millers, moths—dry flies—Thomas Chalmers caught upwards of a hundred shad. His story "leaked out"—according to *The Turf, Field & Farm* (March 13, 1874)—but in losing his private paradise Chalmers became a progenitor of American shad fishing.

Beside Holyoke Dam today are two large elevator cars that much resemble their counterparts in office buildings. The analogy extends, as shad are lured in there by a concentrated current and lifted five stories in such numbers that the cars contain more fish than water. During the spring migration, several hundred thousand shad go up in the elevators and swim on out to the north, first passing glass walls and the flattened noses of Massachusetts schoolchildren, who come there by the busful. All that notwithstanding, the water below Holyoke Dam is still what Thomas Chalmers figured it would be: the hottest spot in New England to fish for American shad.

A thousand feet wide, the dam connects Holyoke, on the right bank, to South Hadley, on the left. Urban Holyoke is a fossil American Venice, with mile-long canals running like streets through the city, delivering power to industries that flourished in the century before the century before. In ten places, water shoots down penstocks from the high canals, turns turbines to make electricity, and plunges into the Connecticut River. Confused shad mill around these plunge pools, and fishermen do, too. South Hadley, Massachusetts, across the water, is wooded. Trails come down to the river from suburban streets. A narrow unpaved lane drops through the trees to a clearing made for launching boats. During the spring migration, many schools of shad choose the South Hadley side when the Connecticut is running high over the dam—when "the river is just honkin'."

The speaker is Boyd Kynard—plaid shirt, dark-blue watch cap, the numbers on his Massachusetts fishing license so large that a fish-and-game warden could check on him and not get out of a car. Kynard is sinewy, square-jawed, dark-haired, compact. His eyes are bright, and quick to notice things. He appears to have been indoors on scattered occasions in the past. He has come to the river in South Hadley so early in the morning he's the first on the scene—earlier even than Armand Charest. Kynard lives in Amherst, twelve miles away, and works in Turners Falls, thirty-three miles upriver. He remarks that he is not only the first fisherman on the scene on this May, high-season day but the first person to show up here, every year, at the start of the spring migration—earlier even than Armand Charest.

A van of some age rumbles down to the river, swings around, backs, and parks among the sycamores, ironwoods, and locusts. The driver does not step out but instead disappears into the back of the van and begins a series of activities visible only in the rocking of the chassis. Something like origami is going on in there, as hooks and hinges link unfolding parts and the van turns into a store. A sunroof pops up, as vent. Paired doors in one side fold back against the body, each bright with shad darts, striper jigs, willow-leaf blades, and other lures. A sales counter spans the opening—Armand Charest at the counter, ready for business. All around him are shelves of shad darts—varied, variegated, in great numbers and in every size and sparkling color. Charest is alert, incisive, weightless, and wiry. Even his glasses have wire rims. You will never see better shad darts than the ones he has in that van. They're all of his own making. "Willow-leaf blades" is Connecticut River dialect for flutter spoons.

Of shad caught by sport fishermen in the Connecticut River, eighty per cent are caught in Massachusetts, and at least eighty per cent of the shad caught in Massachusetts are from Thomas Chalmers' paradise, here in the purview of Armand Charest. Opportunely, Charest's trade has expanded into striper jigs, because striped bass have lately become populous in the river. Personally, I have to admit that I would be less inclined to fish for stripers with jigs than with trinitrotoluene. I look upon stripers as I look upon the worst ilk of editor. Stripers eat the young of shad.

Kynard asks Charest if he notices much difference between shad fishermen and striper fishermen.

Charest says, "Shad fishermen are polite."

Charest looks out on the river, and up toward the widespread dam, where the water is falling in discrete curtains like an immense roaring bar code. Then he amplifies his comment, saying, "Shad fishermen are polite. They're educated. They include a lot of women. Striper fishermen are rude. They're obnoxious. They're meat fishermen. No women."

Kynard says, "They're basically your wrestling crowd."

Charest says, "They have missing teeth."

Kynard says, "They're kick-ass fishermen."

I purchase half a dozen very small roundhead darts by Armand Charest. He looks me over with approval. The colors I choose are miscellaneous. Kynard wants to know what colors have been working well in recent days in the river. Charest mentions red-and-yellow. I give it as my opinion that the fish are hitting or they aren't—color doesn't matter.

Through Charest's wire-rims comes the look that Carl Gustav Jung would have had if Jung had sold shad darts. Armand Charest says, "It matters to the fisherman."

Nearer the dam, Kynard and I pull on chest waders and enter the river. We're up to our waists, casting. After an hour, I've caught two little blueback herring, but I can't get near a shad. It must be the color. I change darts, from chartreuse to red-and-white—to no effect—and watch cormorants riding the current. I catch, and grudgingly release, a beautiful young striper scarcely a foot in length, but I still can't get near a shad, while Kynard's darts, on four-pound test, are flying. They seem to go halfway to Holyoke, and he's hooking into roe shad. Whatever else he is, the man is all fisherman, and, if it can be said of certain people—in Norman Maclean's phrase—that they are able to "think like a fish," the description is tailored to Boyd Kynard.

He's had a roe on the line for twenty minutes. She bulldogs in the current, jumps, bulldogs again. My admiration of his skill is somewhat diminished by green corrosive envy. He looks around laconically while the fish races crossriver. He says, "The settlers called them white salmon, because of the way they leap."

I ask, "What color you using?"

He answers, "Red-and-white."

His fish jumps again but does not interrupt his train of thought. "When it's early in the season and there's a lot of turbidity, I want something really flashy and silvery, or gold, that catches whatever light it can. Later on, as the water clears up, I think what makes the biggest difference is the size. You see guys out here throwing great big darts in clear water—they're not going to do any good." As he handles his rod, his interest seems high but his level of concern low. If the fish breaks off, the fish breaks off. This is not his first prom.

"They're beautiful fish," he remarks, as the present one rolls, flashes, and dives. "Especially the first wave to come up. With their big silvery scales, they're lovely animals."

It was to Boyd Kynard that I sent scales from my two-hour-and-thirty-five-minute, three-year-old roe shad—and, from time to time, to Boyd Kynard that I have shown other scales from shad that behaved unusually or seemed anomalously small. Shad scales, like overlapping shingles, are only about twenty-five per cent exposed. The exposed part is the opaque silver. The hidden, anterior part is translucent and bears the tree-ring-like annuli that—in the late nineteen-nineties—began to yield enhanced information through new techniques in the chemical analysis of microelements. For example, different rivers contain differing quantities of selenium. The selenium in an annulus of a shad scale can be used to identify the home river of the shad. "Even areas within the same river," Kynard has told me. "They're doing this with Atlantic salmon now. They can actually tell you where in the river—or in which tributary—a particular scale was grown. The scale is a growing tissue that is affected by the environment around it; so when we take it, we have a book. It has a freshwater and a saltwater part. You can follow a shad to the Bay of Fundy. You can relate the chemistry of the scale to the environment that the animal did its growing in—the actual spatial location. Biologists in Canada tag fish and get letters from Connecticut, New Jersey, and so forth. The shad is carrying the same story on its back." In close approximation, the scale records the date of birth and the date of ocean entry. The successive annuli record the successive years at sea. Then comes the spawning mark on the first annulus that records a return to the river.

After fishing until noon that day in South Hadley, we went up the wooded slope and into a small restaurant of the type that stakes its reputation on unique meat loaf. Like all other shad fishermen, we discussed—as we had before and would again—the behavior of American shad. With this difference: Kynard is a behaviorist at the S. O. Conte Anadromous Fish Research Center, in Turners Falls, the only laboratory of its kind in the world. He is the author of numerous scientific papers on—among other things—sturgeon and shad. His early-season, cold-weather visits to Holyoke Dam largely have to do with the fish elevator and what may be coming into it, but he always has his rod in the car.

"They're fish with emotional problems," he said. "You can lift them out of the water a matter of seconds and they just die, the stress is so great. I've never handled another species like that. It may be that their potassium level goes down. In any case, some sort of chemical imbalance occurs and it's irreversible. They literally die of fright."

Since they've been in the ocean maybe five years, and were only about four inches long when they left fresh water after their first summer, I could not imagine what goes on in their heads when they come back and take on the rush of a river—its sudden variations, its limited range of depths, its floods, its blocking structures. "What do they think when they come upon a riffle or a rapid?"

"They never keep going. They look it over. They're going to

bunch up any time anything confronts them. Rapids. A bridge pier. Otherwise, they're strung out in a line. They're afraid of variation. They're afraid of the unknown. They get used to a particular environment, and if it changes they have problems. They've had this nice river with uniform laminar flow; it's deep, the light is the same. They're down near the bottom. That's where they swim—in the bottom third. I've done some studies on that. They're down where they have just a little bit of light but everything is very predictable. They go right up the channel. Now they get to a shallow-water area with riffles, white water. Everything is changing. And they have problems. Different fish respond differently to variation. Salmon move very cautiously. When they get to something like that, they will delay, too, but they figure it out a lot quicker. Shad—they're like the extreme for having an adverse reaction, for stopping when presented with change. They swim around in circles. Even a half-submerged log will create a riffle in the water, and, when shad come up to it, it stops them. They just circle around, thinking, Oh my goodness, I'm in such big trouble. I'm so confused. I'm so confused. They're a schooling species and very flighty. They don't like to do things on their own. From the moment those guys are hatched until the day they die, they are always in a school."

Their schooling is more than mass hysteria. It has hydrodynamic advantages. Like geese in their V formation, like bikers in a pack, the schools get along on less energy than their individual members would expend if they were swimming on their own. Vortices that come off bird, fish, and biker help draw followers along in the way that eddies behind rocks in rapids will pull a canoe or a fish upstream. "Their individual oxygen consumption is lower when they're in schools," Kynard said. "If a school becomes small, the amount of oxygen they use per individual is going to go up. But I think it's mostly psychological. They're really reactive as a school."

A railroad runs along the Delaware in the seventy-five miles where the river is the border between New York and Pennsylvania. I told him I had never felt a shad hit a dart while a train was going by. I have waited out the tremor of as many as five engines pulling upward of a hundred and forty cars—many of them double-decker—while my casts were limp in the river. The shad sense the presence of trains through their lateral lines—networks of pressure-sensitive tubes on either side of the head. Kynard said, "When a train is going by, that lateral line is just jumping—sending messages, Help! Help! Help! Avoid! Run! Run!" When you're standing in the river, shad will swim right into your leg. They're not afraid, because they think you're a rock or a tree. But a masked friend of mine who swims in the river shooting fish with a spear-gun—killing rainbows, walleyes, and bass for his table—tells me that he has never been able to approach shad close enough to hit one.

They are sensitive to any type of change, from a passing shadow to a developing storm. When a full moon rises over spawning shad, as soon as the light hits the water they stop spawning. Light—more than anything else except temperature—prompts their behavior. Without it, they are disoriented, but with those big absorptive eyes they don't need much. "When it's dark, these guys will be almost immobile. They'll hold where there's no current, or very slow current. If light intensity gets above a critical thresh-old—about ten lux, which is less than a candle—they can begin to use it for orientation, and they will move into swifter water. They have a zone in which they can function—too little or too much is outside the zone. By the middle of the day, you will find them avoiding bright light and staying over in the shadow."

From the perspective of a shad, nothing shoots forth light quite as much as white water on a bright day—one more reason to stop and think twice about a rapid. "They don't see in the way that we see," Kynard continued. "They make a chemical called rhodopsin that is sensitive to light. The more light, the more rhodopsin is used up." Shad normally, and successfully, avoid bright light. They stay deep enough in the ocean. They stay low in the river. "But when they want to come up rapids they have to come into shallow water, where they have this bright bright bright light—of fifty, sixty thousand lux. That's what it is! I think so much light is coming in there that it uses up all the rhodopsin, and now they're essentially blind. And now it's exactly the way it was at night. They cannot stay in fast water. I think that's why they have difficulty going up long rapids in the middle of the day."

They move upstream at first light—an optimal time, when muscles are rested. And resolutely they move in the afternoon. Kynard guesses that the falling light reminds them that another day is ending and they've got to get on with their mission. "That drive to get upstream is strong. It must be particularly forceful when they sense that they are losing light."

This reminds me of what I do all day (nothing). I sharpen imaginary pencils and look out real windows. The light of a computer screen seems far too bright to me. I kill hours, hoping for distraction, and complain bitterly when distraction occurs. Three, four, five P.M. Nothing whatever accomplished. The day coiling like a spring. Nothing is worse than a lost day. Panic rises, takes over, and I write until I go home at seven, thinking like a shad.

When daylight drops in the evening, the fish turn and retreat from rapids, because they can't maintain orientation. "They go back down, but not far. They find the very first deep slow-water area. That's where they stay. They just kind of settle down to the bottom. Get down to a lower velocity. Get in the current, where they can just maintain position. Let the lateral line take care of keeping them up, and not moving downstream." As if they were treading water, they wait out the night.

"Do they sleep?"

"They rest. That's as close as they come to sleep. Some fish settle to the bottom, and you can come up to them at night. You can hit 'em. They're out of it. Shad are never out of it. Even at night. We've looked at them with infrared. Their eyes are moving."

"Those fish you can go up to and touch—would you say that they are sleeping?"

"Yes. They're out. If you're a predator, they're toast."

"For example."

"Yellow perch. Sticklebacks. All the centrarchids—basses, crappies. Their eyes and brains are not connected with the outside world. There's probably a better word for it, but it's certainly sleep. They're resting on the bottom—two fins and the tail."

If night comes upon a school of shad in a long and quiet reach of the river, they will, sometimes, continue to migrate upstream. "Telemetry studies have found that these guys do move at night, on the bottoms of rivers. In the first place, velocities down there are low. The shad are orienting with their lateral lines. They can do that. They have incredible lateral-line senses. That's how they move upstream at night."

These generalizations about the behavior of American shad are valid only to the point where they give way to individual characteristics, he suggested. "Shad vary. They're as individual as people. If you had fifty people in a room and asked them to do something, there would be fifty different ways of doing it. It's the same with fish. Some shad fight harder than others—wherever they are in the river. I'm a behaviorist. To tease out the variation in behavior, you tag twenty or thirty fish and see what they do." He once tagged "a bunch of shad" below Holyoke Dam, with its controlled tailrace, its elevators—its high-tech methods of manipulating nature. He wanted to see what the bunch would do. Some individuals figured it out quickly and went on upstream. Others took many days. Others hung around for weeks, never figured it out, and went back downriver to spawn.

"We see that in the Delaware," I remarked. "Some fish quit at the first riffle. Others go on and on."

"Oh, you've got to know it," Kynard said. "Some phenotypes are just better at doing that sort of thing than others."

"So they're not particularly clever or smart?"

"I don't know if they're clever. I'm not sure they're smart. They're persistent. With a few exceptions, they're persistent. They never give up."

"What are they living on?" I asked him. "I've looked in hundreds of shad stomachs. I like to slit open the stomach and look inside. Usually, it's clean as a whistle. I've never seen anything of any size in a shad's stomach."

"Neither have I."

"Once in a while, I find something like little bits of grass or algae."

"I've never interpreted that as food."

"How does it get in there?"

"Incidentally."

"Oh."

"When a shad comes into a river, after living on zooplankton in the ocean, it has fixed storage reserves—fat reserves, muscle mass. Those are at a peak for that fish, because a shad never eats on the spawning run. In April, there are essentially no zooplankton in the river. A shad loses up to forty per cent of its somatic body weight. In mass, it's half the fish that entered the river."

Shad that come out of the Gulf of St. Lawrence go upriver past Quebec City and through the Lachine Rapids at Montreal and on to the Ottawa River, a distance of four hundred and fifty miles. Some shad do that—but not all shad that enter the St. Lawrence River. Shad out of the Gulf of Maine—before being occluded by dams a couple of centuries ago—went a hundred and seventy miles up the Penobscot River to Millinocket, where they encountered the natural dam called Grand Falls. Less than two miles below Grand Falls is a broad pool in the river that is still known as Shad Pond. The historic range of shad in the Connecticut—something over two hundred river miles, including a hundred of the border miles of Vermont and New Hampshire—is inconvenienced and ultimately shut down by five dams, of which Holyoke is the first. The free-flowing Delaware is the only main-stem major river in the forty-eight contiguous American states that is not blocked by a dam. A large proportion of the spring migration seems to prefer to spawn between the Delaware Water Gap and Minisink Island—a piece of river two hundred and ten to two hundred and forty-five miles from the sea buoy. Considerable numbers, though, continue. Those that reach the head of the river, at Hancock, New York, have ascended three hundred and thirty miles, yet many of them keep on going. They go up the Delaware's tributary branches and swim on into a dendritic shrine—the streams of sacred origin of American fly fishing. They go up the Beaver Kill to the Willowemoc and sail through the trout at the Junction Pool. What an experience it must be for a trout to see these argent zeppelins go by. Shad have been known to go on up the Willowemoc to the Little Beaver Kill, passing the Catskill Fly Fishing Center and Museum, at Livingston Manor. According to Ed Van Put, a regional fisheries technician, shad have been seen a mile up the Little Beaver Kill, four hundred miles from the ocean, where they were stopped by a ten-foot waterfall.

I told that story to Boyd Kynard.

He said, "These guys are the Olympic fish. It has to do with swimming abilities, with response to new environments. This is your athlete fish."

Shad vary, right enough. I thought of my own Olympic fish—two and a half hours on the line at Lambertville. Had I not interfered, she would have gone up to the Little Beaver Kill, jumped that waterfall, jumped the Catskill divide, swum up the Hudson to Lake Champlain and down the Richelieu River to Montreal, gone up the Ottawa to Lake Nipissing and down the French River into Lake Huron and on across Superior and up the Pigeon River and on to the Lake of the Woods and Lake Winnipeg and Reindeer Lake and Lake Athabasca and the Great Slave Lake (doing the Methye Portage in a heavy rain) and down the Mackenzie to the Rat, and up the Rat to the Porcupine, and down the Porcupine to the Yukon River, and down the Yukon River to the Bering Sea. It's a shame I ate her.

I asked Kynard why shad would go all the way from the Atlantic Ocean to a Catskill mountain brook when they could copulate in New Jersey. Why would shad in the Connecticut River, which could have their sex in Hartford, fight their way into an elevator car, ignore the creature comforts of the Holyoke Pool, and—at Turners Falls and Vernon—scale a couple of fish ladders to get to Bellows Falls?

He said, "I think I know the answer. I have a hypothesis, anyway. This is what, to me, seems to drive the whole migration. There must be a big selective advantage in going upstream, and in putting your offspring upstream, or you wouldn't do it, would you? The farther up you go, the less energy you have, the more obstacles you encounter. So what's the advantage to the offspring? We have a little bit of data on this. I think they're putting their offspring at the head of the chow line."

Tributaries bring zooplankton into rivers. Plankton are what fingerling and juvenile shad eat. Plankton, for that matter, are what shad eat in all their adult years. They are ram ventilators—swimming with their mouths open, using the force of swimming to pull water across their gills. The gills remove oxygen from the water. Meanwhile, plankton are trapped in the long tines of the gill rakers. One September, when large numbers of juvenile shad were in the Holyoke Pool—the thirty-odd miles of impounded water between Holyoke Dam and Turners Falls—Kynard and a graduate student monitored the plankton that came into the pool from upriver. (The spawning run, at that time, was stopped at Turners Falls.) The study showed a whole lot of plankton in the river at Turners Falls, of which nothing was left at Holyoke. "The zooplankton had been grazed by all those shad in the Holyoke Pool. So my hypothesis is that what keeps these guys going farther and farther, when there are clear disadvantages to doing so, has to be an advantage for progeny. And the one advantage to progeny that we have documented is that there's more food—zooplankton—upstream for concentrations of juvenile shad than there is downstream. So, put your offspring at the head of the chow line. This hypothesis relies on the very well documented fact that the larger you are as a prey species the better off you are. Even one extra millimetre will confer a survival advantage to you in the face of predation. When juvenile shad move down the river, they're subject to all sorts of riverine predators that eat them—smallmouth bass in particular."

"What else eats them?"

"Walleyes. White perch. Stripers. These guys—the juvenile shad—are coming down by the hundreds of millions, and they're all very tender and bite size."

In spring, sexually mature shad begin to enter their home rivers when the water temperature rises through six degrees Celsius, and they spawn when the temperature is between sixteen and twenty-two (sixty to seventy Fahrenheit). So, in effect, they have brackets around them. In the Connecticut River, they have, on average, forty-five days to make their run and complete the ritual sexing of their eggs.

In Kynard's words, "When they enter a river, the clock is ticking. They have varying degrees of energy, varying degrees of swimming ability. They're not feeding, so they have an unrenewable energy reserve that will take them only so far up the river, depending also on delays, water velocity (how hard they have to swim to get there), and water temperature. It is fairly well established that when water temperature gets to twenty-one they slow down, and by twenty-two they stop. They look for a suitable place to spawn. It's a race against time. If you're a shad, you take every opportunity to get as far upstream as you can, past every obstacle, before the water temperature reaches twenty-one degrees. The joker is that you never know what the environment is going to throw at you. You can have the fifty-year flood. You can have low water. Through it all, you have to keep going, and go as fast and as far upstream as you can, because that's the only way your offspring have any chance to have an advantage."

When the Delaware River is just honkin', I told him, I have discovered that I can catch shad on people's lawns. After extreme and sustained rains—water over the banks—the center of the stream is a lethal rage of gray rolling waves. A couple of hundred miles above Philadelphia, I'm standing on somebody's lawn, in fairly calm but turbid water three feet deep. This is not quixotic. The fish—completely frustrated, anxious to go as far as possible— are up on the lawn, too. Kynard explains: "Come a big rain, the whole migration will stop for two weeks. Trying to save energy in slow water, they aren't doing anything—they're just hanging on. Out in the river, not only is the current heavy but turbidity is such that the shad can't go to the low slow water, because there's not enough light down there. They have no choice. They have to hang out way over to the side, maintain position, and just hope like hell it doesn't keep raining."

Out of our waders and into Kynard's office, we had been through a fair amount of this dialogue at the S. O. Conte Anadromous Fish Research Center, in Turners Falls, a small community in northern Massachusetts enabled by a dam built in 1798 at a natural pitch of the Connecticut River. Built to intercept logs, it also blocked the migration of fish, setting a fateful precedent as the first main-stem dam on a major river in North America. Thomas & Thomas bamboo fly rods are made at the intake end of the power canal there, and the Conte lab, two miles down, is not far from a generating station where the canal water spills through turbines and back to the river. Below Thomas & Thomas, a modest cluster of antique industrial structures soon gives way to open ground, forested at the edges, in which the swift current of the canal slows and spreads into something like a lake, flanked by a road but—in the better part of a mile—only a low pair of buildings, the seventeen-million-dollar Conte lab, nestled into the canal's right bank. Named in part for Silvio Conte, the Massachusetts congressman who made it happen, the lab was Boyd Kynard's idea. It was built by the Department of the Interior and modelled on a lab on the Columbia River that is now a parking lot. It was also named for anadromous fish, which live in oceans and spawn in fresh water. Nimbly, all other possibilities have been covered in language that would entertain W. S. Gilbert. If you live in fresh water but go out into the ocean to spawn, you are catadromous. Anadromous means "running up." Catadromous means "running down." If you are anadromous or catadromous, you are also diadromous. And if you're a fish that goes from fresh water to salt water, or salt water to fresh water, to eat or to survive drought but not to procreate, you are amphidromous.

Ordinarily, ichthyologists visit fish. At the Conte lab, it's the other way around. "Without a lab, we could not do experimental work; all we could do was field work," Kynard explained. After shad arrive at Turners Falls, a selected number might go into one of three long concrete flumes that suggest the containment chambers in a nuclear-fuel reprocessing plant. The fish hop uphill and upcurrent in pool-and-weir fishways built of wood and jigsawed into experimental geometries—open Vs, inviting trapezoids. Above each pool—each step of the ladder—is an antenna. The shad are wired and are broadcasting to the antennae, which are related to a computer. Using fly-tying vises, Dr. Alex Haro and Ted Castro-Santos, a graduate student, have bound No. 8 fishhooks to small cylindrical microchip tags in exactly the way you bind bucktail to a shad dart. The microchip rigs resemble shad darts. Haro and Castro-Santos hook them into the back end of the shad's dorsal fins. The shad don't seem to mind, possibly because they are each and all veterans of Holyoke Dam, showing raw spots and missing scales from the thrashing ride in the elevator.

The Ph.D.s on the lab's staff are also adjunct professors at the University of Massachusetts, in Amherst. Alex Haro wrote his doctoral dissertation on American eels, which are not ignored in the anadromous-fish lab, the fact notwithstanding that they are catadromous. Dr. Steve McCormick and Dr. Joe Zydlewski study salt-excreting cells in gills, and the rest of the complex physiology in transitions between river and sea. As one of McCormick's Ph.D. candidates intent on learning how much energy migrating shad burn away as they swim, Jill Leonard developed the laboratory's swimming respirometer—a vertical toroid tube about the size and shape of a truck tire, in which water flows around like river current and can be sped up or slowed down. Built into the respirometer's uppermost arc is a clear-plastic horizontal chamber, sized for one shad, in which the incumbent specimen swims in place under eyeball-to-eyeball scrutiny, taking on whatever current Leonard chooses. She measures, among other things, oxygen depletion— the oxygen requirements of shad at different swimming speeds.

In the natural Connecticut, down through steep woods from the power canal, some of these people fish for shad, in a place they described as uncommon. Site unseen, I made a date to go with Steve McCormick at six-thirty one morning in late May. From my fishing diaries, this is the entry for that day: "Their place is called the Rock Dam, an imposing diabase ledge between the left bank and a large island. In the ledge close to the bank is a narrow gap, like an open door. You can cast a fly line across the confined river as it comes through that slot and drops into a twenty-foot pool. Beyond the pool is a pond eddy. Steve McCormick had to leave at eight. Having caught salmon smolts in Turners Falls and equipped them with acoustic tags, he went off to listen to the salmon in Hartford and beyond. Others from the Conte lab fishing at the Rock Dam this morning were Joe Zydlewski, Joe Kunkel, and Gabe Gries. At one point, as many as nine fishermen were clustered there. Gries is an ecologist who works on juvenile salmon. He caught a shad. Joe Zydlewski took it—he wanted the gills. Joe Kunkel is doing a study with McCormick and Zydlewski to see how gill morphology changes as shad come into the river. I used a fly rod and a spinning rod. I used a flutter spoon. I used darts. I used lead-core leader. I used my brain, to the extent that it was working, and once again I could not get a shad out of the Connecticut River. It's as if I were a rejectee, an alien. The Rock Dam is as tight and intimate as it is natural and beautiful. Everybody else was fishing from dry ground in sneakers, while I was dressed up in neoprene stocking waders, sand guards, L.L. Bean felt-soled boots, and an Orvis vest bearing the orange-and-green emblem of the Delaware River Shad Fishermen's Association. I looked like a hapless astronaut, while these scientists stood on the ledge in their bluejeans, catching shad."


Kynard, as attentive to sturgeons as he is to shad, likes to point out that sturgeons are Cretaceous. That is, the species has existed in the world a hundred million years. This causes him to yawn in the direction of the crossopterygian Coelacanthidae, so-called living fossils (also dating from the Cretaceous) that have turned up rarely in modern seas, inconveniencing Webster's Second International, which describes them as "extinct." Kynard says, "Biologists hunt the world for a coelacanth, and sturgeons are right here. When dinosaurs were walking around in shallow water, they were stepping on sturgeons."

Sturgeons run up to spawn in most American coastal rivers. In Nova Scotia, I have seen them—seven feet long—trapped in shad weirs in the Minas Basin. They inhabit tubs in the Conte lab. The experiments of Erika Henyey, one of Kynard's grad students, are meant to show how they orient to bottom structures in rivers—shortnose sturgeons, Atlantic sturgeons, highly endangered pallid sturgeons. The fish anatomist Willy Bemis, of the University of Massachusetts, has said of Kynard and his graduate students, "He doesn't hang around if they're not good. He's stiff. As a result, it's a distinction to have been trained by him. Moreover, he is the very best field biologist I've ever known. You can go anywhere with Boyd. He'll teach you to observe things you would never have seen by yourself and that other people either aren't able or willing to teach you. The animal sign. The little scrape in a stream. He's a real honest-to-God naturalist. He might not tell you where to fish with a fishing rod, but he'll tell you what you need to know to get started. When you're out there stomping around with him, it's like being out there when you're fourteen."

When Boyd Kynard was fourteen, he fished with a cane pole, "a little short six- or seven-foot cane pole," he says, "which I would go out and cut in the swamps—cut my own cane poles, cure my own cane poles." Sometimes, he cut big ones: "Thirteen, fourteen feet; drying them was a long process, seeing what kind of action they had."

"No reel?"

"No reel. I just pulled fish straight up and out. There was native cane in canebrakes all over the swamps. You pick exactly the kind of pole you want, put eyes on it, and wade out into the oxbows and lower a minnow from the pole."

Kynard does not talk Massachusetts. A shad is not a piece of broken crockery. A bod to him does not suggest a poet. In his adult life, though, he has lived in the Pacific Northwest, in the desert Southwest, and in enough other places so that his phrases emerge in a phonic palimpsest. It takes a while to hear your way through them and into Mississippi.

With a few feet of fixed line on those homemade poles, he was fishing in the meandering rivers of the central part of the state. He fished the Strong, the Yazoo, and, most often, the Pearl. He trapped. He kept snakes in his back yard. The Pearl was two miles from his home, in north Jackson. He would go there on his bicycle. Alone, or with others, he camped there. He was on the river twelve months a year. "It's a serious river. It was the nearest wilderness. The rest of it was farms. Crude farms. Once you got to the Pearl, that was it, there was nobody lived there, it wasn't anything but snakes and alligators and fish and water and trees and swamp." He caught bass, crappies, catfish. There were sturgeons in the Pearl. Paddlefish. Gar. He was fifteen when he hooked his first bowfin.

"Bowfin?"

"Think of a coelacanth. A primitive, voracious fish. Twenty-five to thirty pounds. You'll hook a lot more than you'll ever land. The inside of their mouth is solid bone, with not much to hook onto. Lower a minnow in the oxbows, and my God Almighty you're like five feet away from these fish. You'd be in there with these monster fish, and when they'd grab ahold you weren't sure who had ahold of who." From a canoe, he was lowering a minnow when he attracted that first bowfin. "He weighed at least thirty. I got him up near the surface, and he was running at the boat—right underneath the surface, running right for the boat. All I could do was hold the pole up. His head was like seven inches thick. You're in a canoe and a fish is charging and you wouldn't normally be afraid. But that guy was so big and so aggressive. He bent the rod right under and broke the line. That made me a bowfin fisherman."

"When did it dawn on you that you were never going to leave this field?"

"Quite early. When we moved to Jackson—from Bruce, Mississippi, a small lumber town—I saw my first tropical-fish store. This was 1950. I was twelve. In north Jackson, there were very few stores, but a guy opened a tropical-fish store. We hadn't been there three weeks when he came. The place stood alone—this small, old building, no others around it. I had never known of anybody who had fish in captivity or used fish for anything other than to eat. You know, catch and eat—that's what you did with fish. And here was this little tiny store, like six feet wide and ten feet long. I walked in, and there's these little beautiful fish. I remember thinking, You can buy fish in a store! You gotta be kidding me. You know what I did that summer? I mastered the techniques of not only housing and caring for them but breeding them. I would go down to the pickle factory and get five-gallon pickle jars. I learned to put a kerosene-soaked string around a pickle jar. You light it, and it expands the glass under the string. You just take the top right off. I must have made fifteen or twenty aquariums, and I used them for breeding different pairs. See, I'm so cheap I would buy two fish at the tropical-fish store, and in two months I'd have forty. I was selling them to other kids. I knew a good thing when I saw it."

He bred zebra danios. ("They were my egg-layers.") He bred swordtails, mollies, guppies. He sold them for ten cents apiece, undercutting the tropical-fish man by fifty per cent. This went on for three years. "Ask guys who work with fish for a living if they raised fish when they were young. You can't just look at one and say, 'There's a fish.' You really have to want to get under those fishes' skins. You really have to understand how to make a situation that fish want to breed in. This implies a great deal of understanding, even for zebra danios. I knew when I was in the eighth grade that I wanted to be a biologist."

"Did you eat the fish you caught?"

"Of course. The bowfins were real cottony and had a lot of bones in them. You had to marinate those guys."

Catfish were a whole different thing.

"We would camp out on a beach. There were lots of beautiful sand beaches on the river. You always set out catfish trotlines. Trotlines and Southerners are almost inseparable. We'd put chicken livers and gizzards on there, for channel catfish—oh, goodness! We had the fire going. When we'd catch 'em, we'd skin 'em down, fillet 'em, throw 'em right there on the fire—I mean the fish was not even fifteen minutes out of the water, and if you've eaten fish like that it's a whole different thing. We'd just do that all night."

When he was seventeen, he became a Y-camp counsellor, on the swiftly flowing Strong River, where he taught canoeing, camping, tree identification, and survival skills, and led overnight canoe trips twenty miles down the Strong to its junction with the Pearl, and fifteen more down the slower, wider Pearl. There "your attention switched to catfish." Five miles below the junction was an immense limestone outcrop ("with layers of quartzite, white and crystalline") that knocked the river right back where it came from—bent it around like the head of a paper clip. At the curve, opposite the outcrop, was the steepest sandbar he would ever see—"as vertical a sandbar as you can pile up sand." The water in the curve was "probably forty or fifty feet deep." Kynard and the others were in fifteen-foot Grumman canoes—a hundred per cent aluminum from their molded seats and machined thwarts to their flotation chambers. Traversing the deep curve, Kynard and the others heard an unearthly, weird sound. The air was still, the current silent, but out of somewhere—what else but the river?—came deep down-register tones, halfway across the scale between bull and bullfrog. They camped on top of the outcrop. Kynard took a Grumman, went out, and heard the sound again. He decided that it was coming through the water, and that it was being picked up and amplified by the flotation chambers—in effect, sealed drums—in the bow and stern of the canoe. After he had crossed the deep curve, the sound was gone. He turned around, went back, and heard it again. He gave some thought to bowfin, but more to catfish. "I know catfish make sounds. They have a bone that they rub against their air bladder. You can take a channel catfish out of water, and he'll sit there making sounds. I, of course, had brought my trotlines. I baited them with chicken parts, and caught two of the biggest catfish I'd ever seen. That must have been some concentration of fish." For years, in Grumman canoes, he listened in other places. Nowhere but in that one place has he ever heard the catfish chorus.

After three years in the Marine Corps, Kynard majored in English at Millsaps College, Jackson, and double-majored in biology. A moment was fast arriving when, as a biologist, he would have to decide between fish and mammals. It was not a long moment. "Fish lend themselves to getting up close and personal," he says. "I want to be able to understand as closely as I can what's going on with these guys. Fish—because of their limited sensory ability and limited ability to get away from you—would lend themselves to an up-close-and-personal approach more than, say, a beaver would."

His choice was reinforced by eighteen postgraduate months at the Gulf Coast Research Laboratory, in Ocean Springs, Mississippi. During this period, he married Janice Ray, whom he had met at Millsaps. (Their daughter, Kari, is a journalist. Their son, Brian, is a field technician at the Conte lab.) After Ocean Springs, Kynard went into a master's program at Mississippi State, where he worked on the behavior of mosquito fish and their physiological resistance to DDT. Somewhere along the line, he came upon a book called "Behavioral Aspects of Ecology," by Peter Klopfer, found himself reading the whole of it in one night, and decided that behavior was going to be his field. "I was ready to be imprinted."

Imprinted and advised. His "major professor," a herpetologist who happened to come from Oregon, said to him, "Boyd, you're interested in evolution, and individuals, and behavior. You're not going to be able to find that in the South. I think you've got to get out."

Kynard studied journals to see who was doing what on the behavioral ecology of fish. The field seemed to be concentrated in Honolulu, Miami, and Seattle. The School of Fisheries at the University of Washington was the largest and oldest in the United States. Kynard spent five and a half years there, completing a doctoral dissertation on the behavioral ecology of the threespine stickleback. He did his field work in a kayak on a glacial lake in the foothills of the eastern Cascades. He had a microscope, preserving jars, and other lab equipment in the kayak. He had covered the deck with a small platform he could lie on. After observing a fish long enough to note any idiosyncrasies, he would "collect him and collect his nest."

Within six years, he was a tenured professor at the University of Arizona, in Tucson, where he created the undergraduate fisheries program and developed a strong ambition to establish a desert-fish institute. Arizona was not interested. In 1978, ignoring his tenure, he joined the United States Fish and Wildlife Service, and was assigned to a unit in Massachusetts attached to the state university. He had never seen a shad. He was there to work in marine fisheries, but after he saw a shad he transferred into migratory fish. His work on shad and sturgeon has ranged, for the most part, between northern Connecticut and southern Vermont, but has led him in related ways to China, Brazil, Romania, Puerto Rico, and most shad rivers on the two sides of North America. In interior Puerto Rico, where flash floods—"flashy beyond belief"—can turn a stream into frothing "liquid mud," various fish have developed an ability to go back and forth from fresh to salt as often and as rapidly as they need to. In Pennsylvania and Maryland, Kynard helped the shad specialist Richard St. Pierre work out the restoration program that has to make its way through four huge dams in the Susquehanna River. As a representative of the United States government, he has worked with "high-level conservation officials" in China to illuminate the life histories of migrating Chinese fish. His research in Brazil has been similar. Willy Bemis has said, "When most people are confronted with new environments, their eyes glaze over. It's all too much for a while. My impression is that Boyd goes into a new environment and begins making original observations immediately."

Kynard is the only American in the Danube Delta Research Institute. When I went shad fishing with him in South Hadley in May, 1999, he was still feeling traces of jet lag after flying home from Romania. Carrying 55–75-kilohertz hydrophones, he had spent three weeks tracking sturgeon up the Danube, with Dr. Radu Suciu and a three-man Romanian support team. Kynard was the river pilot. It was his boat. He had bought it in Arkansas and shipped it to Romania in a forty-five-foot box. The Romanians named it Sam, because it came from America. It had a seventy-five-horsepower outboard motor. Telling me some of this as he stood in the Connecticut that morning casting darts for shad, he said, "All my trips come back with some kinds of stories; they just don't include a war."

Above river kilometre 130 is a zone of intense commercial fishing on the Danube, a drift gill-net fishery, where Kynard and company picked up—mainly from Gypsy fishermen—forty-four sturgeons on the spawning run. They were stellate sturgeons, averaging four and a half feet in length and fifteen to thirty pounds. In addition to fitting them with ultrasonic telemetry tags, it was highly advisable to get them out of the heaviest commercial gill-netting zone before releasing them back into the river. On Sam, which was six feet wide and twenty feet long, they could carry only six of the big fish at a time. They made a canvas sling, pinched it off at the two ends like a brioche, rigged it to a twelve-volt pump that kept water in it, slung it from gunwale to gunwale, and carried six sturgeons upstream to river kilometre 178. They turned around and went back for more. When it was time for lunch, they ate green onions, feta, salami, bread, and jam. The Danube there is the border between Romania and Ukraine. They made the seven round trips in two days. When it was time for dinner, they ate green onions, feta, salami, bread, and jam. A hundred miles up the Danube from the Black Sea, all forty-four wired sturgeons went back into the river and most took off upstream. Kynard and the Romanians had no idea where stellates spawn in the Danube. Their purpose was to find out.

Going up the river, they stopped at one-kilometre intervals and put the hydrophones over the side. The hydrophones, with their long arms, were like boom mikes on a movie stage. There was no sound from the sturgeons. Kynard heard only the soft rustle of sediment moving in the river. A 0–1,000-hertz hydrophone is so sensitive that it can hear sand grains in motion, even in very quietly moving water, as Kynard would demonstrate to Willy Bemis, me, and others one day in Willy's boat in the Holyoke Pool. A relaxing and soothing sound, not unlike the recorded surf played above the cribs of infants, it was audible geomorphology—you were listening to mountains on their way to the sea. The sound is the signature of rivers, Kynard said. The Danube's differs from the Yangtze's, the Yangtze's from the Connecticut's. He had never heard the Yukon River. With its great load of glacial flour—jagged particles of fresh-ground rock—the Yukon would sound like a chain saw.

At the Danube River's kilometre 250, he had not caught up with the sturgeons. Before long, the Danube, having crossed eastern Romania, became the boundary between Romania and Bulgaria. At river kilometre 500, he had still not heard the sturgeons, nor at 600. The Danube is a braided river, full of islands, and Sam the fishing boat tracked all channels and both sides of islands as well as the left and right banks. In all, Kynard figures, he tracked about fifteen hundred kilometres, stopping once a kilometre to listen for the fish. Kynard and company camped out all the way. Each morning for breakfast, they had green onions, feta, salami, bread, and jam.

This was at the height of the 1998–99 Kosovo war, when the North Atlantic Treaty Organization was bombing Serbia intensely. Danube kilometre 830 is the Serbian border. On the east side of the river, Romania continues, but on the west side Bulgaria ends and Serbia begins. When Sam had progressed as far as Calafat (Romania) and Vidin (Bulgaria), which flank the Danube at kilometre 815, the hydrophones had still heard nothing from the sturgeons' acoustic tags. Spawning sturgeons swim side by side in pairs. In Kynard's words, "They have a form of communication that is probably tactile." The male has a large anal fin, which cups the milt. The milt and the caviar are blended by the current. Ichthyologists would not call the eggs caviar. A single female sturgeon may carry a million five hundred thousand eggs. Sturgeons engaged in sex and simultaneously broadcasting to hydrophones will outbolero "Bolero."

As the boat had come ever nearer to Serbia, other traffic had diminished on the river. Along the Bulgarian side were towers, in which were guards equipped with machine guns and telescopes. "The Bulgarians were not happy about the hydrophones on their side of the river." When the guards reached for the telescopes, it was not clear—from the water—if they were reaching for the telescopes or the guns. Sam had a cabin enclosure and looked pretty much like a fishing boat, but Kynard, in earphones sitting by a receiver with a hydrophone shaft sticking out a window into the water, created a somewhat martial impression. In a specialized way, he had become known up and down the Danube, but not to these Bulgarian tower guards. Even the Hungarians, isolated by dams and far to the north, were aware of his Romanian project. They had asked him to come to Hungary and track the sterlet sturgeon, a freshwater species, because sterlet is good caviar. Kaluga sturgeon, pallid sturgeon—there are numerous species of sturgeon and four genuses, three of which are subjects of studies by Kynard. See Bemis, W. E., and B. Kynard (1997), "Sturgeon Rivers: An Introduction to Acipenseriform Biogeography and Life History," *Environmental Biology of Fishes* 48:167–183. The acipenseriform sturgeons are the most typical and common: in North America, the shortnose, Atlantic, lake, white, and green; the sevruga and beluga in, for example, the Black and Caspian Seas. At Galati, on the Romanian Danube, Kynard spoke at a 1998 symposium involving all the Danube countries. He advocated a Danube River compact for sturgeon conservation.

In Calafat and Vidin in May, 1999, there was not much going for the compact. The Romanian border military at Calafat told Kynard and company not to proceed, and made them sign a paper stating, in effect, their awareness that NATO was attacking more than fish. They pushed on. Kynard listened to the water, hearing nothing. As the boat drew closer to the Serbian border, absolutely all other activity disappeared. More kilometres, more silence. They kept going, and stopping to listen. "The river was deserted. There were no boats—zero. It was a war zone." They kept going, and stopping to listen, until they heard bombs.

Emplaced in bedrock between Romania and Serbia, at river kilometre 985, is a dam called Iron Gate II. Nothing swims past it. Having failed to catch up with his forty-four sturgeons, Kynard decided that they might have gone on to spawn at the dam. He speculates, "Maybe all sturgeon-spawning in the Danube is in Serbia, because they spawn over rocky bottoms, from gravel upward. Basically, the war stopped me from finding out."

# THREE

# AMENDING NATURE

On the Pamunkey River, in earliest Virginia, a cockarouse was any Pamunkey who could wade into the river and cinch a noose over a sturgeon's tail, and then hang on, even if the sturgeon hauled him under water, and ultimately bring the fish to the riverbank. Atlantic sturgeon in the Pamunkey River were eight feet long. They came up in spring with the run of shad.

The tribe numbered a thousand then. Sixty live on the Pamunkey reservation now—twelve hundred acres in an oxbow bend of the river, in the tidewater plain not far from Richmond. They slow-cook shad in two sheets of foil, six hours at two hundred and fifty degrees, dissolving the smaller bones. They scramble shad roe in their scrambling eggs—a whole set of roe with two eggs. Season it with salt and pepper only. Mix it well, and fry it. You leave Rose Garden on Route 113 and go southwest five or six miles through a network of small roads with names like Powhatan Trail and Pocahontas Trail. You pass near Powhatan's grave. It is not known if Powhatan ever was a cockarouse or how he liked his shad. His brother Opechancanoe was the leader of the Pamunkey tribe, while Powhatan ruled over many peoples as a kind of tyrant king. Powhatan was described as a tall, well-proportioned man with a sour look, and he presided over the Powhatan Confederacy—among whose thirty-odd tribes the Pamunkeys were the largest and most powerful. At night, he posted four tall guards at the corners of his house, with orders to call out to each other—one to the next one, round and round—while he slept. And while his daughter Pocahontas slept. English colonials named the river York, but the Pamunkeys rejected the idea and have gone on rejecting it for several centuries—the Pamunkey becomes the York only in its last thirty miles. (The Powhatan River, a little south, became the James.) In 1614, Pocahontas was baptized Rebecca in order to marry the colonist John Rolfe. He took Rebecca home to England. She met King James and Queen Anne. Rebecca died in Gravesend at the age of twenty-two.

Her name Pocahontas lives on among women of her tribe, whose houses range from suburban brick colonials with two-car garages to wooden places that seem run-down, rural, and old. They are spread among fields of cotton, running to the river's edge. The Pamunkeys' seventeenth-century treaty with the colonial government of Virginia stated that the tribe was to "enjoy their wonted conveniences of oystering, fishing and gathering tuccahoe, curtenemons, wildoats, rushes, puckone, or anything else for their natural support, not useful to the English . . ." Evidently not useful to the English was the American shad. By the nineteenth century, the spring migration had become a commercial asset for the natives as well as a subsistence resource. Shad became so significant in the tribal economy that—in 1918—the Pamunkeys set up a shad hatchery "to put fish back into the river." This was foresight on a Nostradamian scale. For something like seven decades while runs declined in East Coast rivers for various reasons, including stream pollution and ocean intercept fisheries (commercial boats offshore), shad continued to flourish in the Pamunkey River. Toward the end of the twentieth century, Maryland closed its waters of the Chesapeake Bay to shad fishing, and soon the Potomac and all rivers farther down in Virginia were closed as well, with the exception of tribal subsistence fishing in the Pamunkey. Alarmed by the declines in neighboring rivers, the Pamunkeys tore down the original hatchery and built a much larger one.

It is a plain gray building on pilings—a long dock behind it, reaching into the quiet current of a meander bend. This was an October day, off-season—I was stopping by on my way to Norfolk—and no one was there. Ivy Bradley soon arrived in his pickup—a tall, whitish-haired, strong-looking man who had lived on the reservation all his life and was among the managers of the hatchery. Retired, he had long commuted to Richmond, where he installed sprinkler systems in large new buildings. He said that when the shad come up the river he and the others go out in johnboats with drift nets six hundred feet long.

The river is about a quarter of a mile wide, thirty to forty feet deep. They have six boats, fifteen nets, all working at once. They fish a mile of the river, going both ways with the ebb and the flow. The salt line is far downriver but the fresh waters around the reservation are pushed up and pulled down by the ocean tides. Shad are milling when they spawn, in early to late evening, so that is when the boats are out and the nets are in the river—over the spawning beds of Lester Manor Reach, of Docks Island Reach, of Rockahock Reach, of Lay Landing Reach. In a very good session, Ivy Bradley said, the nets will trap eighty female spawners. "When the tide stops, and the net is vertical, that's when the most fish are caught."

They strip the fish right there in the boats, pinching the body behind the head and sliding their fingers toward the anus as if they are squeezing pastry from tubes. In this way, they draw roe and milt, and they admix the two in a plastic bucket. The milt is so white it looks like crème anglaise. The roe is often likened to applesauce. They bring the buckets to the hatchery and let them stand for an hour. The mixture swells, as the barely visible eggs become diaphanous amber pearls. Three litres—a hundred thousand eggs—go into hatching jars on the sides of tanks. Four days later, sac fry appear and fall into the tanks, where they absorb their sacs and are then fed microscopic shrimp. On any given day in spring, the hatchery is nurturing two and a half million shad, he said—in all, about seven million in the eight-week season. Their survival rate indoors is at least twenty times what it would be in the river. They live in the tanks seventeen days, and are now and again "dyed" or "marked" with tetracycline, which is absorbed in calcium structures, notably the hard calcareous bodies known as otoliths, in the shads' inner ears. Otoliths have daily growth rings, so you can write on them a kind of bar code with tetracycline, and if you know how to read the otolith you can tell, among other things, where a shad comes from and the day on which it was born. At the age of three weeks, Bradley told me, the fry are released through the bottoms of the tanks and descend through pipes to the Pamunkey River.

I asked him if he ate shad roe. "Salted real good," he said. "And wrapped in bacon. And wrapped in wax paper. Deep fried."

The first time I had seen sexual secretions expressed from the bodies of captured shad was years before at Smithfield Beach, on the Pennsylvania side of the Delaware River, just above Tocks Island. This was below the Kittatinny ridge and near the improbable gap where the river has severed the spine of the deformed Appalachians—a scene that inspired some of the finest work of the so-called Hudson River School. But shad spawn at night, the johnboats were lighted by twelve-volt batteries, and all was dark above the trees. Under the eye of Richard St. Pierre, of the U.S. Fish and Wildlife Service, a team of biologists hung gill nets in the river, all parallel to the current—eleven six-foot-high nets, each two hundred feet long. Placed at several distances from shore and held up by floats, they resembled lanes for racing shells. Because spawning shad go back and forth crosscurrent while other fish are travelling upstream and down, these axial underwater fences select the shad. From time to time, we went out in the johnboats to pick the nets, where the lanes zigged and zagged from the pressure of fish. They were dumped into tubs of clear water, which was quickly reddened by their damaged gills. The Delaware teems with fish of countless species. In four hours, we collected one catfish, one sucker, and sixty American shad.

Ashore, under floodlights, the roe shad were squeezed over bowls, which rapidly accumulated the pulsing jets of eggs. After the eggs stopped coming, the fish were tossed into a large waste receptacle. In the paired ovaries of a big female shad—her roe sacs—there might be three hundred thousand eggs. Rare specimens have carried twice that, and the average is a quarter of a million. There at Smithfield Beach, if a fish was "green" and nothing came forth when she was stripped, she went into the receptacle. A fish whose eggs have not ripened is known as a green roe, a green fish, a hard shad. Eggs ripen outward from the innermost part of the roe sac. The ripe eggs pass through a tube along the sac that leads to the anus. The roe shad spawns when she is ready. Spawning takes place in different places across a sequence of nights, while the sacs progressively ripen and deplete. So even a "good ripe fish"—being stripped by human hands—would yield little more than forty thousand eggs, and the rest, with the mother, went into the can. The plan, St. Pierre said, was "to shoot for a million eggs"—in the season, ten million eggs in ten nights of stripping. The aim of this annual endeavor was—courtesy of the Delaware— to revive the run in the Susquehanna River.

The buck shad are always ripe, like buck rabbits and buck fruit flies, not to mention other species close to home. One buck shad could fertilize the river, or so it seems, as his white stream goes over the eggs in the bowl. Stir with index finger. Each egg has a microscopic aperture. One sperm enters, and the aperture seals.

As the eggs swelled up golden, and clear as glass beads, St. Pierre said, "Applesauce turns to pearls. If they're white, they're dead, and if they're red they're no good." For an hour, the bowls were immersed in floating tubs designed to bathe the eggs gently in flow from the river.

I asked him to what extent the spring migration is affected by people who take shad from the river. At the time, in the Delaware, commercial fishing was taking fifty thousand shad, sport fishermen were keeping about sixteen thousand shad (and damaging a very large unknown number), and biologists were removing fifteen hundred.

"If fifty per cent of the run make it to spawning, you're o.k.," he said.

"Do they spawn in tributaries?"

"Large ones, yes. If it looks like a mountain trout stream, no. If it's broad and sluggish, yes. Generally, shad are main-stem spawners. Everything about them is temperature-controlled—when they move, when they stop, when they spawn, where they go, when they strike and don't strike."

They like to spawn over gravels and sands, in four to eight feet of water moving less than a foot a second. As they spawn, the males, at the surface, are splashing. They spread their cloud of milt around the emerging eggs. When fertilized and swollen, the eggs are slightly denser than water. Slowly, they sink. On the bottom, they roll along, bounce along, for several days—the time depending, as ever, on temperature—before sac fry emerge, and soon become larval shad.

Salmon, after homing to their natal rivers, do not copulate just anywhere, as shad seem to by comparison. Salmon go back to the exact spot where they were born, and move rocks around in order to protect their eggs in fortresses called redds. While shad hatch in a few days, salmon eggs, buried under gravel, stay in the redd all winter and hatch the following spring. Larval salmon stay in the redd. Moreover, young salmon stay around their birthplace for two years before taking off for the sea—plenty of time for detailed imprinting. Shad come down from the Gulf of Maine, and find the right river, but they do not form close identification with one place in the river. If a salmon was born in a hatchery, as a returning adult it will climb a fish ladder trying to get back into the hatchery.

Shad larvae, in their millions, darken the river and look like one-inch eels. Minnows eat them. Shiners eat them. Ninety per cent of fish in the river eat shad, and ninety per cent of what's in other fishes' stomachs will be larval shad. "After thirty to forty days, they go through metamorphosis and look like fish-shaped animals," St. Pierre said. Fish-shaped animals look even more delicious than one-inch eels.

I asked St. Pierre what sort of diseases he had encountered in studying the species.

He said, "We have never found a disease in a wild shad. But remember, we're trained to look for trout diseases. We've never found a trout disease in a shad."

His degree in fisheries science was from the University of Virginia, and he went into the science as a direct result of the fishing and scuba diving he did as a kid in Florida. Trim, six feet, he had closely cut hair, an intent narrow face, a soft low voice and contemplative manner. He had arrived early at Smithfield Beach and had fished with a hook and line until seven. When he works in other rivers, he takes his six-pound test and ultra-light. Below Troy and Albany, the mile-wide Hudson can look hopeless for fishing from the bank, but it failed to intimidate St. Pierre. "They don't know what they've got," he said. Across the river from Catskill, he fished one evening from a ferry dock, where, despite the great breadth of water, sufficient current ran close to the eastern shore. Using a big dart for a long cast, he caught a nine-pound, nine-ounce roe shad. It was twenty-eight inches long and twenty-eight inches in maximum circumference. It was somewhat heavier than the New York record shad. But St. Pierre is "not into that sort of thing" and did not report it.

Soon after midnight at Smithfield Beach, the last of more than a million eggs went into a plastic bag and were ready for shipment. There were five bags, each with five litres of eggs, and a college kid in a station wagon took off with them for Thompsontown, on the Juniata River. There are nine shad hatcheries in the United States, and Pennsylvania's is in Thompsontown, where people would be waiting when the eggs arrived at four in the morning. Incubated at sixty degrees, they would hatch in six days. Two-thirds of the young shad would be stocked in the Juniata, a major tributary of the Susquehanna, and the remaining third would go to Conowingo, the first dam above the Chesapeake Bay. If you are trying to re-store American shad in a depleted river system, there is no better way to do it. In the nineteen-eighties, an attempt was made to plant adult shad from the Hudson River in the uppermost Susque-hanna, near Tunkhannock, Pennsylvania, and Owego, New York. In two days, the fish were out of the Susquehanna, swimming two hundred miles and tumbling down the spillways of four dams. "We've seen fish move a hundred miles a day in the Susquehanna in the wrong direction," St. Pierre acknowledges. "If you put an adult shad in a strange river, the fish knows it's in the wrong place and takes off. It just boogies."

St. Pierre has sent eggs to Thompsontown from places a great deal more distant than Smithfield Beach. For example, the Colum-bia River. To help meet the voracious requirements of the Susque-hanna shad rehabilitation program, he has FedExed eggs from the West Coast to Pennsylvania. Something like five million shad come up the Columbia in spring, the largest shad run anywhere. They go a hundred and forty-six miles upstream before they encounter one of the world's largest concrete structures. They stop to think it over. They have been likened to a crowd waiting for an escalator, which, literally, a lot of them are. The ladders at Bonneville Dam can accommodate more than a hundred thousand shad a day, and one or two million go on to spawn upstream. The majority spawns below Bonneville, and shad fishermen are all but shoulder to shoulder among the big boulders on the tailrace side, casting heavy darts on eight-pound test into the ten-mile current. Every so often a fly fisherman appears and stands off downstream, where the backcasting of his dense ten-weight sinking line won't attract a lawyer.

The American shad does not derive from these American waters. The species originated in the rivers of eastern North America, and first appeared in the West in 1871, two years after completion of the transcontinental railroad, when Seth Green, of the New York Fish Commission, came over the Sierra Nevada by train with four milk cans full of baby shad from the Hudson River. Seth Green could cast a dry fly a hundred feet. An aquacultural pioneer, he was in his fifth season of hatching shad. He had worried the fish across the continent, trying to keep their environment healthy. In Chicago, he tried the drinking water and found it too oily. Chicago water, though, had Omaha water beat to death. In Omaha, Seth Green filled a bucket with water and poured it into another bucket, then poured it back, and poured again—bucket to bucket—until he had oxygenated and purified the water. On he went, five years before Little Bighorn, through the homeland of Cheyenne and Sioux, where a heat wave was hostile to the shad. The train carried ice cut in winter. Gently, gingerly, his fingers turning red, Seth Green flicked ice water into the milk cans, keeping temperatures down around eighty degrees. Two thousand shad died, but ten thousand made it to Sacramento, and by stagecoach up the Sacramento River a hundred and fifty miles to Tehama, where Green let them go.

He liked their chances in all environmental respects but one.

There was something alarming about thousands of millions of cubic yards of the Sierra Nevada being flushed off the mountains by giant nozzles working gold. The ocean was brown at the Golden Gate. Enough material was going into the Yuba River to fill the Erie Canal. Washed-down rock, gravel, sand, and mud choked the American River. The American and the Yuba were tributaries of the Sacramento River. The mining detritus had raised the Sacramento seven feet. Seth Green planted the fry in the Sacramento. He reported to the New York commission: "I can only say that if they do not have shad in the Pacific Ocean there will be but one cause, the roily water, caused by washing the mountains down for gold. However, I think the fish will get through all right." Shad deal well with turbidity. The shad would make it. They'd be back in four years. A reward was posted—fifty dollars!—for the first adult shad caught in California. According to Volume I of the "Bulletin of the United States Fish Commission" (1881), Baltimore Harry caught the first shad.

Baltimore Harry's fish had come home to California, but by no means did all the transplants behave in the traditional way. They spread out. They rapidly invaded other rivers. They not only went up the Feather, the Yuba, the American, the Mokelumne, the San Joaquin, they also went up coastal rivers far from the Golden Gate. They went up the Russian, the Eel, the Klamath, the Trinity. In the words of the 1887 Report of the Commissioner, United States Commission of Fish and Fisheries, they upended the "dictum of fish-culture that fish plants in a river would return to it when mature for the purpose of spawning." Actually, one or two per cent of Eastern shad stray to other rivers, and a similar small percentage began the expansion in the West. Gradually, they spread south to and beyond San Diego and north to the Rogue, the Siuslaw, the Coos, the Umpqua, the Millicoma. They went up the Columbia (where they were also transplanted, in 1885). They went into Puget Sound. In Canada, they went up the Fraser River. They found the Alaskan archipelago. Eventually, they established home rivers in Siberia. Maybe they were looking for the Hudson. Less than fifty years after Seth Green crossed the continent with his milk cans in the train, an annual six million pounds of shad were being commercially landed in California.

The species took longer to attract Western anglers, but the sport accelerated in the years that followed the Second World War. About the first place that shad see a shad dart after coming through the San Francisco bays and into the Sacramento River is at the Minnow Hole—five hundred yards of the Sacramento River near the Sacramento Zoo. Most anglers are fishing from the shore there. Roughly one in four is in a boat. Collectively, in an average season, they might catch about forty thousand shad, half the number caught by anglers in the whole of the Sacramento River. They kill and keep ninety per cent.

Shad anglers from the East Coast are struck speechless when they encounter these Western numbers. Three million shad coming in at San Francisco! Five million shad on their way to Bonneville Dam! To find that many shad in the Delaware River you'd have to turn time back a century and more. On the Willamette River in Portland, they see boats side by side from one bank to the other. This is known as a hog line, according to Lenox Dick in his West Coast primer, "Experience the World of Shad Fishing" (Frank Amato Publications, Portland, 1996). Travelling East Coast shad fishermen have taken pictures of hog lines in Oregon and later shown them breathlessly—and a little wickedly—to Armand Charest at his shad-dart stand in Holyoke.

Lenox Dick is an M.D. who lives in Vancouver, Washington, and does most of his shad fishing in a boat in front of his house. The Columbia River is a mile wide there, but the channel is close to the Washington bank. Sometimes his Labrador retriever, for the sheer sport of it, swims in place beside the boat—a strenuous standoff with a mighty current. During the 2002 migration, I fished there with Dr. Dick and his friend Paul Johnston, an all-seasons, all-species Columbia River fisherman to whom the doctor—his shad book notwithstanding—deferred. To get down three fathoms in that current and flap something past the noses of shad, Johnston used a rig out of Rube Goldberg by Alexander Calder. It involved a swivel on one end of a drop line and, on the other end, a lead sphere about the size of a cherry tomato. His main line went through the swivel, which could slide up and down but was blocked by another swivel, from which his leader led to a small dart with a flexible tail of sparkling plastic. He called this mobile a "slider rig," and summarized it, saying, "Your main line goes through your drop." In the turbid river under gray cloud in morning rain, the shad were up in the water column and the lure seemed to be below them. They were within reach of the fly line I· was using, with its long sink-tip and lead-core leader. When the sun came out in the afternoon, the shad descended—right into Johnston's slider rig, one after another and another. To my surprise, they were twenty to thirty per cent smaller than Delaware River shad.

Tall and rangy, Lenox Dick had once been a medical missionary in Africa, had long practiced in Portland, and was now eighty-six years old. The next morning, he and I drove east up the Columbia Gorge and stopped off at Bonneville Dam. Nearly half a mile of fishermen, of two sexes and four colors, were lined up below the tailrace. Many were using poles ten feet long. We made our way down the riprap basalt to the edge of the surging river. With seven-foot rods, six-pound test, and split shot larger than chick-peas, we made some long heaves. Dr. Dick hung up his dart on his first cast. He tied on another, and soon was cursing a new snag. However, as he put it later, "the snag took off." We fished there only half an hour, but I had some snags that took off, too. In the Columbia River at Bonneville Dam, Dr. Dick and I were catching shad. We also watched them swimming past picture windows in an indoor amphitheater at the top of the Bonneville ladders. They had climbed sixty feet.

We crossed into Oregon and went up the Deschutes River, where he has a shack on the left bank, approachable only on foot or by boat. The Deschutes, in its canyon, describes itself in flights of white water. The river at the time was exceptionally high. After loading up a McKenzie boat with piles of gear, Dr. Dick at the oars fought across at an angle and then continued upstream, muttering all the while about his failing strength now that he's in sight of ninety. I'm not a trout fisherman, not a dry-fly fisherman, anywhere, let alone in a big Western river crowded with brush, deep near the edge, and racing wall-to-wall. Author, also, of "The Art and Science of Fly Fishing" (Amato, Portland, 1993), Dr. Dick was full of tactical and tactful suggestions. He teaches the subject to organized groups. Thanks to him, I caught five rainbows. A day or two later, he left for Wyoming to fish the Green River. In three weeks, he was off to Iceland in pursuit of Atlantic salmon. Fish or no fish, when I grow up I want to be like him.

In Oregon's storied Umpqua River, shad come in after the steelhead run, like ninth-inning pitchers coming in to finish. In the Russian River, in California, fly fishermen make their way upstream from the Hilton pool to the Summerhome Park pool, as Carl Ludeman once did, to cast for shad with a red-white-and-silver fly of his invention, known today as the Ludeman Shad Fly. Using a No. 22 Ludeman fly, a really brilliant caster can hook and land a five-pound shad. A 22 hook is the size used by fly tiers on which to imitate a mosquito.

Bump-net shad fishing developed in the California delta, and has not been adopted by the rest of the world. The California delta itself is a rare phenomenon. It is the common delta of two big rivers—the Sacramento and the San Joaquin. Moreover, it has formed in the Great Central Valley, in the middle of California,

and discharges its flow into the San Francisco bays. Of world rivers
with common deltas, there seem to be no more than the Kennebec
and the Androscoggin, the Ganges and the Brahmaputra, the
Tigris and the Euphrates, the Sacramento and the San Joaquin.
The deltaic landscape—west of Lodi, east of Pittsburg, thirty miles
south of Sacramento—is a polderland of high dikes and low or-
chards, where you look up at big ships sliding by above the trees. If
you were driving on the dikes, you looked down over fields of corn,
fields of asparagus, fields darkened by multitudes of sandhill
cranes. You passed Chinese towns with false-front stores. You
passed Al the Wop's restaurant and bar, famous for its steak with
peanut butter. In this milieu, someone figured out that a slowly
moving boat could be much like a pregnant shad. With nets made
of chicken wire on long handles, bumpers went out in small out-
boards, notably on the North Fork of the Mokelumne River off
Dead Horse Island and Staten Island, not far from where the
Mokelumne joins the San Joaquin. When shad spawn, they will often swim high in the water, breaking the surface in a movement
known as washing. Males will sometimes turn and butt the females, possibly to help express some eggs. Among the bumpers of
the California delta, this process was not ignored. The wash of a
slowly turning prop attracted shad. The long-handled, stiff nets
were held in the water near the wash. Buck shad came along and
bumped the net. They thought the boat was a roe shad. They were
spawning with the boat. The person on the handle had about a
tenth of a second to react perfectly and flip the fish aboard. Not as
many people are as good at it now, but at the meridian of bump-
net shad fishing they caught, in a season, ten thousand shad.

Shad fishing is good in the Yuba River, the American River, the
Feather River, with darts, spoons, or flies, and even naked flashing
hooks. Going up the Yuba River the shad run is blocked by Da-
guerre Point Dam. In the American River the shad run is blocked
by Nimbus Dam, in the Sacramento by Red Bluff Diversion Dam,

in the San Joaquin by Mendota Dam. In the Feather River, the shad run stops at a fish barrier close to Oroville Dam.

Driven by desire to place their offspring as far upstream as they are able to, the shad that migrate by ladder into Columbia waters above Bonneville Dam are looking up a river that is further plugged by The Dalles Dam, John Day Dam, McNary Dam, Chief Joseph Dam, Grand Coulee Dam.

In major rivers of East Coast America, the migrations are blocked by seventy-eight dams. The first ones up from the ocean tend to concentrate shad fishing, as in New England at Holyoke Dam. The Hudson, drowned in its fjord to Albany, is dammed at Troy, and the migration piles up there. The Susquehanna is blocked ten miles from its mouth and shad fishing is illegal in the Susquehanna. Alone, as noted, is the Delaware, with its two hundred miles of shad fishing above tidewater at Trenton. In several places, there are wing dams, also called pier dams—walls that reach into the river from the two sides but don't meet. Angled downstream, they concentrate and deepen the channel, and were built in the nineteenth century to help float rafts of logs. High in Catskill tributaries are three dams built to enhance New York City's water system, but from mile 1, at Hancock, New York, to the sea buoy at Lewes, Delaware, the river flows free. When you come home to the Delaware from the confines of other rivers, you feel a patent sense of relief as you move about in the absence of dams.

For some years, shad were picked up below Conowingo Dam, in the Susquehanna River, and put in trucks full of water that was swirling in circles to create in the fish a sense that they were migrating inside the truck. And they were. They rode fifty-eight miles, passing four dams, and were let back into the river. This was known as trap-and-transport. There were as many as ten trucks. One year, they carried fifty-six thousand shad. The Susquehanna dams now have elevators.

On the Rappahannock River, in Virginia, brigades carry shad

in buckets from tailrace to pool around Embrey Dam. In April, 2000, Virginia's United States Senators—John Warner and Charles Robb—were among some fifty people carrying the buckets. They were there to help proclaim the imminent removal of Embrey Dam at a cost to the federal government of ten million dollars, opening a hundred and seventy miles of spawning ground in the Rappahannock's main stem and tributaries, such as the Rapidan. The fifty-odd people in the bucket brigade carried twelve American shad around the dam. You have to start somewhere. Senator Warner was wearing a fishing vest. His own.

Toward the end of the twentieth century, the once unthinkable notion of destroying dams went through a surprisingly swift trajectory from the quixotic to the feasible. As I began collecting material on this one anadromous species, and became ever more aware of historic migrations and the extent to which they had been stifled, reduced, or absolutely cut off, the most obvious of solutions never seriously occurred to me: Get rid of the dam. What had seemed unthinkable, however, rapidly arose as a groundswell of voices, all across the country, calling for the riddance of dams. After the federal government ordered the destruction of a significant dam in the capital of Maine—at the head of tidewater, in a nationally venerated river, restoring spawning grounds above—I decided to go up there and watch the dam go out, and return soon afterward to the rejuvenated river.

# FOUR

# FAREWELL TO
# THE NINETEENTH CENTURY

With John McPhedran, I carried a canoe around a ballfield in Waterville, Maine, and on into woods. The terrain fell away there sharply. The boat was heavy but its skin was indestructible, and we dragged it, bumping on roots. So much for the loving care reserved for canvas, bark, and Kevlar canoes. This one had no need of it. Its makers promote its type with pictures that show one being thrown off the roof of their factory in Old Town. So we twitched it downhill like a log. On the threshold of the year 2000, this was just one of the countless ways of saying farewell to the nineteenth century.

A few days earlier, we would not have had to choose a model so tough. We put it into Messalonskee Stream, which carried us into the Kennebec River, which, in this stretch, had suddenly lost about five million tons of water as a result of deliberate demolition. Fifteen miles downstream, in Augusta, Edwards Dam, two stories high and more than nine hundred feet wide, had been breached on the first of July.

There were rapids at the mouth of Messalonskee Stream, but they had been there in pre-Columbian time. Just above the dam's impoundment, they suggested what its depth had concealed. A blue heron tried to lead us through the rapids, or seemed to, in a series of short, nosy flights down the left bank. A kingfisher watched. The Augusta Water Power Company blocked the river in the year that Martin Van Buren replaced Andrew Jackson as President of the United States. It was the year of the Panic of 1837, when real estate collapsed, banks failed like duckpins, and homeless people died in the streets. The first steam railroad was nine years old. Oberlin, the first coeducational American college, was four years old. If you could afford Buffaloe's Oil, you used it in your hair to fight baldness. In Augusta, primarily thanks to the new dam, some people could afford Buffaloe's Oil. The dam powered seven sawmills, a gristmill, and a machine shop. Incidentally, it had a fish ladder.

Beside the second rip we came to was a sofa bed, its skirts showing the stains of fallen water. We expected more of the same. We expected grocery carts. This, after all, was not Township 13, Range 11, of the North Woods, where nearly half the State of Maine consists of nameless unorganized townships. This was settled, supermarket Maine, but in the fifteen river miles upstream of Augusta we would see one beer can, no grocery carts, and three tires. Now we saw a mallard, a pewee, goldfinches. We heard song sparrows, a wood thrush, a veery. I wouldn't know a veery from a blue-winged warbler, but John McPhedran is acute on birds. I had known him since he was seventeen, seventeen years before. Since then, he had become a botanist, a general field naturalist, and a freelance water-quality consultant working for the Maine Department of Transportation. We saw sticking up from a large and newly emergent river boulder an iron bolt fully an inch and a half in diameter and capped with a head like a big iron mushroom. I knew what that dated from—the log drives of the Kennebec, which began in colonial times and came to an end in 1976. Put a chain around that bolt and you could stop a raft of logs.

We saw no white pines, very long gone as the masts of ships. Or spruce, for that matter. We saw deciduous trees. In fall, the river's walls would be afire in oranges and reds, but now, in summer, the leaves seemed too bright, too light for Maine. Among them were few houses—in fifteen otherwise uncivilized miles, a total of three nervous houses peeping through narrow slots in the trees. This seemed to report a population that had turned its back on the river, which it had, for the better part of a century, because the river was cluttered with the debris of log drives, becessed with community waste, spiked with industrial toxins. Square-rigged ships once came up into the fresh Kennebec to carry its pure ice down the east coasts of both Americas and around Cape Horn to San Francisco, and even across the Pacific, but by the nineteen-forties and fifties the Kennebec had developed such a chronic reek that windows in unairconditioned offices in the Capitol of Maine— six hundred yards from the river—were kept tight shut in summer. After the Clean Water Act of 1972, the Kennebec, like so many American rivers, steadily and enduringly cleared, and the scene was set for the dam destruction of 1999 and the restoration of this part of the river.

We looked down through clear water, color of pale tea, at a variously rocky and gravelly bottom. In Maritime Canada, I had recently fished over a scene like that in a place locally known as the Shad Bar. Shad like to spawn over that kind of riverbed. In this river, 1837 was not a good year for anadromous fish. Something like a million American shad came up the Kennebec before the dam at Augusta stopped them. Immemorially, the Kennebecs themselves speared Atlantic salmon below falls upriver. The fish ladder at the Augusta dam may have helped to some extent, but it disappeared in a flood in 1838, not to be replaced.

We saw and heard three crows charily screaming at a red-tailed hawk—a sedentary drama enacted in a dying tree. A spotted sandpiper watched as well, from a newly dried rock in the fallen stream. Like a scale model of the Yukon River, the Kennebec was unfolding before us not in multiple twists and turns but in sizable segments, long reaches—a bend, a mile here, another bend, two miles there. They quickly added up to Six-Mile Falls, a rapid that was covered over by the rising impoundment in 1837, and until just a few days ago had been an engulfed series of bedrock ledges under the still-water pool. In 1826, the United States Engineer Department surveyed the Kennebec River and mapped Six-Mile Falls, so named because they were six miles downstream from Ticonic Falls, at Waterville. The engineers' report (1828) would preserve that name, if nothing else, while the surf-like sound and the roil of white water were taken away for a hundred and sixty-two years. Six-Mile Falls, the army engineers reported, were "three ledges of rock forming three distinct pitches." Downriver, we heard them now—that sound of gravel pouring on a tin drum. You don't need Sockdolager, the Upset Rapid, or Snake River Canyon to pick you up with that sound. Any riffle, let alone a small rapid, will do. I can feel adrenaline when I fill a glass of water.

Six-Mile Falls was a white riverscape of rock and plunge pools, small souse holes, tightly coiled eddies, and noisy, staired cascades. As we approached, we had to stand up and look for the thread of the river. The place was making scenery lifted from the dead. For six, seven, eight generations, it had been as withdrawn from the world as Debussy's *cathédrale engloutie,* but now, as in the time long gone, it was making its own music. Its higher rock, in broad, flat segments, was covered with filamentous algae, which under water have the look of long grass, combed straight by current. These algae were in thick brown mats, opened to the sky by the breaching of the dam and on their way to removal by the wind. We picked what seemed to be the most promising chute. The canoe slipped through it. We spun around and hung in an eddy. From riverbank to riverbank, water was falling in a hundred different ways. The truly moving fact that this scene, now restored, had been occluded for so much historic time was in an instant wiped from my mind by an even more stirring thought. Migrating fish "bag up" at the base of any rapid. You could be here during the spring migration and catch the milling shad.

From the bateaux of Colonel Benedict Arnold, coming up the Kennebec River, these impeding ledges of rock would have looked about as they again do now, and the bateaux surely had no choice but to bag up here, too. There were two hundred and twenty of them, newly made of green and shrinking pine, and eleven hundred Revolutionary soldiers, some in the bateaux, some on foot along the banks, collecting at places like Six-Mile Falls to portage the boats or haul them up the rapids. Local farmers came, with oxen, to help. Passing through here in September, 1775, Arnold's was the inspiring expedition that attempted to capture Quebec, meanwhile encountering so much cold, swamp, snow, and hunger that the soldiers—who included Henry Dearborn, of New Hampshire; Daniel Morgan, of Virginia; Aaron Burr, of New Jersey— boiled their own moccasins for soup.

Thirteen years before the arrival of the Pilgrims at Plymouth Rock, the first English settlement on the Kennebec River was established. Flowing straight south from what would become known as Moosehead Lake, the Kennebec was the central thoroughfare of Maine. When the Plymouth Colony was eight years old (1628), Plymouth set up its own trading post on the Kennebec—forty miles inland from the ocean, at a place known to the Kennebecs as Cushnoc. According to the Abenakis, of whom the Kennebecs were a band, *cushnoc* meant "head of tide" or "where the tide stops." The tide stopped at a rapids squeezed by Cushnoc Island. Ocean ships were stopped there, too. Traders continued upriver in smaller boats. This moment in any major river—the site of the first rapids above the sea—is known universally as the fall line and is an obvious place for a city. Richmond, Washington, Trenton, Troy, and Montreal grew at the fall line of rivers. Fort Western was built on the fall line of the Kennebec—on the left bank, close to Cushnoc Island—in 1754. As early as 1785, settlers there were speaking of the island, the rapids, the ledges, the gravels as a suitable site for a dam, and in 1797 the island, the fort, the native village, and the white settlement became the Township of Augusta in the Massachusetts district of Maine. In red brick and white clapboard, among state buildings of Maine granite, Augusta is still a town—larger than Montpelier, smaller than Juneau.

At about six A.M. on July 1, 1999, the first of more than a thousand spectators began to collect above the eastern end of the Augusta dam, in a place known locally as the Tree-Free Parking Lot. Tree-Free Fiber is a bankrupt company that recycled paper. The view was immediate, across three hundred yards of barrage—called Edwards Dam since the eighteen-eighties, when the Edwards Manufacturing Company bought it and was soon operating a hundred thousand spindles and employing a thousand people in one of the largest cotton mills in the world. The dam was veiled now in falling water, an exception being a gap at the west end, where sixty feet had been dismantled and removed. A curvilinear cofferdam, convex to the current of the river, ran like a short causeway from the west shore to the broken end of the dam, cupping the wound and holding back the river.

The crowd gathered in suits, ties, and combat fatigues, sandals, sneakers, boots, and backpacks—babies in the backpacks. There were port-a-potties, T-shirts for sale, booths of brochures—Trout Unlimited, American Rivers, Salvation Army Emergency Disaster Services. There was a row of television cameras. A helicopter preëmpted the sound of the river. With "Muddy Water" and "River" and a banjo and a guitar and a pennywhistle, a trio called Schooner Fare tried to compete. Two fixed-wing planes, one of them on floats, flew in circles even tighter than the chopper's. The people had come to hear the Secretary of the Interior, the

Governor of Maine, and the Mayor of Augusta—but mainly to witness the freeing of the Kennebec, the breaching of the dam.

To dam-allergic conservationists, the idea is insufficiently satisfying that hydroelectric-power turbines spare the atmosphere by reducing the burning of fuels—a standpoint I had first attempted to describe nearly thirty-five years before:

> In the view of conservationists, there is something special about dams, something—as conservation problems go—that is disproportionately and metaphysically sinister. The outermost circle of the Devil's world seems to be a moat filled mainly with DDT. Next to it is a moat of burning gasoline. Within that is a ring of pinheads each covered with a million people—and so on past phalanxed bulldozers and bicuspid chain saws into the absolute epicenter of Hell on earth, where stands a dam. The implications of the dam exceed its true level in the scale of environmental catastrophes. Conservationists who can hold themselves in reasonable check before new oil spills and fresh megalopolises mysteriously go insane at even the thought of a dam. The conservation movement is a mystical and religious force, and possibly the reaction to dams is so violent because rivers are the ultimate metaphors of existence, and dams destroy rivers. Humiliating nature, a dam is evil—placed and solid.

During the energy crisis of 1973 and thereabout, the conservationists kept their viewpoint somewhat muffled while small-scale hydroelectric enterprises blossomed by the hundreds at small existing dams and helped meet a national need. By 1986, though, long lines at gas stations were in long-term memory and the environmental movement made a literal breakthrough on dams. The Federal Energy Regulatory Commission, which had before then been instructed to promote unequivocally the development of hydroelectric dams, was now instructed, by an amended Federal Power Act, to give "equal consideration" to wildlife, recreation, environmental quality, and related factors when renewing licenses or granting new ones. At Edwards Dam, in Augusta, Maine, for example, ocean fish coming upriver to spawn—such as Atlantic sturgeon, Atlantic salmon, and American shad—had received essentially no consideration for sixteen decades: they could not get past the fall line to their historical birthing grounds above the dam. Disturbed by the plight of American shad in another New England river, in 1849, Henry David Thoreau described them "patiently, almost pathetically, with instinct not to be discouraged, not to be *reasoned* with, revisiting their old haunts, as if their stern fates would relent, and still met by the Corporation with its dam. Poor shad! where is thy redress? When Nature gave thee instinct, gave she thee the heart to bear thy fate?" Thoreau would have been thrilled to know that the answer to his questions would one day be handed down by a federal agency called FERC.

Prodded by activists' lawyers, the commission soon developed what amounted to a retroactive statement of environmental impact. Edwards Dam had been making electricity since 1913—lately, 3.5 megawatts, scarcely enough to light the warehouse at L.L. Bean. The license was up for renewal. Since "needed and appropriate" fishways would cost three times as much as removing the dam—and the power it produced was hardly a redeeming factor—the commission ordered the Edwards Manufacturing Company to shut down its turbines, deconstruct the dam, and restore to a natural, free-flowing state the public waterway the company had used for profit.

This was the first big dam in a major river to be ordered out of existence by the federal government while the owner was left holding a wet application. In a national way, the Tree-Free Parking Lot was full of people who hoped for more, manifestly including

Rebecca Wodder and Margaret Bowman, of American Rivers, who would afterward raise glasses of champagne in celebration of "the new era of dam removal"; Amos Eno, of the National Fish and Wildlife Foundation; Todd Ambs, of the River Alliance of Wisconsin; Mike Lopushinsky, of New York Rivers United; and—from Arizona—Pam Hyde, of Glen Canyon Institute, dedicated to the breaching of Glen Canyon Dam in the Colorado River. They sat on folding chairs as if on a ship's deck for a formal surrender. For the victors, this was Yorktown, Cornwallis sulking in his tent. It was not a great moment for the National Hydropower Association, despite its reminders that eleven per cent of the national energy pool keeps three hundred and thirty-five million tons of carbon dioxide out of the air. It was not a great moment for wistful Augustans, lining the riverbank, who remembered the water-powered mills that had nurtured their town. Dieter Bradbury, of the Portland *Press Herald,* later wrote that he had seen "part of Augusta's rich industrial heritage slowly drain into the Atlantic."

To some environmentalists, hydropower seemed cleaner than the ultimate deal by which the cost of removal was effected. The owner's way out was to give the dam to the State of Maine. The state's way out was a many-back scratcher in which the Bath Iron Works, thirty miles down the Kennebec, and a consortium of hydropower stations up the Kennebec jointly provided more than seven million dollars—or enough to eradicate the dam with four million left over for restoration programs involving fish.

Bath Iron Works. If the Kennebec was historically rich in salmon, sturgeon, and shad, it was no less so in ships. The first was built in 1607. In the forty miles of the tidal river, thousands followed. The Hesperus, wrecked multiguously by Henry Wadsworth Longfellow, was built in Pittston, on the freshwater Kennebec. Bath was once the fourth-largest seaport in the United States. The Bath Iron Works carried the tradition from the age of sail into the age of steel, and continues to build destroyers for the United

States Navy. Exasperated with the inefficiencies of building new hulls on inclined ground, the shipyard desired to fill in seventeen acres of the Kennebec and build new drydocks. With the concurrence of the State of Maine and the Kennebec Coalition of environmental groups, the Iron Works contributed two and a half million to the razing of Edwards Dam, and, unopposed by environmentalists, went on to build the drydocks. The Kennebec Hydro Developers Group added nearly five million to help see Edwards gone. Their reward would be postponements of up to fifteen years in the requirement to install fish passages at their dams. Jonathan Carter, who once was a Green Party candidate for governor of Maine and had become the executive director of the Forest Ecology Network, told the Kennebec *Journal*, "By following the money trail and the inside dealing, the hoopla becomes clouded by sellouts, buyouts, and trade-offs, which set very dangerous precedents."

Maine's first governor (1820) was William King, a Kennebec shipbuilder, and also farmer, miller, sawyer, storekeeper, banker. A French traveller mistook him for an authentic king (according to the Kennebec poet Robert P. Tristram Coffin). In any case, King was known for being "as independent as a hog on ice." This set of facts seemed to cluster about Maine's incumbent governor—the Independent Angus King—as he rose to speak in the Tree-Free Parking Lot. He had tousled hair. He had a sandy mustache, medical in nature, and he wore a red-and-gold tie covered with blue fish. Having secured seven million dollars for the cause, he now lifted things to a loftier stratum than the lubricated trade-offs in his Kennebec River Comprehensive Hydropower Settlement Accord. Speaking without notes, he mentioned POP. He defined POP. He described the promise of its cybertronic effects in connecting entire communities to the World Wide Web, and he said that POP would be to the twenty-first century what the community dam had been to the nineteenth. It was time for the dam to go.

A year earlier, a short way downstream on the same riverbank, Bruce Babbitt, the Secretary of the Interior, had said, "This is not a call to remove all, most, or even many dams. But this is a challenge to dam owners and operators to defend themselves, to demonstrate by hard facts, not by sentiment or myth, that the continued operation of a dam is in the public interest economically and environmentally." In the months that followed, the ancestral truism "As Maine goes, so goes the nation" was frequently invoked by people proclaiming a new national momentum in sentiment toward removal of dams. And now, in an open-collar faded-brick Madras shirt, Bruce Babbitt looked across the crowd before him and counted the television cameras. He remarked on the considerable number of reporters, who had travelled from cities in four time zones. "They're not coming just to celebrate good news," he said. "I'm here to tell you, that's not what the American press is about. Reporters are here because they know this is the beginning of something that is going to affect the entire nation. It's a manifestation of who we are: neighbors living in a democracy. Before the Clean Water Act of 1972, the river was so polluted that it turned buildings black and literally peeled the paint off the walls. For healthy rivers and fisheries, the removal sets an important precedent. You're going to look back in years hence and say, 'It all began right here on this riverbank.'" Later in the day, Babbitt waxed almost Biblical, adding, "It's about coming together to restore the waters, recognizing that the rivers in turn have the power to restore our communities."

Begging his pardon, but from where I was sitting it all seemed to be about fish. Another speaker—among ten or so before and after King and Babbitt—spoke with reverence of a deceased state legislator who had helped lead the cause against the dam: "Wherever he is, I hope he's hooked to an Atlantic salmon on a fly rod somewhere," said the speaker, as if the purpose of destroying the dam was not so much to benefit as to barb fish. An economic study that might have been carried forward by a day trader had determined that forty-eight million dollars would be brought to the river by sport fishermen soon after the dam was gone. In the eighteenth century, Kennebec salmon were so abundant that farmers hiring help typically had to promise not to feed them salmon more than once a day. And now the eighteenth century—POP!—was coming back to the river.

Lewis Flagg, who was in the crowd, had told me that he expected as many as seven hundred and twenty-five thousand shad to be spawning north of Augusta in fifteen years or so. Flagg was the director of the Stock Enhancement Division of Maine's Department of Marine Resources. He enumerated the biological advantages of removing a dam—any dam. (1) It gets rid of obstructions to migration. (2) It restores natural habitat. (3) The river resumes the natural variations of its flow. (4) The siltation of spawning and feeding habitat ceases in what had been the impounded pool. (5) It gets rid of debris. (6) It gets rid of unnatural temperatures downstream. (7) It removes turbines that kill juvenile fish. Unless you're a stocked trout in the cold water downstream from a dam in Arkansas, the rationale for dam removal is quite compelling from a fish's point of view.

Schools of striped bass had been seen by construction workers nosing up to Edwards Dam that morning. A big Atlantic salmon broached and—two feet out of water—just hung there, watching. A high-school bell was mounted on a post near the microphones, and Babbitt, King, and others—on schedule with the speeches and the downstream recession of the morning tide—began to ring it. And ring it. Evan Richert, of the Maine State Planning Office, shouted into the microphones, "Set the fishery free!" He did not say, "Set free the river!"

On the cofferdam near the west bank sat Reggie Barnes, of Alton, Maine, at the levers of a Caterpillar 345 backhoe with a two-and-a-half-yard bucket and a thirty-nine-foot ground-level reach.

Even from across the river, it looked Cretaceous, its head above the trees. Facing east, it swung right, and it bit a few tons of gravel. After swinging farther to the right and dropping the load, it went back for more. It was eating the cofferdam. It ate from south to north, toward the restrained water. Swing left. Bite. Swing right. Drop. Swing left. Bite. The machine was opening a chasm, and the north end of the chasm was becoming a pillar of gravel separating air from water. Bite. The pillar thinned. Frankly, I had not imagined this moment in history to be dramatic—the engineering was so extensive, monumental, and controlled. I mean, a Stuka wasn't dropping one on the crest and flying off to Frankfurt. But this backhoe, positioned on the very structure it was consuming— swinging to and fro on the inboard end of the cofferdam—was hypnotizing a thousand people. It hadn't far to go. The bucket had not reached water before water reached the bucket. From a thousand feet away, even through binoculars, not much could be seen yet but occasional splashes in motion, south. They were occasional enough to cause Reggie Barnes to roll his treads and get the big backhoe out of there, fast. It scooted off the cofferdam and partway up a hill. A bottle of champagne had been cracked on the bucket before it all began, and now from beneath a mass of hard hats came a cheer that might have been audible in Portland. While the hard hats watched and the Nature Conservancy watched with the leaders of American Rivers, the licks and splashes increased in frequency and height above the cofferdam, which was now being eaten by the Kennebec River.

Rapidly, it widened and deepened its advantage. It became a chocolate torrent. It shot through the gap in the western end of the dam itself and smashed into the foundation wall of the gatehouse, once the entry to the power canal. The foundation wall of the gatehouse consisted of very large blocks of granite. The liberated currents caromed off it and angled into the lower river. A milky brown plume spread through the clear water there and nearly reached the eastern shore, a thousand feet away. In eight minutes, the Kennebec, completely in charge of everything now, melted down the cofferdam until a channel had opened seventy feet wide. The rage of high water seemed to fly through the air before hitting the granite wall and exploding back into the river. In the Tree-Free Parking Lot, the assembled phalanges of the environmental movement were standing as one, standing on their chairs for a line of sight through a forest of elbows apexed with binoculars, framing Babbitt on a cell phone before the frothing river. The volume of the rapids grew. After the initial blowout of sediments, the thundering water turned white and the slicks were cordovan glass. The Kennebec River in Augusta, after a hundred and sixty-two years in the slammer, was walking.

And twelve days thereafter, in the Old Town canoe about halfway from Waterville to Augusta, we passed a concrete boat launch that had launched its last boat. Its lower lip was many yards back from the river and much higher than the surface of the water. Broad shingle flats had become exposed here and there, but mainly the banks of the river were so steep that evidence of the breaching was confined to the two sides. Small, hanging streams and small, hanging falls were cutting fresh canyons to the river. A kingbird went over us, a bald eagle, a cedar waxwing. A cormorant swam past us, and two beavers off the left bank slapped and disappeared. Standing high in the river now like stockade towers were the rock-filled cribs of the log drives. Made from trees with a hundred and twenty rings, they disciplined the flow of logs. This stretch of river had a parklike appearance, with no structures but these emblems of the history of Maine. An island, high and elongate, sat up like a warship on its hull of rock, with twenty-three towers leading to it and five away from its downstream end. When dams are built, the complaints of inundated communities gradually gurgle into silence, and when dams are destroyed—evidently—complaints in fresh demeanor come to life. An ecosystem sixteen decades old was being destroyed, no matter that it was significantly man-made. Seriously threatened were the yellow lampmussel and the tidewater mucket. On the day of the breaching of the dam, volunteers from Nokomis High School worked feverishly all afternoon moving mussels and muckets from mudbanks to deep water while baby lampreys squirmed in the muck around them. In the absence of Edwards Dam, some people thought, carp and other untouchable species might get into tributary streams. When the State of Maine proposed building a small dam in a tributary to block the carp, letters to editors shouted ironic derision. A citizen of Augusta called the Edwards Dam breaching the "blunder of the century." Noting that the damsite was actually a fine place for a much higher dam and more hydroelectric power, another writer ridiculed a government "pushed by environmental wackos." In less than a year, in the spring of the next migration, fishermen would be catching five-pound shad in the Kennebec above Augusta.

Dams are said to last, on average, about fifty years. At the time, one of four American dams was that old and eighty-five per cent would be by 2020. In the state of Washington, the Federal Energy Regulatory Commission told Condit Dam on the White Salmon River that fishlifts would soon be required. Condit is four hundred and seventy-one feet long and a hundred and twenty-three feet high. Removing the dam is cheaper than installing fishlifts. The owner agreed to remove it in 2006. On the Elwha River, where two dams also block salmon, the government has bought the dams in order to remove them. The Army Corps of Engineers is weighing the fate of four dams on the Snake River. They date from the nineteen-sixties and seventies, they are half to three-quarters of a mile wide, they irrigate thirty-six thousand acres, and they make enough power to light Seattle. From Pasco, Washington, to Lewiston, Idaho, they block a hundred and forty miles of river, and the price of their removal is a billion dollars. Nonetheless, if all methods of assisting fish migrations fail—if the salmon population continues to decline—the four dams may be removed. The Corps of Engineers, like any bureaucratic agency, has no higher agendum than its own survival. It can survive as well removing dams as building them.

On Fossil Creek, in Arizona, a paradise of rock ledges and travertine pools, it's 5.6 megawatts versus the Gila topminnow and the razorback sucker. Embrey Dam, on the Rappahannock River, in Virginia, has about the same height and width as Edwards had in Augusta and cuts off a hundred miles of historical spawning grounds of shad. While the cost of removing the dam is four million dollars, the cost of fish passage would be 10.2, so the dam is coming out. The shad migration on the Neponset River, in and near Boston, has been cut off variously since 1634. The Army Corps of Engineers has been studying the feasibility of removing the Neponset's two dams. A dam on Malibu Creek, in California, is a hundred feet high, and the reservoir behind it is completely landfilled with silt. It is seventy-five years old. A rare species of steelhead used to run up there. Savage Rapids Dam on the Rogue River, in Oregon, is thirty-nine feet high, four hundred and sixty-four feet wide, and was built more than eighty years ago to help small farmers whose farms are now real-estate subdivisions. The endangered Colorado pikeminnow would be considerably less endangered following the removal of Price-Stubb Dam, on the Colorado River, which was built for irrigation before the First World War and has not watered anything since 1919.

Since 1960, some two hundred small-river dams have been removed in the United States, nowhere as feverishly as in Wisconsin, where the Slabtown Dam, on the Bark River, was destroyed in 1992; the Wonewoc Dam, on the Baraboo River, in 1996; the Hayman Falls Dam, on the Embarrass River, in 1995; the Readstown Dam, on the Kickapoo River, in 1985; the Mellen Dam, on the

Bad River, in 1967. Baraboo was Barabeau once. A barabeau is a sturgeon. The tribes called the river Ocoochery (Plenty of Fishes). Wisconsin has deconstructed more than seventy-five dams, ranging in height up to sixty feet and length to four hundred and fifty.

There are sixty-six thousand river dams in the United States five or more feet high. The highest—Oroville, on the Feather River—is seven hundred and seventy feet high. The greatest producer of power is Grand Coulee Dam, on the Columbia River, making six thousand megawatts. American Rivers once said that the power made at Edwards could be saved "by replacing seventy-five thousand lightbulbs with energy-efficient bulbs." Grand Coulee appears safe, unless someone comes along with a hundred and thirty-two million lightbulbs.

To be completely free, the Kennebec River will have a more than metaphorically uphill struggle. In its watershed above Augusta are at least a hundred dams, ten in the main stem from Waterville to Moosehead Lake. In the resurrected rapids of this stretch above Augusta, its fifteen miles seemed both modest and momentous. It was about the length of Manhattan Island. A lot of fish could spawn there. In its possibilities as a state park, its beauty and seclusion, it rallied the nineteenth century. From no river in the country of the Kennebec's size or stature had a dam ever been removed. On the fresh current, we rounded a final bend. Down the long thoroughfare of water and trees we now saw—three and a half miles away and rising from mid-river like the blade of a gunsight—the bronze and granite Capitol of Maine. To left and right, above the trees, were the spires of two churches. With John's father, Alexander McPhedran, we had scouted early in the morning for a place to end the trip, and, with some difficulty, had found one, about a quarter of a mile through woods from a small roadside park. We had left a white-birch log on a rock to mark the spot. Seeing it now, a mile down, John McPhedran rummaged in his pack, removed a cell phone, and asked his father to pick us up.

# SPAWNING AND THE OUTMIGRATION

In the days before the dam was breached, more than three million larval shad had been poured into the Kennebec at Sydney and Waterville to pass the summer and be imprinted in the renewed spawning grounds. Another million would soon follow. Stocked by the state, they were coming from a private hatchery in Waldoboro, some thirty miles to the southeast, where fertilized eggs are obtained in a manner strikingly different from the fatal strippings at Smithfield Beach and the Pamunkey reservation. Sam Chapman, in his Waldoboro Shad Hatchery, induces a soothing counterclockwise flow in big cylindrical tanks and puts full-grown, swimming shad in there to have sex while he watches. I wanted to watch, too. I went over from Augusta. Spring after spring on the Delaware, on quiet evenings at dusk, I had sat on a boulder cleaning shad and looking downstream across half a mile of what seemed like Olympic rings not quite overlapping—ritual circles in the river, drawn on the surface by paired shad in tight coils. Since the view stopped at the surface, I wondered how they went about what they were doing.

In squarish green ponds on the edge of open country, black clouds of larval shad raced for cover in suddenly emerging sunlight. "If they can stay away from bright sunlight, they will," Chapman said. "If a pond is green, they'll get down in it. If a pond is clear, they'll school right on the surface, having nowhere to go to get away from the light. As these fish develop in the eggs, one of the first things you notice is the development of the eye, so light must play an important role in this fish's life."

There were three ponds—in effect, some of the shipping docks of the business. Beside the ponds were two metal buildings, like the hangar and machine shop of a very small airport. The larger building was three stories tall and cavernous inside—a single space, with a stairway in one corner that led to a high platform where observers could lean on a railing and look down from close proximity into an uncovered tank fifteen feet in diameter. Large dark shapes flashing silver were swimming there, schooled up and steady in concentric skeins, when Chapman took me to the platform at four in the afternoon. They were swimming against the current, clockwise—swimming high to low in the water column, randomly changing depths. Now and again, the high ones broke the surface slightly with their dorsals or tails. Rarely, they snapped at bubbles, as if the bubbles were shad darts. The scene was calm, cool, and migrational—expert swimmers moving into current, instinctively moving upstream, not evidently rattled by Chapman's closed circuit. Every so often, as the afternoon lengthened, a single shad would break the spell, looping around to swim against the crowd. Chapman said, "Normally, during the daylight hours, the fish are going to be swimming around the tank pretty well in a parallel fashion. They're all uniformly swimming, and there's not much deviation from the given path. It's like running track. Later, you see individuals break out of that pattern, break the line, and go from one track to the other."

Eventually, some shad began to alter the pattern further by exploding forward and passing the rest of the school at extreme high speed. Twice, three times, they would whip around before settling down to cruise as before. When they started this "burst-speed swimming," as Chapman called it, he said, "I'm guessing. It must be five o'clock."

It was 4:55. Burst-speed swimming is the first real sign of the orgiastic pageant to come. The schooling discipline is closing down for the day and the sexual intent is rising. The tank had something over a hundred shad in it, and by six o'clock they were beginning to swim in a miscellaneous, improvisational, free-form way.

Chapman, in shorts and a T-shirt, is a stocky man with short dark hair, with down-East inflections, down-East humor, and legs that would not look amiss in the National Football League. I asked him where he got the fish.

They had recently come out of the Gulf of Maine and into the Saco River, he said—seventy-five miles down the road. They were trapped at the fishlift at Cataract Falls, and the Maine Department of Marine Fisheries—his customer and client—trucked them to Waldoboro. They would go back to the Saco in the same trucks. He had used fish in years past from the Connecticut River, but he was wary of them because of the beating they had taken in the fish elevator at Holyoke Dam. He said, "You wouldn't bring a sick cow in to breed it." Since the season began, he had received more than five hundred shad from the Saco.

I asked him the temperature of the water.

About seventy-five degrees Fahrenheit. Its blue coloring was from something called Aquashade, which is used to color ponds on golf courses. Aquashade also inhibits the growth of algae. Its effect in the Waldoboro tank is to calm down the shad.

By seven, the light was beginning to fall, and the shad were loosely carouselling, milling as well, some doing tight whirling turns, or downcurrent loops, at all levels in the tank, dorsals and caudals occasionally splashing the surface. At seven-thirty, Chapman went down to ground level and closed a large overhead door at one end of the building. It was as if the sun had dropped behind riverbank trees. The milling intensified. Chapman had hung a seven-watt bulb in a reflector tilted toward the ceiling, and gradually this extremely low source became the only light. Watching the fish in the dark was like waiting for water to boil.

The smaller shapes were males, the larger ones females. A smaller one slid his nose past the tail of a larger one and moved it along her body. She bolted, sprinting around the tank. He followed, just as fast. "I think she is dribbling eggs and giving off a hormone," Chapman said. "That attracts him. He's ready. She isn't. So she takes off, and he gives chase. I call this phase 'aggressive one-on-one.' "

The satyr chases began occurring frequently, with a lot of thrashing on the surface, and while that was going on other fish went off to one side and swam in small circles, just as in the National Basketball Association when four players clear the floor so the fifth can go one-on-one. As twilight deepened into night, the aggressive one-on-one became, in Chapman's term, a "passive one-on-one." Doing a kind of play-by-play, he said, "It's almost like a water ballet, with two and sometimes more fish swimming in synchrony, actually touching—each fish vibrating, male and female."

The essence of the passive one-on-one is that she is now as receptive as he is aroused. While making their tight circles—maybe two feet in diameter—they paired closely, nose to gill, and they vibrated. Sometimes they were splashing at the surface, and sometimes they were a little bit down. They kept moving rapidly, side by side, like a couple of skywriters, trailing gametes—eggs and milt. "It's just a short dalliance," Chapman said. A pair would finish in an extremely tight arc, a fiddlehead flourish.

This had an effect. It was democopulation. It stirred the rest of the school. Gradually, they formed their own pairs, and the general orgy got under way, veiled in clouds of white sperm. In 1879, in a small volume called "Fish Hatching and Fish Catching," R. Barnwell Roosevelt and Seth Green rubbed words together to evoke the ambience of this moment in the spawning beds of the natural world: "They seek out some rocky ledge where there is a gentle current, and uniting in pairs press their vents together and extrude the spawn and milt in a spasm of amatory pleasure."

Chapman's shad were now milling, as they do while they spawn in a river. While most seemed to vibrate against one another, others went alone to vibrate against the side of the tank or against the plastic standpipe in the center, swimming in a tight spiral, quivering against the pipe to shake out eggs.

"Once you get enough hormones and gametes in the water it triggers a school-spawning response," Chapman said. "Now they're going at normal speed, not trying to get away from one another. When they're expressing the gametes, they go through some kind of rotational or bumping motion, and this is when the eggs and sperm are coming out. It doesn't take a one-on-one. They can do it all by themselves. I've seen the sperm so thick it was like looking into a milk jug."

By ten-thirty or so, in the seven watts of light, the evening's activity had reached the high end of its crescendo and was beginning to quiet down. It doesn't always end so early. "Oftentimes I'll come in and check at ten o'clock—and I've had it for the day, you know—and I'll check it and there's no eggs. Then I come in the next day and there's as much as a litre and a half of eggs. They're young eggs. You can tell just by looking at the degree of development. Some of them are just a few hours old, so they were given off in the wee hours."

As in a river, the indoor spawning in Waldoboro can go on for weeks and take place every night. One year, the same group of shad spawned every evening from the third week of June to the middle of August. The eggs slowly sink and go into a drain and down into collection bags. Chapman culls the best eggs with a two-millimetre sieve, rejecting up to seventy-five per cent. Even so he ends up with about ten times as many eggs as he would if he were squeezing them out of the fish on his own. From a single evening's spawning, he might collect a hundred thousand eggs, at sixty thousand eggs per litre. Like shad, most fish are oviparous—that is, their eggs go into the water and are fertilized externally. While one female shad has, say, two hundred and fifty thousand eggs, a female giant bluefin tuna will carry in her sacs about forty million eggs. Maybe one or two of those forty million becomes an adult giant bluefin. Shad eggs in the wild do better than that. But not much better.

Chapman describes himself as a man with a "blue thumb." His wife, Carolyn, who works side by side with him, has one, too. She raised lobsters, oysters, and marine worms at the University of Maine's Darling Marine Center, in Walpole, on the Damariscotta River. She was from Rockland. They met when they were teenaged. After majoring in botany at the university, Sam, too, went to work at the Marine Center, where he became an aquaculture specialist and discovered his talent for "building things that animals lived in." The animals were lobsters, clams, oysters, scallops, and mussels. When Sam and Carolyn were in their early forties, they left the Marine Center to follow their own ideas and raise fish in Waldoboro. They began with smelts, advanced to alewives, and escalated to shad.

Growing up in Waldoboro, Sam had understood the effects a dam could have on the life of a river. His home river, the Medomak (it rhymes with "atomic"), was only sixteen miles long and was dammed in eight places. Its name means "where fresh meets salt," but it could not have been been more discouraging to anadromous fish. In part as a result of dialogue with Sam, a Waldoboro farmer who raised sheep by the river created in his will the Lloyd L. Davis Anadromous Fish Trust. In June 1990, Sam applied to the Fish Trust for travel money and got seven hundred dollars for a trip to Smithfield Beach, on the Delaware River, and the hatchery in Thompsontown, on the Juniata. The following season, he went to the Connecticut River, collected shad eggs, and hatched shad fry in his garage in Waldoboro. "I didn't know a thing about them," he told me now. "If you want to get funding, you do something other people aren't doing." Sam and Carolyn, in their second summer, hatched a million shad. He sold them to the Department of Marine Resources, which had listed shad second after Atlantic salmon in its restoration endeavors. For the Chapmans, each succeeding season proved as good as or better than the last. They sent larval shad in huge numbers to the Androscoggin, the Sebasticook, the Saco, and the Kennebec, and they kept not a few for the Medomak.

At the Manning Hatchery in the state of Maryland, where adult shad also spawn in tanks, biologists developed a way of injecting the fish with hormones in order to accelerate maturation of the eggs, enhancing greatly the yield of larval shad. Sam and Carolyn tried the method but found it "too hard on the fish—you can feel the shad fighting the handling, with their muscles quivering as if they were being jolted by electric shocks." For the spawning Waldoboro shad, a night in the tank can be rough enough without a traumatic injection. "They'll go around very fast and quite often they'll ram the side of the tank, and it kills one or both of the fish. If they hit it a sideways blow, they'll become stunned, and they'll swim around for a while with their jaws locked open. There was quite a bit of activity last night—chasing each other, going like bullets—and I thought at times they were going to pop right up out of the side of the tank. They're big-river fish, and at times they need to be in a big river, meaning that if they turn and really go for it here they might hit the side, like birds hitting a plate-glass window." You see a number of noses bruised red. You see an eyeball bulging. Suddenly, a pair takes off, burst-speed swimming. They hit the side of the tank, rupture their kidneys, and fall to the bottom.

The most obvious characteristic in shads' behavior, he said, is their nervousness. "If they're in a tank outside in sunlight, just step near the tank and they all bang into the other side." Even indoors, the Chapmans are careful not to move rapidly. One day, Sam and Carolyn were talking and she inadvertently draped a white filter bag over the rim of a tank. The fish, in waves, banged into the far side, then came back and banged into the near side. A ringing telephone has caused them to bang one side and then the other. Once, when Sam injected some roe shad with tetracycline, nineteen out of twenty died from the stress of being held down. "I was too busy digging graves to count," he told me. "Those females don't take much. It doesn't take much stress to put them down."

Almost in afterthought, he remarked that the U.S. Fish and Wildlife Service—considering the costs of everything from boats and gasoline to waders, lures, and rods—had computed the dollar value in the Northeast of one shad caught in one day from a boat ($45) and from shore ($22.50). "If you've got seven hundred and fifty thousand shad in the Kennebec River and the catch rate is ten per cent, they're worth three million to six million dollars. Multiply that by all the rivers in Maine, and the value of a restored shad fishery is huge. But not as huge as some things. Try duck meat, try woodcock, if you want to see a big number."

Drifting on the Delaware in the evening, I sometimes go down through the flat shallows and the rings of spawning shad. Their dorsal fins—out of water like shark fins, like conning towers—are sketching out the rings, males hanging close to females, nose to gill. This is in June, usually, but the spawning begins in May and goes on into July. Some individuals mate and move on upriver, mate again and move upriver. Others seem to choose a deep pool and stay in it, day after day for a week or two, going off into pebbly, sandy shallows to copulate at night. They will even mate in the daytime if the day is dark enough with clouds and rain. The spawning grounds are known to fishermen as shad wallows.

People on the river still say that when the Dutchman's breeches bloom, it's time to go for shad. Or when forsythia blooms. And, of course, when the shadbush blooms. Almost everyone mentions the shadbush, but few as gracefully as the fish-and-fishing encyclopedist A. J. McClane: "The shad comes into New England's rivers when the shadbush blossoms in clusters of white flowers and a mottled brown caddis or shadfly emerges in great clouds from the water to dance in a warming sun." The biologist, like the shad, will prefer to note the temperature of the water. While schools come into the river when the water gets up beyond forty Fahrenheit, and spawning begins around seventy, the fish are so individual and idiosyncratic that even after the shadbush has turned from white to green—in the middle of May at the height of the spring migration—they are everywhere in a river from sea to source. Radio-tagging has shown that they can go thirty miles in a day if they want to. They may not want to. The migration, at its peak, is bewilderingly spread out. While shad are still being netted by commercial fishermen in Delaware Bay, the vanguard of the run is three hundred miles upriver.

Since shad seem to require a large critical mass in order to detonate successful spawning, they go into the slow shallows in considerable numbers and make those endless Olympic rings. After fishing since April to invisible fish, a fisherman could ask pardon if he feels a little lust himself on seeing the circles in the river. I will confess that I have paddled to the edge of shad wallows and permitted a small dart, presented by a fly line, to drift into one of those sun-and-planetary systems. Whatever else might be made of it, to do that—to cast a ⅟₃₂-ounce dart into that scene—is to know what it is to be ignored. Try again. Again. The dart is in front of their noses, ignored. The various fish are like collected crop dusters working the same field. Very rarely, a buck will hit the dart, perhaps to protect the spawning ring. The buck is usually furious, as who, copulating, would not be if yanked out of bed on a barbed bit of wire? The buck leaps, flips end over end, dives, races, sounds. One ran so far with my line that the backing was about to expire. I stopped the line and the hook flew out of the fish.

If you drive to the upper Delaware from central New Jersey, as I do frequently in spring, you go around the end of Jenny Jump Mountain, and, on Route 46 in Manunka Chunk, first glimpse the river. It tells you sometimes more than you hoped to know. Early on, it may be high, fast, and wide, its riffles drowned where no one could stand, and later it is low and channeled, its anatomy exposed. When you see scaffolding there—as you do every year—you know that your season is over. The scaffolding stands in the river, far out from either bank. Weighted and firm to the bottom, it rises maybe three feet above the river's surface and is capped with wooden planks. Bow hunters stand on these platforms and shoot arrows at shad.

A week or so before, a bow hunter could have stood on one of those platforms and shot all day, hitting nothing. A bow hunter could sooner stop a ray of light than a high-season swimming shad. But now, at the end of time, the archers are able to hit them because the shad have slowed way down. They are languid as they swim, their bodies in sinuous motion, the big forked tails slowly sweeping. I stopped there to eat a sandwich one day, and saw three men standing like Saracens on three mid-river parapets. They were peering into the water, bows drawn. Their arrows were connected to lines that were connected to reels. Suddenly an arrow entered the water. The bowman reeled in and lifted up a big shad pierced straight through. After withdrawing the arrow, he dropped the shad in the river. The evident purpose of the line was to enable the archer to retrieve the arrow. Shoot and release.

People speak of a "mud taste" in shad taken in late season. They say the shad "taste of the river." They do taste different, sometimes, but they have not been eating and the taste is not from the river. Fasting since they left the ocean, they have sustained their energy by depleting their own bodies. "Someone is calling it mud taste for lack of a better term," Boyd Kynard has remarked. "It's off taste—from oil depletion, muscle breakdown."

Like Atlantic salmon, shad spawn and die; and like Atlantic salmon, some shad spawn and do not die. The correlation with latitude is distinct. In the St. Johns River in Florida—the southern extreme of the range of the species—they all die. Below Cape Fear, North Carolina, spawned-out shad, with few exceptions, die. In the rivers of the middle states—in the Delaware, the Hudson, the Connecticut—roughly fifty per cent die. In the rivers of Maine and Canada, most shad spawn, go back to the ocean, and return in later years to spawn again. Typically, a doomed roe shad in Florida carries twice as many eggs as a northerly roe shad that spawns and survives.

In the Delaware, as in other Middle Atlantic rivers, shad that survive turn and go downstream very soon after spawning. Fishermen call them downrunners. Of their number, fewer than ten per cent will return another year to spawn again. In Maine rivers, about a third of the migration will come back and spawn again, some of them four or five times. The shad in West Coast rivers survive and repeat in percentages comparable to Maine's. (All Pacific salmon, after spawning, die.) Generally, shad that are repeat spawners are larger than virgin shad. A six-pound roe is experienced; a three-and-a-half-pound roe is almost certainly a virgin. Almost. The Delaware River's eleven-pound one-ounce, all-time-record shad was a seven-year-old virgin.

When the fish slow down and in themselves declare the end of the season, you can stand on a rock in the river and watch them go by. These are the ghost days. The fish, always in single file as they climb into faster water and advance the migration, are gray and spectral. But they keep going. You can dangle a dart in their path and watch them in hundreds swim past and ignore it, but if you throw out a proper cast and let it swing downcurrent an occasional shad will hit. They may be tired but they're not defeated. One evening in late June, standing in white water, I lost three out of five as—with ten thumbs and dimwitted—I impatiently thought I could horse them into an undersized net. They had let themselves be reeled in as if they were docile. They rebelled when the line was short. One was a big roe shad. Her resistance was about fifty per cent of what it would have been a couple of weeks earlier. She somersaulted three or four times but did not clear the surface, flipping instead like a racing swimmer. That day's diary says, "She was, in two senses, a depleted roe. But keep perspective on the struggle she put up. Half a shad is twice a trout."

Below Holyoke Dam, Armand Charest once told me about a fisherman at the end of the season who caught a shad that had been lying dead on the bottom of the Connecticut River. The dart was hooked perfectly in its lip. I could not quite match that feat, but thirty miles upstream, at the Rock Dam in Turners Falls at the end of one season, I did hook into a roe shad that died on the line. It thrashed around for a couple of minutes but did not move in the net, or thereafter. I thought of the matter of "mud taste" and was wary of its future on the table. I wondered if the flesh would be deteriorated, and was a little wary about baking the fish. That night, nonetheless, I stuffed it and baked it. Even that specimen was, indisputably, *Alosa sapidissima.* Its specific name means "most savory."

Shad fry and fingerlings are eaten, evidently, by just about every kind of predator that can get its mouth around them, while shad in turn prey all their lives only on the animal titbits collectively known as zooplankton. After four or five days growing in eggs, shad fry hatch out into the river by the hundreds of millions, and are decimated immediately by minnows, shiners, and almost any small fish that happens to be around—eaten alive even as they are still absorbing their own yolk sacs. About five weeks later—as larvae in cloudy black masses—they are consumed in even greater numbers. Small wonder that some parents are instinctively driven to place their young as far upstream as they possibly can, to be nearer sources of zooplankton, where they might gain a slight advantage in speed and size over others they will join. As juveniles —two, three, four inches long across the summer—they look remarkably like miniature adult shad in every detail but their huge, disproportional eyes.

Juveniles spend the summer in and around their birthplace. When the planet orbits far enough to lower the water temperature to sixty degrees, nearly all of them move downstream, joining others and then others and millions of others in the great mass transfer of energy known to science as the outmigration. A small number of juveniles hold in the river all winter, as do a few adult shad. But nearly all juveniles join the outmigration. Temperature is not the only factor drawing them toward the ocean. Cellular structures within them have changed, and they are losing their ability to live in fresh water.

Now comes a scene that in aesthetic appeal all but equals the circles of June. Everyone who is still on the water in very late summer and early fall (long since fishing for something else) remarks on the dimpling of the baby shad. They are coming down the river in galactic schools, and at dusk especially they will turn the water white. They dimple, dapple, leap into the air. They seem like a squall of silver rain. It has long been said that they are jumping for insects. What the human eye sees, as it observes the dimpling of the shad on the blue river bordered with turning leaves, is early Impressionism rooted in the Hudson River School—the peace and the quiet of Nature with touches of silvery motion in it, an Arcadian pastoral vision. To a side-scan sonar, it looks like this: bronze-backs that can take in two and more shadlings in one swallow are coming up under the juvenile shad and eating them from below. That would make you dimple. A bronzeback is a smallmouth bass. In complete terror, the young shad are struggling for the top of the water column, and many leap into the air. Boyd Kynard, who has done some of the sonar studies, says the fish that lead the dimpling are coming from the bottom of the school. Others follow, while the school as a whole tries to turn itself inside out and upward. "The predators attack only those individuals in the low part of the school. So the school struggles within itself for the higher positions, and dimpling results. It's a survival mechanism."

Historically, American shad encountered few predators in Northeastern rivers. For most of the nineteenth century and back through all of colonial time, the rivers in autumn were sluggish with fingerling shad. Kynard calls this the "precentrarchid community." Centrarchids include sunfish, crappies, and black bass (a term that incorporates smallmouths and largemouths). Centrarchids are native to the American South, and were introduced into the Hudson and the Connecticut. There were some in the Delaware but more were stocked. Channel catfish also gobble up juvenile shad, as do pike, perch, and muskellunge. Sturgeons gorge on them, and so do striped bass. At the turn of the twenty-first century, the striper populations were strongly on the rise in the Connecticut, the Hudson, and the Delaware. In fall, they were resident in the main-stem Delaware from mile 1 to the sea buoy. Of the overall effect of every kind of bass on shad, Kynard says, "They really hammer 'em."

Human beings do not much alter the outmigration. The shadlings get past dams. I will confess that when I left Waldoboro I went down to L.L. Bean—at Sam Chapman's suggestion—and bought some artificial mosquitoes on No. 22 hooks. They were so well tied they seemed to be ready to drink from your arm. On a 6X

tippet, you lay the mosquito on the river and pull it along the surface where it cuts a miniature wake. Pow! Zap! The tenderest of
shad are fighting for your mosquito. You hook, land, and pocket six
or seven, and, as soon as you can, sauté them in butter. You cook
the whole four-inch fish—head on, scales on, fins intact. And that's
what you eat—innards and outards, head and tail, the whole baby
shad. Sapidissima!

The bright-red copious blood of a shad looks like human blood
and has in it about the same level of salt as there is in human
blood—roughly a third as much as in sea water. The fresh water in
a river will have salt in it, too, but precious little—about a thou-
sandth of what is in the sea. Since the salt in a fish's blood is drawn
and replenished from the fish's environment, a fish in fresh water
has to hoard the salt it takes up, while a fish in the ocean must get
rid of more salt than it keeps. If this is the same fish, it obviously
needs a reversible talent, an osmotic adjustability that can meet
such radical change.

The process by which the young shad move from fresh water
to salt water is incompletely understood, but if you wanted to edge
up to this scientific frontier you might call on Steve McCormick
at the S. O. Conte lab in Turners Falls. A fish physiologist whose
Ph.D. is from a program run jointly by the Massachusetts Institute
of Technology and the Woods Hole Oceanographic Institution,
McCormick grew up in suburban Schenectady, and was not at first
your obvious future biologist. When he went fishing with his father, he asked his father to bait the hook and remove any fish that
happened to get on it. In the company of a grandfather, he did develop an affection for crabbing off piers in Virginia, and fishing for
croakers and spot. He has written numerous scientific papers on
osmoregulation, as fresh-salt transitioning is called—often in co-

authorship with his Conte-lab colleagues Joe Zydlewski, Joe Kunkel, and Boyd Kynard. McCormick once wrote out for me an explanation of the physiology of osmoregulation:

> When in fresh water, fish are always losing ions and gaining water from the environment. To counteract this, they actively take up salts across the gills, while the kidney produces large amounts of a dilute urine. In sea water, fish are gaining ions and losing water to the environment. In spite of being surrounded by water, they are constantly trying to prevent dehydration. To do this, they drink sea water and transport both salt and water across the gut into the blood. Excess salts are secreted across the gill, and urine production by the kidney decreases. When fish make the transition from fresh water to seawater they must reverse the "pumping" mechanisms of the gill from salt uptake to salt secretion.

I asked him what happens when shad return from the ocean. When does salinity change occur? "We don't know," he answered, explaining that it is not clear whether shad come into their rivers on homing instinct alone, or from physiological necessity as a result of a renewed cellular and osmotic need to be in fresh water. He said, "The fish is doing what it wants to do, and whether it is following its physiological limitations, or whether it's just innate behavior—we can't really tease those two apart. To understand the physiology we have to have more controlled conditions, and we haven't done that at all, with adults. Hormones that are involved in triggering spawning may be involved in triggering their ability to go back into fresh water, but we don't know."

It occurred to me, parenthetically, to ask him what we literally mean when we say of someone that he drinks like a fish. In a given period of time, how much water goes into the mouth and over the

gills of a shad? He said there had been no studies on this particular fish, but an extrapolation from rainbow trout provides a con-
servative estimate, i.e., "when swimming fast or recovering from
exercise" even a little buck shad will take in ten quarts a minute.

If larval shad are experimentally immersed in sea water, they
die. If juvenile shad are removed from a river in summer and put
into sea water, they survive. "Right at the larval-juvenile metamorphosis, when they take on the appearance of full-grown shad, that's
the time when they develop their salinity tolerance," McCormick
said. "That's a couple of months before they normally migrate. It
was Joe Zydlewski who determined this, when he was a student in
my lab." Possibly the salinity tolerance develops early because
some shad spawn near their river's salt line, and the young, in high
water, could be washed down and go to sea prematurely. With dual
capability—salt and fresh—they could get themselves back across
the line. Or zone. The fresh-salt change in a river differs with years
and seasons. Some rivers have very sharp salt wedges, and in others the change is more gradual. Shad tend to be in larger rivers,
where the change is not abrupt.

Salmon of all species can go back into fresh water at any time
in their lives. The mechanism is always there. As a result, biologists
believe that salmon evolved from ancestors that lived in fresh water, acquiring in their evolution their ability to go into salt water.
Shad, in this context, are "almost the reverse of salmon," Mc-
Cormick said. "At the end of the outmigration, they actually lose
their fresh-water tolerance." Why they do not retain their juvenile
ability to go back and forth between salt and fresh is an as-yet-
unanswered question. "Since they're spending three or four years
out in the ocean, maybe it's just not economical for them to keep
all those structures developed and sitting there. It's maybe a waste
of energy. That's what we assume is going on. They don't keep
structures that they don't really need."

The structures, principally, are chloride cells in the gills. "We know a lot about these specialized cells," he continued. "We know the hormones that cause their development and the hormones that turn on ion transport when the shad move into sea water. Hormones control their ability to make the change."

When the small silver shad cross from fresh to salt downriver, they leave behind them the stream's iron gauntlet of voracious predators—the black bass, the channel cats, the walleyes, the muskies. However, as they sprint for the blue ocean, bluefish are waiting at the sea buoy. Fish-eating fish go for bright flashing targets. Mackerel scissor into them. Sea trout, stripers, sharks. Tuna eat them by the classroom. If they swim too close to the bottom, flounders suck them in. The juvenile shad that joins the big crowd in the ocean—the yearlings, the twos, the threes, the fours—may swim in the shadow of a six-pound roe, but it is already a stressed, anxious, nerve-shot fish. In the science, a new young fish that survives the trip downriver and emerges into the ocean to join an adult school is known as a recruit.

# A COMPETITIVE ADVANTAGE

Before that recruit sexually matures and returns to its river to spawn, what is its itinerary in the ocean? Until fairly late in the twentieth century, science was unaware of the travels of the species. In 1879, Roosevelt and Green reported "that shad do not roam about the 'vasty deep' in immense shoals, making journeys of thousands of miles, and sending off relays to each river they pass, but that they remain quietly near the streams where they are bred till the time comes for them to leave the ocean, seek the fresh water and complete their duties of procreation." Roosevelt—a novelist and entomologist and a basic figure in American fly fishing—was known in other contexts as Teddy's uncle. When he wrote the book with Seth Green, he was the Commissioner of Fisheries of the State of New York. Their idea about the schools' staying close to home was based on the varying abundance of shad in East Coast rivers, and it served as conventional wisdom for three-quarters of a century. The species' long journeys in the ocean—typically twelve thousand miles from recruit to spawner— were suspected in the nineteenth century but were essentially un- known before 1958, and unclarified before the eighties and nineties.

As early as 1937, the distant recovery of one tagged shad was noted in the scientific literature. Over the next nineteen years, the U.S. Bureau of Fisheries and its successor agency the U.S. Fish and Wildlife Service tagged more than seventeen thousand shad netted in various places. Reporting the results in their 1958 paper "Atlantic Coast Migrations of American Shad," Gerald B. Talbot and James E. Sykes mentioned "very little evidence . . . as to where shad spend the winter months" but a very distinct discovery that shad native to every river congregate in summer in the Gulf of Maine—that is, in the Atlantic bight north of Cape Cod, an area of some thirty-four thousand square miles.

The idea that shad in rivers are functioning within a frame of temperatures had been around since 1884, when it was proposed by Marshall McDonald in a contribution to G. B. Goode's "The Fisheries and Fishery Industries of the United States." Now, after Talbot and Sykes, a specific isotherm began to be seen as the controlling factor in shads' migrations in the ocean as well. They were keeping themselves in a thermal window. As the sea warmed up in spring and summer, they were moving north to stay in that window. In 1972, William C. Leggett, of McGill University, and Richard R. Whitney, of the University of Washington, published a paper called "Water Temperature and the Migrations of American Shad," in which they gave the isotherm as thirteen to eighteen degrees Celsius and tracked it to the Gulf of Maine in July and August and back to the mid-Atlantic bight—Cape Cod to Cape Hatteras—in October, November, and December. They pointed out that ninety per cent of the run at Bonneville Dam occurs when the water temperatures in the Columbia River are between sixteen and nineteen and a half degrees Celsius, and that the water temperature at the peak of the shad run in Holyoke had averaged nineteen and a half degrees Celsius for fifteen years. "The precise correlation between temperature and the timing of the spawning migrations of the shad places the maximum number of adults on the spawning grounds when the temperature is optimum for the survival of eggs and young." These temperatures, they added, apply to most but not all shad. Fourteen shad were once caught by an Atlantic trawler fishing in four-degree water.

Six years later, Richard J. Neves, of the University of Massachusetts, and Linda Depres, of the Northeast Fisheries Center Woods Hole Laboratory, presented the results of a series of bottom-trawl surveys in a paper called "The Oceanic Migration of American Shad, *Alosa sapidissima,* Along the Atlantic Coast." In ten years of surveys, they said, not so much as one shad had been picked up in autumn months south of New York. Yet the schools were found at that latitude in winter, and off Hatteras in spring. In a general way, Neves and Depres confirmed the thermal window but observed that shad are vertical migrators as well as horizontal migrators, moving through a variety of temperatures in search of planktonic food. In the ocean, they primarily consume large copepods, euphausids, mysids, and zoobenthos. The zoobenthos and the mysids speak of greater depths. Shad feed anywhere, high or low, migrating from bottom to surface with the presence of zooplankton. But they're closer to the bottom during daylight hours.

In the middle nineteen-seventies, a young Canadian ichthyologist named Mike Dadswell—aware that a corporation set up by the Nova Scotia government and supported by Ottawa planned to exploit the tides of the Bay of Fundy by sending them through an epic barrage filled with hydroelectric turbines—began to wonder about the effect it would have on creatures that might pass through the barrage with the water, especially shad. Dadswell worked for the Canadian government but he was wondering on his own. He worked in New Brunswick at the St. Andrews Biological Station of the Department of Fisheries and Oceans, and he went up to Fundy's northern end whenever he could, to set out gill nets from boats, chat up local fishermen, and learn to deal with quicksand holes if he was walking the flats in waders. ("Flip off your shoulder straps and swim out onto the mud.") Eventually, he got government support for research in both the Cumberland and Minas basins—the uppermost reaches of Fundy, where the tidal range is the most dramatic. When the tide is out, the exposed mudflats, brick red, can be a thousand metres wide; when the tide is in, the same muds are under seven fathoms of water (the height of a four-story building). The Bay of Fundy is finger-shaped and a hundred and twenty miles long. The tide range increases from the open to the closed, northern end. A good spring tide in the Minas and Cumberland basins can bring on a difference approaching sixty feet. Atmospheric high pressure can move low tide down by as much as a foot, making the flats even larger. This is the scene where the unwatered seafloor reaches out to the horizon, the focal point a fishing boat, lying on its side. Dadswell has spoken wistfully of the "three-inch tides of Tahiti."

He is now a professor of biology at Acadia University, in Wolfville, on the shore of the Minas Basin, and his home is across the peninsula, on Nova Scotia's open-Atlantic coast. He raises scallops there, and is busiest in September, when they spawn. The device he uses for collecting scallop larvae is a mesh bag containing a tumbleweed mass of monofilament fishing line—sort of a bagful of backlash—set in the ocean. Scallop larvae settle onto the monofilament, stringing themselves like pearls. He attaches many such bags to a long-line, and the sheltered waters of Mahone Bay wash through them for a year. The scallops grow, and when they are about a half-inch across, they drop off the line—but they can't get out of the bag. In this way, Dadswell has developed a marine farm of half a million scallops. It is no longer clear whether his aquaculture supplements his income as a professor or his academic income supplements the farm. About fifty, he has short graying black hair and a neatly trimmed black-and-white beard. He wears bluejeans and T-shirts with fish on them. He and his family own eight boats, from canoes upward. In J24s, he was once a competitor in the Canadian sailing championships. Because his father was a career officer in the Royal Canadian Air Force, he moved around a lot when he was young, but grew up primarily in Huntsville, Ontario, more than four hundred miles from the ocean, playing lacrosse. To teach his four courses in marine biology and supervise the work of graduate students, he commutes fifty miles or so, across Nova Scotia. He commutes in a pickup with his gun and his dog. Being a professor, he is not always pressed, and sometimes stops to hunt.

Dadswell knew the literature, of course, about the summer congregations in the Gulf of Maine, when he began his studies of shad in Fundy's upper basins, and he was fairly sure they were not local but had travelled long distances to be there. Shad populations had been rising sharply in U.S. eastern rivers. They were also on the rise in the Bay of Fundy. If he could relate these two facts, then he could demonstrate that hydropower's potential effect on the shad was an international matter, and an ecological question more than two thousand miles long. Over seven seasons in the Cumberland and Minas basins, Dadswell and various colleagues and assistants tagged thirteen thousand five hundred and eighty shad. The tags resembled small plastic arrows and were inserted just under the dorsal fin. Science swims on. Each tagged fish carried its own serial number and promised the finder a reward.

In the first summer—1979—they tagged five hundred and fifty shad, and waited. September. November. January. No returns. Dadswell, at the St. Andrews Biological Station, was beginning to wonder what could have happened, and he was still wondering, one day in February, when his telephone rang and a male voice addressed him: "Howdy. Ah'm from Welaka, Florduh. Ah got wunna yawls shad down hyuh." Dadswell enjoys reproducing the moment, largely overcoming the balsam in his drawl.

Over the years of the study, he would hear from eight hundred and twenty-seven people, nearly all of them shad fishermen. He would hear from Verdell Felter, of Lehighton, Pennsylvania, who caught MD06318 "on a black-and-white-with-white-tail shad dart" at Smithfield Beach on the Delaware River. Dadswell sent Felter three dollars. He sent three dollars to the Atlantic Seafood Company, of Mayport, Florida, which had processed and sold MD01604. Ronda Armstrong, of Atlantic Beach, Florida, got six dollars for reporting two fish, and Lee Walley, of Birdsboro, Pennsylvania, got three dollars after catching and reporting a seven-pound roe shad, more than two feet long, sporting the fluorescent orange. MD00558 was caught by a New Jersey man who wrote, "I was very happy to have caught a fish with it's history it may have. Also I beleave NJ Division of Fish and Game would appreciate this data also." One of Dadswell's shad was netted by Fred Lewis at his commercial shad fishery in Lambertville, New Jersey. In Canada, Dadswell has since caught shad tagged by Lewis. MD05533 was caught in a gill net in Palatka, Florida, on the St. Johns River, by a commercial fisherman named John J. Sullivan. And in February, 1980, after Irvin Stanley, also of Palatka, reported catching MD01625, Dadswell wrote to him, in part, "Dear Mr. Irvin . . . The fish you captured traveled about 1700 miles since last September."

Dadswell heard from Nain in Labrador, from the Pee Dee River in South Carolina, from the Ogeechee River in Georgia, and Rivière des Prairies behind Montreal Island. He heard from the St. Marys River (the Atlantic boundary of Georgia and Florida), the Satilla River, the Altamaha River, the Savannah River, the Edisto River, the Santee River, the Cape Fear River, the Neuse River, the Pamlico River, the Roanoke River, the Chowan River, the James River, the Pamunkey River, the Rappahannock River, the Potomac River, the Susquehanna River, the Hudson River, the Connecticut River, the St. John River, the Miramichi River, the St. Lawrence River. Among others. The shad he tagged in summer in the Cumberland Basin and the Minas Basin of the Bay of Fundy had gone out to and were reported from every historical shad river in North America. He and his colleagues had established something previously unknown: that the American shad as an essentially entire and convening species not only migrates to the Gulf of Maine in summer but keeps on going into the Bay of Fundy and circulates through its uppermost basins.

Dadswell has a friend named Peter Hicklin who tagged semipalmated sandpipers in Chignecto Bay and the Minas Basin—special-performance birds that come down from Arctic Alaska and Arctic Canada in mid-summer, and stop over in upper Fundy to stuff themselves with mud shrimp and build the fat that will carry them nonstop to South America. One sandpiper can eat forty thousand mud shrimp in one day. The bird's weight doubles in ten days. A few become so bloated they can't fly. You see hundreds of thousands packed together near water's edge at high tide, and out on the flats near the line of receding water. Hicklin's story not only parallels Dadswell's but equals it in political pertinence, because any human artifact that would damage the shad's ecology would surely decimate the fuel that supplies the birds' intercontinental flights. Hicklin tagged many hundreds of them, Dadswell told me, and "never got a tag back." Eventually, he persuaded the government to send him to the mouth of the Orinoco River, where he went from island to island visiting the homes of fishermen, and found a favorite souvenir—the bands he had attached to the legs of the birds.

"In the northern hemisphere, if you stand facing the sea, the major current flow in estuaries always comes in on the left side and goes out on the right side," Dadswell remarked one summer day, in a lecture I heard him give in Digby, beside the Annapolis Basin. The Bay of Fundy is a large estuary. As you face down it toward its open end, its residual currents come in on the left, and run northeast up the Nova Scotia side, then swing through the complicated upper end always in a counterclockwise direction, and exit on the right, down the coasts of New Brunswick and Maine. The counterclockwise motion is a result of the Coriolis force, which derives from the planet's rotation and spins northern waters counterclockwise not only through estuaries but also down the drains of bathtubs and sinks. Shad swim with the residual currents—in spring and early summer on the Nova Scotia side, and in late summer and early fall on the New Brunswick side, going the other way. The shad use the current to guide them around the bay. Shad on their way to spawning grounds up Fundy rivers are the first to appear in the bay in spring, followed by the great nonspawning migration. In Dadswell's studies, he has not come upon a single exception to the counterclockwise route.

Of all the possibilities between the north coast of Labrador and the St. Johns River in Florida—historically, the thermal brackets of the species—why would the American shad be collectively drawn, as to nowhere else, to the Bay of Fundy? Dadswell clicks onto a screen a photographic slide of a steep-rising Fundian coast, cobble beaches exposed at low tide. In the large zone between high and low tide, rockweed grows in dark-green profusion, and it grows in exceptional abundance in the Bay of Fundy because of the vast acreage of the intertidal zone. It is the familiar form of seaweed that has little floats spaced along it in pairs. These are air bladders that lift rockweed in the water, where it bobs slowly, undulates, and sways. At low tide, it lies on the beach, a wet mat. It has no predators. It is slightly toxic to small creatures that might otherwise graze it bare. It grows, and goes on growing, and nothing stops it. Where does all the carbon go that is locked up in this plant? The tops of the rockweed are broken off by the motions of the water. The loose pieces float in great quantity in the bay. Washed ashore, they lie piled at the high-tide lines as wrack—in effect, a compost heap. Fly larvae chew on it, and reduce it to SLS.

"SLS? Begging your pardon, what is that?"

Dadswell says, "Shit-like substance—brown, squishy, no smell." Ebbing tides carry the SLS into the waters of the bay, where it nourishes phytoplankton that are eaten by copepods that are eaten by shad, moving the carbon up the food chain. And this biological richness of the Bay of Fundy is one reason why the shad are there, in Dadswell's conception.

Spartina grass—cordgrass—is a dominant plant of the tidal marshes, growing along the U.S. Atlantic coast in sometimes vast prairies, five, ten miles wide. Its roots reach down into the ooze and mine nutrients. When the grass dies and crumbles, it becomes high-protein detritus. The marsh is a soup of microscopic animals and plants. Reaching northward, spartina grass seems to stop at Cape Cod. It is everywhere down the coast but nowhere up the coast, with one exception. It leaps from Cape Cod four hundred miles to the shores of the Minas Basin, where spartina grows in a vast isolated colony. Water temperature rises as you go from the open to the closed end of Fundy. The sun, baking on the mudflats at low tide, warms the ecosystem there, warms the water, and allows the grass to flourish at the edges. Spartina, like the rockweed, breaks off, breaks apart, and ultimately nourishes invertebrates and phytoplankton.

In the ocean in daytime, other things equal, shad will generally prefer depths between a hundred and fifty and seven hundred feet—far enough down for them to find their level of "preferred light intensity." They come up the Bay of Fundy into progressively shallower and increasingly cloudy water. When they ride the flood tides into the northern basins—opaque with suspended mud—they can comfortably rise near the surface within the same range of light. They are thus vulnerable to anything human beings might do to them, but take the human factor away and they are left with an edge over most other swimmers. As ram ventilators, swimming with their mouths open and water washing through their gill rakers as if through long-toothed fine-toothed combs, they can eat with no difficulty in the dark, even if the darkness is caused by mud. Turbidity seems to be a large reason why shad go into the north-

Fundy basins. The turbid waters are rich in zooplankton. "A filter-feeding planktivore such as a shad could prey on this food source while sight-oriented planktivores would be less able," Dadswell and his colleagues wrote in their initial paper, in 1981. "Our studies indicate virtually no other large pelagic fish utilize Cumberland Basin, suggesting that turbidity may provide shad with a competitive advantage."

Dadswell and his colleagues said it was possible that shad had been coming there in all the six thousand years since the turbid habitat developed in the wake of receding ice. Evidently, what Talbot and Sykes discerned in 1958 as schools summering in the Gulf of Maine were actually shad travelling in and out of the Bay of Fundy.

The question remained: Where do they go for the winter? By 1987—all tag returns in and analyzed—Dadswell and company decided that "three distinct aggregations" occur in the winter Atlantic: a modest one on the Scotia Shelf (which is an area of comparatively warm water off Maine and Nova Scotia that is accommodating to shad from far-northern rivers), a major one in the mid-Atlantic bight (shad from the Delaware, Hudson, and Connecticut congregating with others off the Virginia Capes), and the third off Florida. They also concluded and proposed that shad move through their geographic cycles drawn and guided not only by thermal sensitivity but also by a sophisticated complexity of other instruments. Their 1987 scientific paper—"Influences of Origin, Life History, and Chance on the Atlantic Coast Migration of American Shad"—arrives at this intriguing sentence: "Evidence also suggests that American shad alternate between extrinsic and intrinsic cues to direct migration, depending on their physiological state, and at times may use a bicoordinate navigation system with map, compass, and clock."

"Extrinsic?"

"Temperature, light intensity."

"Intrinsic?"

"Sexually reproductive. Ready to spawn."

"Physiological state?

"Ripe or not ripe."

"Bicoordinate?"

"They're offshore. There are no real cues. They seem to know the way. They must have a genetic map in their heads that tells them where to go."

South to north at the end of winter, the migrations approach the rivers. In the mid-Atlantic bight, they part like lines of graduating seniors, going left or right to their rivers, homing on olfactory clues. Having been out in the ocean three to six years, they need keen olfactory memories, and some of them miss. In studies of wild Pacific salmon, as many as six and a half per cent have missed their ancestral rivers and gone to novel streams. Striped bass are less erratic, but one in a hundred strays—or goes astray, as the case may be. Nearly all shad are faithful to their home rivers, but not a hundred per cent. A shad Dadswell once tagged in a Nova Scotia river was found spawned out in Chesapeake Bay. Another was captured in a different Nova Scotia river. The numbers are low but not unremarkable, like the divorce rate among pheasants.

In the ocean, after the spawning migrations disappear into the continent, the young and otherwise nonspawning shad, in their vast numbers, are left with nothing much to do. They just make their way toward the Bay of Fundy, easily averaging fifteen miles a day, ram ventilating, and sucking up plankton. Survivors of the spawning runs will follow. Some shad bypass Fundy and make their destination the north coast of Labrador or the upper estuary of the St. Lawrence. In the latter, tide-stirred turbidities and regional oceanographic conditions are much like those in the upper end of Fundy. "In Labrador, there's no turbid water," Dadswell says. "They don't go shallow. In Labrador and Newfoundland, incidentally, shad are known as king herring." The numbers suggest that for every visit they make to Labrador or the St. Lawrence estuary, they go in two summers to the Bay of Fundy. "There's no way to sort them out easily," he comments. "But virtually every American shad born on the East Coast of North America goes to the upper Bay of Fundy at some point in its life cycle."

The migration will linger there as much as four months—mid-June to mid-October. As many as a million shad may be in the Minas Basin on a summer high tide. The Bay of Fundy as a whole will contain in summer eighty per cent of the total number of eastern American shad. Mike Dadswell figures that number to be about thirty million shad.

I had been given the name of James Webb, a commercial shad fisherman in the Minas Basin, and had called him from my home in New Jersey to ask if I could arrange to watch him at work. He was a weir fisherman, meaning that he trapped shad. I had no idea how he did it. As the date he suggested drew near, I began to worry about seasickness, which had severely threatened me now and again on small fishing boats. A few miles east of Atlantic City, while working on an earlier story, I became so queasy on the heaving swells that my pencil couldn't find my notebook. All my life I had heard stories of the tidal whirls and chopping seas of the Bay of Fundy. What would happen to my pencil there? I confided this worry to George Hackl, in New Hampshire, who is a lifetime friend and a pharmaceutical savant. In his bottomless empathy, he express mailed to me a pair of Sea-Bands—tight elastic bracelets ("The Only Clinically Tested Wristband") manufactured in England. On the inside surface of each bracelet was a hard-plastic hemisphere a half-inch in diameter. If you positioned the plastic pressure point a short way up your inner wrist and between the two central tendons—and did so on both arms—you could ride the bowsprit of the Hesperus in the winter North Atlantic.

At Cove Road and Trunk Highway 2 in Upper Economy, Nova Scotia, was Webb's neat, yellow frame house, and a small wooden sign: FRESH FISH. He told me it was about time to go check the "ware," as he pronounced it, and I should get up behind him on his Honda three-wheeler. Hooked to it was a small cart. We went south on Cove Road and through woods to the top of a steep and cobbled slope that afforded us an aerial view over Cobequid Bay, the innermost finger of the Minas Basin. Five miles across, it was reddish-brown with turbidity, and rapidly dropping. This was not as apparent at first as it was a short time later, when a very long thin black line—the top of the weir—preternaturally appeared all at once at the surface. Before long, a vertical foot of the weir was exposed. Soon, three feet, four feet. And presently the vast mudded plain—the brick-red flats—materialized as the water drained away. The weir, more than a hundred yards distant, appeared to be a solid fence. Webb remarked that it was seven feet high at its center, and gradually diminished to five feet at its ends. As if the scene had been painted by Salvador Dali, the fence stood there incongruously on the naked floor of an arm of the ocean. It was three thousand feet long.

Generally parallel to the shoreline, it was, geometrically, a wide-open chevron—a V whose two sides had been bent all but flat.

)

The ends were nearer shore than the point of the V—the bend in the fence—which aimed away from us, toward the middle of the basin. To deflect currents and improve the efficacity of the trap, the two ends curled a little, so that the shoreline and the three-thousand-foot weir looked something like this:

\}

You could straighten up that slash a little, but for government work the image will do.

e

n  \}  s

w

The Minas Basin tapers east and heads near Truro. Upper Economy is about halfway along the north shore. The incoming tide floods east, and carries the shad with it. As the basin tops up, as much as forty-five feet of water will rise around James Webb's fence. When the tide reverses, the shad turn and go with it, moving in a westerly direction—particularly toward the last of the ebbing, when time is growing short. The weir is so strategically placed—with respect to the currents, to the bathymetry, to the tidal channel—that shad swim between it and the shore. But the shoreline now is moving steadily toward the weir. The shad try to swim past its western end, but the dropping water has closed the western end. It's a three-thousand-foot sprint back to the eastern end, but that would be futile. The dropping water has simultaneously closed the eastern end. The water's edge moves ever closer to the V until only a shallow pocket contains the captured fish.

Webb started up the Honda and got ready to go out to the weir. The long cobbled slope that had given us our aerial view was actually an inclined beach. The Honda had stopped just short of a black line of rockweed wrack, where water had been lapping only hours before. Our high lookoff was at the top of the intertidal zone, the edge of the absent bay.

The terrain behind us was forested. As the last of the tide had been disappearing, Webb had told me that the weir was made of woven brush. Without so much as a nail, it was made entirely of young trees. In winter—four months earlier—he had cut down about four thousand trees. Two inches and more in diameter, they had been twelve, fifteen, eighteen feet tall. He had hauled them here to the edge of the forest and bay, and in April took them as needed out onto the flats.

Spruce were best for the stakes—the fence posts—because spruce will "give when the current is strong." Firs are brittle ("They'll break with heavy runs of tide"). But when you are cutting four thousand trees you sometimes have to take what you can get. The weir's stakes were eighty-five per cent spruce and fifteen per cent fir.

At low tide, he would go out onto the flats with a sixteen-pound mallet, stand on the top of a precariously tall sawhorse, and drive the sharpened stakes as much as four feet into the bottom of the bay. His wife, gingerly praising his accuracy, held on to the stakes. He started at the point of the V, after choosing the spot with an experienced look around. He did not use a transit or any other surveying or measuring equipment—just his own height (five feet, eight inches) and his own eyes, repeatedly glancing at landmarks, assessing the subtle contours of the basin, and judging the diminution of the height of the stakes so that all nine hundred of them would emerge on the descending water's surface in essentially the same moment. He placed them three and a half feet apart—five hundred stakes for the east wing, four hundred stakes for the west wing ("the fishing wing"). He could work only two and a half hours per tide, driving twenty-five or thirty stakes. Sometimes, he worked in a thirty-mile wind.

When all nine hundred were standing, he began weaving brush, with the help of his two sons. There was a softwood layer and a hardwood layer—softwoods at the bottom, because they formed an almost impenetrable thicket. Again, spruce was best. It was bushier and more flexible. It went in the middle, and fir filled things out toward the ends. It was a little like weaving a basket. Each tree would go inside one stake, outside the next one, and its butt would lock against the third. Each wing mirrored the other. The butts of the trees were all outboard, and the tops pointed in toward the V. After two courses of evergreens, he wove maple, cherry, alder, and birch ("wire birch, limby birch") into the upper stratum of the weir—an intricately angled, echelon composition. He had been doing this for twenty-five years, after picking up the technique from his father. Each winter, the storms and rafting ice of the Minas Basin completely destroyed his weir. He had to pick a new site—because the old ground was too much disturbed—and start over again each spring. Sometimes, a storm would wreck a weir in the process of construction.

"Why fish by this method?" I said.

He said, "It's the cheapest way to do it."

We made the long descent down the cobble beach to the flats. This was my initial voyage into the Bay of Fundy—aboard a Honda three-wheeler towing not a skiff but a cart, over wet but reasonably firm ground, with two Sea-Bands in their case in my shirt pocket. I wasn't really feeling the embarrassment. I was too occupied, on the one hand, and too preoccupied, on the other, with a condition less preferable than a queasy stomach. I had come down with Lyme disease three weeks before, and come down—on the eve of departing for Canada—with a resulting Bell's palsy. The left side of my face was paralyzed. Half of my forehead was silk smooth, and the other half was filled with ogival arches. If this name means anything to you, I looked like Jack Nicholson. What had been the horizontal line of my mouth was now fixed at a forty-degree tilt. When I tried to drink, a hole formed in one corner. My left eye was frozen open, like an owl's. Seasick, schmeesick. (Fortunately, the condition would clear completely in less than two months.) Soon after James Webb and I reached the pocket of the weir on the flats, a couple of clammers drove out from shore and began to dig beside their old Chevrolet sedans.

We left the Honda, and, in long rubber boots, walked into the V of the weir. Gulls hovered. "The weir never stinks," Webb remarked. "Seagulls, crows, ravens, eagles clean it up." A shallow pool was detained there, with the help of a course of sandbags below the brush ("The bend never goes dry"). Erect, the dorsal fins of shad were above the surface. They were going every which way—tacking, coming about, like the sails of small boats in a confused regatta. In less than two feet of water in the absolute point of the V, a great commotion was being made by an Atlantic sturgeon. It looked like an alligator. It was seven feet long. Near it were two smaller sturgeons. The law said he couldn't keep sturgeons. Also in the pool were June herring ("those little wee tiny greenback fish"), seven or eight gaspereau (also known locally as kayaks, and elsewhere known as alewives), two skates, and two old maids, or windowpanes—flounders with spots. He sometimes traps mackerel, cod, halibut, orangeback crabs, sardines, salmon, small silver hake, smelts, striped bass, toadfish, and porbeagles (the mackerel shark). He can keep one bass a day. All this variety notwithstanding, the structure is known as a shad weir, because trapping American shad is the purpose for which it was built.

Webb waded around with a small hand net—of the sort a trout fisher would use—chasing shad, not always catching one when he dipped the net. "Shad are very fast," he said. "They're touchy and they're quick. You've got to have a scoop net to catch them."

"Do you think they're smart?" I asked him.

"Oh, I guess they're smart," he said. "They lay in the deepest part of the pool."

I said, "If they're so smart, why don't they swim right through the weir when they have a chance? If it's porous enough to let the tide through, shad should be able to get through as well."

He said, "A fish'll go to the water before he'll go to the woods. Birches scare fish. They stop shy."

With surprising agility, he dodged, feinted, and faked the shad, piling them up in a tub. Now and again, he stepped on a flounder, thus discovering it—the natural camouflage of the flounder augmented by the turbid water. The flounder went into the tub. He picked up and kept two gored shad—attacked in the V by gulls. He leases bay bottom from the Department of Fisheries and Oceans for a hundred and thirty dollars a year, and is required by law to tend the weir twice a day at low tide, even if the hour is three A.M. He nets fish by flashlight and the lights of his "bike," as he calls the Honda. In the "dark of the tide" he'll catch more fish than by day. Shad he does not sell locally go to Eastern Sea Products, in Scoudoc, New Brunswick. "They are shipped to foreign countries. They glaze freeze it and ship it out." A large part of the by-catch he sells for lobster bait.

In the flats around us were dotted lines of protruding shafts of wood. They were the skeletal remains of previous weirs. There were many, and there was no orderly sequence about them, but he could point to any one of them and call off its year. The more recent ones stuck up like corn stubble. And one archaeological outline, seventeen years old, looked like the tips of the small intermuscular bones that come up through fillets of shad. The traces of his father's weirs, as much as thirty-five years old, were so faint that to me they were imperceptible until he pointed them out.

I have read since—in various articles and books—that the Algonquian Micmacs, the original people of the region, showed European settlers in the seventeenth or eighteenth century how to catch fish with brush weirs. Other writers see it differently, suggesting that the Micmacs—while expert at trapping fish with wooden fences in freshwater streams—learned from Europeans the craft of building weirs on the intertidal flats of the great bay. Upwards of a thousand years before Christ, Phoenicians in the Mediterranean basin were driving palm branches into the sea bottom forming traps for bluefin tuna. Before Europeans invaded the New World, weirs had been set up for centuries in the Breton flats where the river Rance enters the Gulf of Saint-Malo. The tide range there averages forty feet. To historians like Joleen Gordon ("The Woven Weirs of Minas," Curatorial Report Number 73, Nova Scotia Museum, Halifax, 1993), it seems probable that brush-weir technology was brought to Maritime Canada by the French—by the Acadians, the future Cajuns—who brought it from Mont-Saint-Michel.

In the early nineteenth century, the brush weirs of the Minas Basin trapped as many as a hundred thousand shad on one tide. Salted and packed in barrels, a large percentage of the catch was exported to the United States. Drift nets entered the picture and became dominant after 1840. Toward the end of the century, two-thirds of Canadian shad landings belonged to the Bay of Fundy. The damming and the pollution of American rivers severely cut the numbers after 1900. And now, after another hundred years, seven or eight weirs remained in the Minas Basin. James Webb's is one of two that are made entirely of brush. Some are combinations of trees and nets; and on others gill nets start from the bottom and—like the fencing of a golf driving range—reach twenty feet up tall poles. When the tide is out, shad are hanging so high in the air that fishermen climb long homemade ladders to pick them. If you don't have a Honda, there's always a horse. Mike Dadswell was greatly assisted in his studies by a fisherman named Gerald Lewis, whose pneumatic-tired wagon was pulled on the flats by his horse, Tom. Dadswell, seeking government money to pay for Lewis and Tom, figured that the official imagination might not be able to encompass fishing by horse and wagon. So he measured from the horse's nose to the back of the wagon, and applied for money for a vessel of fourteen feet. The vessel's name? Tom. Engine: one horsepower. Ottawa coughed up ten thousand dollars.

In an ocean system more than two thousand miles long, tined with spawning runs far up countless rivers, anything local that harms this species will be broadly regional in its effect, especially if the locality is in the Bay of Fundy, where nearly all shad go. The tidal-power project conceived by Canadian engineers was an excellent idea in the abstract if not in the environment. The tides of the Minas Basin would yield about three times as much power as Hoover Dam—about five times as much power as a nuclear generating station—if a barrage were constructed from Economy Point to Burncoat Head, sealing off Cobequid Bay. This would be a dam five and a half miles wide with a hundred and forty-eight turbines inside it. They would not make power from the incoming flow of the rising tide. The whole apparatus would function like a pump-storage project. After the incoming tide filled up the inner bay, gates would close, and as the tide ebbed a head would develop—a difference in water level on the two sides of the dam. From the high side, water would drop through the generating turbines.

This was not the sort of thing that could be done just anywhere. You could do it at Mont-Saint-Michel. You could do it in the Solway Firth. You could do it at Turnagain Arm and Cook Inlet and somewhere in the White Sea. There are not many places in the world where the tide range exceeds fifteen feet, and foremost among them is Fundy.

During the years when the proposed barrage was a bold dotted line on the map, it made considerable contributions to natural science, as the government paid for studies of its potential impact. Not only did they detail and illuminate the stories of great migrations (the intercontinental sandpipers, the continental shad) but also they suggested what might become of the migrations after the dam was in place. Turbidity would greatly decline, and with it the abundance of plankton. Amphipods would steeply decline, and with them the avian migrations. Softshell clams (steamer clams) would die by the million. A third of the Canadian clam harvest comes from the Minas Basin. "The day they close the dam, ten thousand acres of the coast of Maine is going under water," Dadswell said. "In Marblehead, basements will flood. Damming the Minas Basin will change the resonance of the Bay of Fundy. The effect will be to raise tides in the Gulf of Maine." Salt water would get into coastal wells, it would run through the storm sewers of Portland. In a world of thick fog, there would be thicker fog.

Meanwhile, back at the barrage, while the ebb tide fell through the twelve dozen turbines, fish would be falling, too. What would happen to them? In Dadswell's words, "It isn't pretty." To find out, he studied a pilot barrage on the Annapolis River, which flows into the Bay of Fundy at about the latitude of Halifax and has a spawning run of a hundred thousand shad. The first hydroelectric tidal power station ever built in North America, it has one turbine. One was enough to show Dadswell what happened to the shad. It contained a propeller. Shad that were not chopped to pieces by the propeller had additional hazards to face. Off the tips of the blades was a zone where waters moved at differing velocities, shearing (like a wind shear) with force enough to tear off shads' heads. From sudden pressure changes near the turbine, their eyes popped, they hemorrhaged at the bases of their fins, and their air bladders exploded. Since a shad's air bladder extends into the braincase, the brains also exploded. Where air produced imploding vapors—the phenomenon known as cavitation—the effect on shad was severe bleeding and the pulping of body tissue, as if they were being killed by dynamite. Dadswell summarized his study, remarking, "Shad are not well designed to go through turbines."

In their ocean migration, individual shad linger in the Minas Basin something like fifty days. Dadswell figured that each fish would go through the barrage ten to twenty times. For every hundred thousand shad to go through the barrage, about thirty-nine thousand would be mutilated. That's just "unacceptably high," the resulting paper concluded. The government agreed. There is no barrage between Burncoat and Economy.

On a freshwater stream about eighteen miles from Cobequid Bay is a small gray building with sides of corrugated metal and a red plywood gable on which is one large hand-painted word with exclamation point: FiSH! The fIsh, in spring, are fresh shad. Up the Shubenacadie River they come, and some run all the way across Nova Scotia to spawn very close to Halifax International Airport. Shoo-ben-ack-uh-dee—the accent is on the middle syllable. Shubenacadie. The small gray building FiSH is a short way up a tributary, and something like two dozen boats cluster on the bank, all but one of them square-ended, fore and aft. The shop belongs to Ralph Meadows, a shad fisherman for fifty years, rowing alone in one of the square-ended boats—twelve feet long, under five feet wide. This is what he does:

He rows up to the big white pine by the 102 bridge, because that is as far as the law lets him go, and he sets his drift net in the water. The net is five feet from top to bottom and is held across the river, like a net across a tennis court, by two staff poles of spruce or fir, weighted at their lower ends.

"Popple don't work good. It sinks."

The net is held down by musket-sized lead balls, and up by orange floats. It is two hundred and ten feet long. He lets it go. It moves downstream on the ebbing tide. He rows.

The stream bends. He rows to the right-bank staff pole. He pulls it even with the other pole.

"The aim of the game is to keep it straight, but you can't do that always. The currents are too strong. You're going to have a bit of an angle."

He goes down the tributary and into the main-stem Shubenacadie. He rows to the left-bank staff pole to pull it even with the other. Seeing a fish hit the net, he rows to the net to pick it.

"At bends, you swing from one staff pole to the other, swing the net. When you see a fish hit, you go get him. If you're out there six hours, you row six hours. You never stop rowing."

He has been doing this since he was fourteen, and he used to go to Black Rock, at the mouth of the river, eighteen miles downstream; and then he would turn around and fish up on the incoming tide, rowing flat out from staff pole to staff pole, thirty-five fathoms apart, all the while rowing to pick the net—thirty-six miles a day.

He is lithe—obviously—and he is matter-of-fact and soft-spoken.

"It takes eight hours to go down to Black Rock, three and a half hours to come back. Nobody does it all anymore. They fish six to eight hours. The tide goes out slower than in. It will rise in one and a half to two hours, that's why it's so swift. The going out tide is much slower."

Racing up the reversible river, the tide is full of debris—branches, logs, whole trees. It is preferable to be travelling with them and not to be getting in their way, especially if you are tending a two-hundred-foot-long net. Past any given point on the bank, the debris that goes by in the morning will go by again in the afternoon, heading the other way. The tide reaches fifty miles up the Shubenacadie. On the day that I visited Ralph Meadows, a dead forty-foot whale was in the river with the branches, logs, and trees. A television news crew from Halifax was running up and down the small roads, trying to find it and tape a whale bite. Their attention span was about an hour, and they failed. If they had waited in one place all day, they would have seen the whale twice.

At the Shubenacadie's more pronounced eddies, Ralph Meadows will vary his method, bending the net around the upstream end of the eddy, then straight downriver.

"Fish are often along the line between the eddy and the current."

As any shad fisherman knows.

When the tide is pouring in, he routinely looks up into what appears to be a rogue wave bearing down upon him, but a rogue wave is random and this one is there every time—the high, rapid flow that sounds like an express train and is known to science as a tidal bore.

"You just meet it. Your boat goes right up into the air. It rides up on top of it. You stay in the middle, not by the bank. The wall of water could throw your boat six, eight feet up the bank, on the rocks. There's places in the river rougher than the bore—whirlpools, breakers."

Drift-netting the Shubenacadie is now a closed fishery. There is a limited number of licenses. To get one, you have to buy somebody out. If you let your license lapse, nobody gets it. The number is down to twenty-five or so.

Meadows sells to a wholesaler who sells to grocery stores. As he rows hour after hour, and fish keep hitting the net, he might pick and put in his boat as many as two hundred shad. Toward the end he is rowing eight hundred pounds of shad.

"A good catch."

Like the rivers of Alaska, the rivers of Maritime Canada can run all day in the mind. Annapolis River, Cloud River, Cat Arm River, Great Rattling Brook. Restigouche. Tetagouche. Margaree. Cascapédia, Patapédia, Matapédia. The Petitcodiac River. The Shubenacadie River. The Miramichi. Emphasizing the final syllable, the people there pronounce it Meer-uh-muh-shee. The Miramichi has multiple branches flaring from its stem like the petals of an iris. Draining most of central New Brunswick, they flow to the Gulf of St. Lawrence at Miramichi Bay. The longest component is the Southwest Miramichi, which rises close to Maine and traverses the whole of the province. The Southwest Miramichi is the most productive Atlantic-salmon river in New Brunswick—the Miramichi of the Miramichis.

I had read years before in *Fly Fishing Quarterly* that shad run up the Miramichi, and that certain anglers were beginning to show an interest in them, but not yet enough to produce a specific shad fly, just a nameless attractor "in orange and silver tinsel pattern on a size 8 hook." *Field & Stream*, at about the same time, mentioned Old River Lodge, in Doaktown, on the Southwest Miramichi, saying that in addition to its preoccupation with salmon it "caters to shad fishermen throughout June; guide Marty Stewart has been successfully pursuing shad on the Miramichi for several years."

Going up there to keep a date with him, I drove out of Nova Scotia and far up into New Brunswick, the last seventy-five miles or so through an all but unbroken stand of trees. You wouldn't call it a forest. Even if they cover thousands of square miles, you can't call trees a forest when they're of uniform size. In differing zones they were of different heights, yes, but this was more farm than forest. Evergreen all the way, it was about as primeval as a stand of winter wheat. Staring into it league on league, I could all but see it rolling through a laser printer.

Nonetheless, it was wooded country. If you were up in the air, you would have to be high to see beyond it. I felt as I moved north that I had left the temperate zone and gone into a cultivated taiga that might not end until I saw a white bear sniffing the edge of a sea. In time, though, the road descended, and descended, and descended more until it debouched into a domestic river valley that would have been at home in Pennsylvania, and a small town under church steeples, with mowed lawns around frame houses, multi-pump petrol emporiums, a curling rink, and an Orvis store. Doak-town. Some salmon fishermen are as familiar with Doaktown as they are with Rome or Paris.

I crossed the river. A two-lane highway paralleled the left bank. Turning off it after six miles, I went down a long unpaved lane to Old River Lodge, and used what was left of the light of the day sitting on the porch of a cabin looking at the Miramichi. The stretch going by was completely flat and placid, softly bucolic. Add a bright poppy and Corot could have signed it. I wrote in my fishing notes: "This beautiful river in its incised valley is not only reminiscent of—it is much like—the upper Delaware in the general region of Equinunk and Callicoon. The flat water shines with reflection, black and green. It is about fifty yards wide. The meadows of the floodplain are like the meadows of Cochecton. Steep hillsides rise with mixed hardwoods and spruce. The spruce are in about the same abundance as the hemlocks of the Delaware. Route 8 runs near but not beside the river, like Route 97 in New York. Route 8 crosses the Miramichi on a long high bridge at Doaktown. A railroad bridge is there, too, and it much resembles the No. 9 Bridge where the Ten Mile River comes into the Delaware at Tusten."

Next day, I spent the morning on the porch, in part because it was illegal for an alien to fish without a guide. Marty Stewart appeared in the early afternoon. Young, athletic, of middle height and trim, he was a good deal less imposing than his green canoe. As the two of us set off downriver, bow and stern, we had to project our voices to be heard. Living rooms are shorter than that canoe. It was twenty-six feet long, twelve inches longer than the fur traders' *canot du nord* that opened the Canadian West. It had a thirty-nine-inch beam, and the planking of the hull was eastern white cedar. The ribs were cedar, too, the gunwales eastern spruce. The canoe was covered with fiberglass cloth. The thwarts were hardwood—birch or maple. I saw the name of the maker on the bow deck and called him a few weeks later—Doug Sharpe, Tide Head, New Brunswick.

"Why twenty-six feet?" I asked him.

"The shorter the boat, the more water you draw."

True. The thing went down riffles as if they weren't there. With that broad beam, the boat was plenty stable.

"You can walk right on the gunwales."

When Marty Stewart and I came to Dean Bar and its world-renowned salmon pool, he said, "This is where we first started experimenting with the shad fishery." Some years back, he and Bill Page and Michael French, all licensed guides, had decided to fill a hiatus in salmon runs by fishing for pleasure for shad. Every spring, they had seen the schools running as much as eighty miles upriver from Miramichi Bay. Dean Bar seemed an ideal place to intercept them. The channel was next to the left bank, and the bar reached on across the river at an angle downstream. It forced the shad into a narrow space as if they were entering a funnel. The guides had no idea if shad would take a fly. They tied white-and-orange combinations, and gave the flies no names. They used tapered leaders nine or ten feet long, down to eight-pound test, which showed a lot of respect for shad. Empirically, they picked up the first fundamental of shad fishing. In Marty's words, "Let the current take the fly downstream, most strikes come as the line becomes taut." To Marty, Bill, and Michael, the sole purpose was "fun." They were not trying to set up anything commercial. "Michael researched it through the U.S. What he read called for long-shank sixes. They didn't work well here." Nothing worked well here, at Dean Bar. "The shad were just moving through, not holding."

We went on downstream, and before long came to the Sutherland Pool, another frisson-maker in the Atlantic-salmon world but not on every lip as (probably) the best place for shad on the Mira-michi, where, in mid-June, Marty Stewart and his companions would see "four or five thousand shad milling around, spawning, between eight and ten in the evening—fifty or sixty shad chasing on the surface, the bucks chasing the hens." In the guides' own nomenclature, the place became the Shad Bar. They discovered that "the shad went after small flies—size 8 or 10—and would take them in the mouth." He said, "Before then, it was just a dip-net fishery—a couple of local ladies, right here on the Shad Bar." The women drifted downriver in canoes at dusk scooping up shad in big salmon nets. The canoes had to be drifting or the bag of the net would pop out in front of the hoop. They collected as many as a hundred and fifty shad in one evening. They sold them commercially, or salted them for their own consumption, or used them for fertilizer. A little farther down the river, dipnetters use flatbottom boats at night with a light that attracts the shad. In markets in Moncton and Fredericton, you see whole, dressed shad. The dip-netters transport them in forty-five-gallon drums and sell them for a dollar and a half apiece. Like Ralph Meadows, of the Shubenacadie, Marty Stewart eats shad baked with turkey stuffing. Marty stuffs a whole fish and bakes it thirty-five minutes at three-fifty. Then he lays it open, and lifts the backbone out, and serves it as an appetizer to be eaten from fingers. He thinks a knife and fork make an awkward approach to the shad's multiple bones. Some people in Doaktown prefer their shad split, sprinkled with paprika and sugar, and smoked.

From the stern of the canoe, Marty Stewart was seeing shad in the river. From the bow, I was seeing water. It was tinted with tannins from the roots of spruce and other trees, washed in by recent rain, but for me—desperately trying to see the fish he saw—the river might as well have been house paint. I had been in this predicament before. I am as completely inept at seeing fish in a river as I am at reading brands on cattle. The author Thomas

McGuane says you don't look for whole fish; you look for parts—light on the tail, the flicking fin—or shadows or chimerical reflections. But Thomas McGuane is half magic and scarcely qualified as a halt leader.

Offhandedly, Marty remarked that there seemed to be a good number of shad in the river. "There's enough to look promising," he said.

"Where are they?"

"They're six feet in front of you."

"I can't see them!"

"There's a whole school of them."

A few moments later, he said, "There's one with a damaged tail."

I would have been happy to fish right then to the invisible fish, but Marty's sense of shad makes catching them an evening occupation. Waiting for the light to fall—and with something else in mind—he moved on. He was looking for salmon. He probably could not imagine that anyone would seriously cross an international border to fish for shad. I guess he thought I ought to be given my money's worth by taking at least a brief shot at a salmon. He had lived all his life on and around the Miramichi. He was a former fly-casting champion. He could keep a fly line folded flat in the air at his shoulder—forward cast, backcast—increasing its distance until he set it on the water ninety-six feet in front of him, leader not included. I had asked him to fish along with me; and he did some casting, but not a lot. He was smoother than a quartz pebble.

At the head of a pool not far downriver, he swung the canoe around and told me to lower the anchor from its extending sprit off the bow. He handed me a nine-foot fly rod with a floating line and said I ought to cast at a little more than a forty-five-degree angle downstream—more downcurrent than crosscurrent, to keep the fly near the surface. Understand: I'm a roughcast fly fisherman, an empirical self-taught duffer. If I were to enroll in an Orvis school, I'd hate to think where I'd end up in the triage. I engage in the art no more than fifty days a year, which is enough, though, to groove a bad swing. And there, in the presence of a champion, in a twenty-six-foot canoe on the Miramichi, with no warm-up and an unfamiliar rod in hand, I felt unsure and untrained.

There, and at several other stops, I cast for about an hour. My loops varied from flat to Ferris wheel. Not always, but not infrequently, my casts were pure terrible, the line settling in an embarrassing heap. Because I was trying to make a thin X with the direction of the canoe, the fly whistled past the anchor rope. As my nervousness increased through time, I went from mostly to all thumbs. Three times, the fly hit the rope and stuck solid.

As we started back upstream, Marty said, "There was a salmon laying there and we didn't quite get down to where he was. Shit."

We went around a couple of bends and came upon a man in waders, newly arrived and in the stream, casting. Two other men were on the bank. Marty noticed a big, holding salmon.

"You cast this time," I said.

With a nod toward the fisherman, Marty said, "He's obviously a paying client. I'm not going to torture him by catching a fish right beside him."

As dusk was beginning, we arrived again at the Shad Bar— three hundred yards of riffling water. We went right up into it and dropped anchor about forty feet from a long black slick on the surface. Marty changed reels, and strung up a high-density seven-weight sinking line. As he did so, he was saying, "A scallop in the river bottom creates a black slick on the surface, and there's usually a roll or a depression there. Fish hold in the scallop. It's a good place to cast. You read a big river differently from a small stream with boulders, ledges, and overhangs. You look for turbulence from sunken rocks. Fish might be below the rocks. You look for chop lines, created by two merging currents. The chop lines make a soft spot in the current, an excellent fish lie."

I had a box of shad flies. He said they were all too large. On a fifteen-pound tippet, he knotted a fly of his own design. It had a gold pheasant crest, orange bott, silver tinsel body, white polar-bear wing, grizzly hackle, and two bead eyes. He said you tie heavy monofilament into the head, slide the beads over the monofila-ment, then melt it "so the beads will settle in firmly." The hook was stainless-steel, size 8. On the Miramichi, no bait is legal but un-weighted artificial flies.

I stood up, he handed me the rod, and I laid the bead eyes and the silver tinsel on the far side of the black slick, at least forty feet abeam. You cast for shad at right angles to the current. Marty said he liked to go a little higher. I went a little higher, hitting the cur-rent at eleven o'clock. The seven-weight high-density sinking line felt a little like a lead pipe and required more arm, but, again, it unrolled over the slick and swung downstream. Suddenly, I had changed into a totally different fisherman, about as nervous as a rock outcrop. I didn't feel like a tentative bumbler. I was doing my thing. On the fourth or fifth cast, I hooked into a shad. It jumped and tail-walked and was all over the river. I worked it to the net— a little buck shad. Three casts later, the line was tight to another buck shad, and when he came in, looking small like the first one, I asked Marty Stewart, "What's the largest shad you've seen?"

"Seven pounds."

"What do you usually see?"

"Three-pound bucks, five-pound hens."

Marty seemed to have relaxed a lot, too. He would never, ever have said it but he may have been feeling in less danger of having his ear torn off.

Thunder was beginning to grumble, northwest of the river. We had gotten by one threat, only to receive another. I laid the fly on the water and watched it swing. I kept some extra line and added it to the cast during the swing. Marty—after a decent interval—made an oblique remark about feeding extra line in after the cast. He wasn't talking directly to me, but I didn't have to be handed a textbook to see that he felt it was like cheating at cards, that all should be included in the throw. I went on casting my way, and you couldn't argue with the incoming shad. I brought in a five-pound roe. I made a dozen more casts, and—under the increasing thunder—brought in another buck shad. I foul-hooked one and lost a couple before we had to run upriver for cover. Marty had described the Miramichi shad run as a "very short evening fishery;" and that, as a matter of light and lightning, had surely been the case, but in one hour of shad fishing I had hooked up with seven shad.

In 1757, a settler named John Witherspoon was captured by Indians in Annapolis Royal and sold to the French, who imprisoned him on the Miramichi. Furtively keeping a journal, he wrote on May 2: "Hear is a fine river in this place for fishen sammon, bearies, trout and what not. But the people are lazey, and lay up nothing for a rainy day." In 1991, when Portland House, of New York, published "Greatest Fishing Locales of North America," the book made passing mention of shad on the Miramichi, calling them "coarse" fish. In two hundred and thirty-four years, Miramichi shad had migrated from "what not" to "coarse," and it seems safe to say that the trip was consistent. Scarce had "Greatest Fishing Locales" been published, however, when a lodge owner or two—impressed by the off-duty discoveries of the young fishing guides—took out ads and in other ways spread promotional word in an attempt to conjure a clientele shad season on the Miramichi, enriching that lull between salmon.

While I was thanking Marty Stewart for our time on the river, I asked him how significant, over the years, guided shad fishing had become. Roughly, how many shad-fishing clients had come to the Miramichi?

He said, "You're it."

"It?"

"It."

He said the all-time number of sports who had come there to fish for shad was one, was me.

# SEVEN

# THE SHAD ALLEY

It has not been long since the Florida peninsula was under water. Covered with sand, it is a limestone platform—like the Bahamas platform, the Yucatán platform. Now that it is up in the air, its topography and drainage patterns are somewhat bizarre. For example, it has an east-west divide and a north-south divide. The shorter one crosses the peninsula at the latitude of Tampa Bay. The longer divide, running down the axis of the peninsula, is known locally as the Ridge. Its high domains—the Apennines of Florida—rise to an altitude of two hundred and forty feet. For a hundred miles, oranges grow on the Ridge in a broad continuous ribbon. Florida is one of the two or three rainiest states in the United States. West of the Ridge, fairly numerous and short little no-fame rivers run to the Gulf—the Manatee River, the Braden River, the Withlacoochee River, the Pithlachascotee River, the Cow Pen Slough. East of the Ridge, however, is an integral world of fresh water that drains to the Atlantic through a single great river—St. Johns—which, in length, is essentially identical to the Savannah River, the Delaware River, and the Hudson River. It begins in St. Johns Marsh less than twenty miles from the open Atlantic and thirty south of Cape Canaveral. It flows north, and meanders, but is generally parallel to the coast for something like three hundred miles. It broadens into at least a dozen large lakes from Lake Hellen Blazes and Lake Washington to Lake Harney,

Lake Monroe, and Lake George. As it approaches Jacksonville, it is a couple of miles wide, but narrows severely to bend right, left, right through the city and go twenty miles east to the ocean.

With the Nain coast of Labrador, this river brackets the historic range of the American shad, north of which the water is all year too cold and south of which the water is always too hot. The St. Johns schools are one rare race of shad—odd, undersized, ineffable, bizarre. Willy Bemis thinks they may be genetically isolated. The distance from the Bay of Fundy to the mouth of their river is fourteen hundred miles. Making the round trip for several years, they swim well over ten thousand miles. When, for the last time, they arrive off Jacksonville in the fall of the year, the ocean there is cooler than the river, and they do not begin the spawning run. Temperatures in the St. Johns in summer are as warm as human blood. While the river slowly cools, the shad mill around and wait. Elsewhere, American shad are biding their time while American rivers warm up. These individuals have a different chip in their heads. Just to get to Jacksonville they have seriously depleted their energy reserves, and when they reach their spawning grounds—a couple of hundred miles up the river—they will have used up as much as eighty per cent. In the Connecticut River, at spawning time, shad will have used up half their energy and have a fifty per cent chance of surviving. That is why in Florida a hundred per cent of them die.

For some reason, in the St. Johns, they hit best in the middle of the day—in bright sunlight, from ten in the morning to four in the afternoon. In the subtropics, shad behave like people on vacation, deliberately doing things in a different way. They'll hit a shad dart on a trolling fly line. In the Northeast, I've never seen anybody trolling for shad with any kind of rig behind a moving boat, let alone a fly line. In Floridian shad fishing, trolling evidently is what the majority do. In January, I went to Coweta County, Georgia, to help Sam Candler lift his canoe to the top of his car. It was already there. In his mind, he was halfway to the St. Johns. I had been in that canoe with him on other rivers. On the Cemocheckobee, he teased a cottonmouth up onto the blade of his paddle. When we went to Florida to fish for shad, we had actually known each other more than thirty years. While Jimmy Carter was Governor of Georgia, he created a Natural Areas Council to identify landscapes that ought to be protected while they were still there to protect. He appointed Sam to the council. In that era, I made an eleven-hundred-mile trip with Sam and his colleague Carol Ruckdeschel, episodically moving around Georgia from one swamp to the next, and from an isolated valley in the mountains of North Georgia to a sea of pitcher plants in the south, before going down the Cemocheckobee. On this shad trip, as it happened, we drove farther than that.

After all these years, he still calls me LYB, short for Little Yankee Bastard. I call him Mr. Candler. We left his farm, near Sharpsburg, and went down through western Georgia into Alabama, stopping on the way at a state park called the Grand Canyon of Georgia, where a visitor center and railinged lookoffs hang precipitously above gullies over a hundred feet deep that are completely unnatural and the result of agricultural erosion. After crossing the Chattahoochee River, we went down through Alabama and across the Florida panhandle to the Gulf Coast at Panama City.

We were there to see Fred Cross, the State of Florida's shad scientist, who, in a textbook example of the subtle ways of government, had recently been transferred from the St. Johns River to the northwest regional office of the Florida Fish and Wildlife Conservation Commission—three hundred miles from the nearest shad. The regional offices were in an estuarial setting under pines and palms twelve miles from the Gulf. We had scarce shaken hands with Fred Cross when we discerned that he was an experimental and practical scientist of the sort Sam and I would be if we were in his shoes—that is, a fisherman. He said, "The shad come through in waves. You can go half an hour without a bump."

I said, "I can go all day."

He said, "Typically our fishery is a middle-of-the-day fishery—a gentleman's fishery—you don't have to get up before dawn. If the fish run strong, you can catch 'em earlier. You get four or five fish a day. Ten or twenty is not unusual. Fifty to sixty fish used to be a good day."

Fred Cross was nearing fifty. He had a mustache and dark, thinning hair. Over Ben Franklin glasses, his regard was guileless and steady, and his bearing at his desk suggested he'd be happier if it were a boat. As early as Thanksgiving, he said, the river could be cool enough for the fish to decide to enter. For Florida shad, cool enough Fahrenheit is around sixty. The run is under way in December. By mid-January, the water has gone down into the fifties. In a rare year, it may drop through the forties, while orange growers turn on their protective microsprinklers. Then the water warms back to spawning levels, and the height of the shad run occurs in what is still the middle of winter, when the flat water of the upper Delaware is frozen over, and ice wrecks the weirs of the Minas Basin.

Fred Cross told us that tides affect the St. Johns as much as a hundred miles upriver, and considerably farther if water levels are low. Even in the stretch that is locally called the Shad Alley the river can be reversible, turning around to flow back toward the south twice a day. The river was low at the moment, he said, but not that low.

The salt-fresh line is not as distinct in the St. Johns as it is in other rivers, largely due to salt deposits near its source—a result of the peninsula's submarine history. In and near the Shad Alley, he told us, the amount of salt in the river water is usually about one part per thousand, or one thirty-fifth of the average amount of salt in the ocean. Even so, that was roughly thirty times as much salt as you would find in most freshwater rivers, imposing one more difference on the physiology of the species, and enhancing the impression that the shad of Florida are a race apart.

The fishery is very popular in the state, Cross said. The *Orlando Sentinel* used to sponsor shad derbies. His dad took him to them in the nineteen-fifties, when he was a kid. The shad were bigger then. Cross was born and raised in Eustis, in Lake County, among the myriad lakes that lie in limestone sinks along the summit of the Ridge. He began his studies in limnology at the University of Florida, in Gainesville, and went on to earn his advanced degree in the subject at the University of Central Florida. "Limnology was the closest thing to fisheries science Florida had," he remarked. In addition to shad, his work as a fisheries biologist has been mainly on centrarchids and sturgeons.

Sam, who had said nothing so far in the course of this interview, stirred slightly in his chair, his beard elevating until it pointed at Fred Cross. Nothing in his soft, rural voice, and nothing in his easeful manner, revealed his cyclonic desire to be on the St. Johns River. "That Shad Alley y'all mentioned. Where exactly was that?"

Sam had guided me to northern pike in Canada, and I him to bass in Pennsylvania. This time we were guiding each other—a zero-sum situation if ever there was one, since neither of us had ever been where we were going. I had with me a roll of maps in the United States Geological Survey's 1:24,000 series—the largest scale of any standard series, one inch equals four-tenths of a mile. I unrolled them in front of Fred Cross. He leafed through the stack, and pulled out only the Osteen quadrangle and the Geneva quadrangle, setting the others aside.

He said, "There are two major areas—the Mullet Lake stretch, from Lake Jessup to Lake Harney, where it's all troll fishing; and the Puzzle Lake stretch, from the discharge end of Puzzle Lake to the Highway 46 bridge, a distance of about four miles. The

Shad Alley is in the Mullet Lake stretch. People fish from boats or from the bank wearing knee-high boots, using fly rods or ultra-light spinning rods. In the Puzzle Lake stretch, when the river is at flood stage it's two miles across, and when it's down you can throw a rock across it. Right now, it's normal low water. Last fall, the water was into the oaks."

While speaking, he had drawn an arrow on the Osteen quadrangle at a place where the river touched a road. He said we could rent a flats skiff there, with outboard. Then he shaded in the Shad Alley—with its S-shaped meander bends and a cutoff oxbow—from the rental dock to Lemon Bluff and Le Fils Slough, less than four miles of the river. Refining things further, he made a series of small X's in spots where shad are sometimes only a little less dense than they would be in the hold of a canning ship. Or so I imagined Sam was imagining. "The St. Johns is a low-gradient river," Cross remarked as he moved his pencil, adding that the Shad Alley is only eight to ten feet above sea level, but the gradient increases there and with it the current. Shad, as lotic spawners, need a certain amount of flow. The river's highest altitude is twenty-five feet. He said the migrating schools were stopped only by a low-head dam near the source. In Florida, the juveniles are called shadeens.

On the Geneva quadrangle, he sketched in fence-line landmarks, made several X's, and wrote "real popular area" at a left-hand bend near Cabbage Slough and Buzzard Roost, south of Route 46.

I asked him the size of the Florida record shad.

He said, "Five point two pounds. The average female is two and a half to three." The Fish and Wildlife Conservation Commission has an annual meeting in Titusville in February, he told us. Always, the conferees take an afternoon off to go shad fishing. "I'll eat a meal or two of roe a year and that's enough for me," he went on. "Very few of us kill fish anymore. The shad's popularity as

catch-and-release, as a fly-rod fish particularly, has jumped tremen-
dously. I wish y'all good luck."

Out of the building and into the car, we drove three hundred
miles without stopping more than five minutes. Out of and back to
Fairbanks, I once drove eight hundred miles in Alaska to fish for
one day for king salmon. This trip was slitting the envelope—so
far, six hundred and thirty miles one-way, to fish for American
shad.

We rented a flats boat, and cast conventionally as we made our
way upstream. Around the first bend, we lost sight of the road, and
in long stretches thereafter—as much as half or three-quarters of a
mile—saw no houses or structures of any kind. The river was intimate, less than a hundred yards across, and edged with lily pads,
hyacinths, and grassy cutbanks, not to mention cabbage palms—
young bulbous cabbage palms, old columnar cabbage palms. Look
up to cast and you saw water turkeys, eagles, hawks, ibises, crows,
egrets, buzzards, Louisiana herons, great blue herons, herring
gulls, kingfishers, and cormorants, identified by Sam. A pileated
woodpecker. We were not in some everglade or even a state park.
Around us were the St. Johns floodplain savannahs. We were
twenty miles northeast of Orlando, and twenty west of the ocean.
At frequent intervals, oranges floated by.

We scouted the river to Lemon Bluff—firm ground ten feet
higher than the river, and lined with cottages and small houses. We
saw longhorn cattle there that looked head-on like sailplanes. We
saw an ornamental citrus tree with lemons, grapefruit, oranges,
and tangerines growing on various branches. Lemon Bluff is a storied place to fish for shad. We fished there, at the mouth of Le Fils
Slough, and caught no shad. We drifted back down the river half a
mile and anchored beside a high cutbank, which Fred Cross had
marked with an X on the map. Flicking a dart from his ultra-light,
Sam brought in a leaping buck shad. With a very small dart on a fly
rod, I brought in a leaping buck shad. Sam got another. With a

spinning rod, I tied on a rig I'd bought from the people who rented us the skiff—a spoon with a shad-dart dropper—and caught two roe shad on one cast. Then Sam had a buck that got off the hook. Under the cutbank the current was particularly evident. When an orange went by, it was moving smartly. We were reading line 1 in the ledger of the slow St. Johns: Where the current is most concentrated, so are the shad.

On the end of our lines, racing crosscurrent, the bright silver fish looked red in the water—a dark herbal red, mainly from cypress tannins.

Sam said, "That color is like Coca-Cola."

I said, "That color is like Pepsi-Cola."

Sam said, "Don't mention Pepsi-Cola. This is a pretty spot."

On a canoe trip in Canada, he once told his children and mine that if you were to pour Pepsi-Cola on the roots of a spruce it would kill it to the ground. His children's great-great-grandfather was the Atlanta pharmacist who developed the Coca-Cola Company.

In settings much like this cutbank under the high grasses on the St. Johns, Sam and I had been in the company of alligators. They had swum under us fast as torpedoes, fizzing like ginger ale. Once, in a skiff on a tidal creek at low water, Sam, standing up, was about to cast a shrimp net when the grasses parted above us. We were right up close to the bank, and its slick mud wall rose five, six feet above our heads, the tide was so low. An extremely large alligator suddenly appeared there, almost directly overhead. It came down the bank fast, went into the water beside the boat and swam off. This cutbank looked so much like the cutbank in the tidal creek that I was waiting for the grass to part. Alligators were there. They were all over the savannahs in the places we fished, Fred Cross later told me on the telephone. But they were not evident, in part because of the mid-winter coolness, and in part because Florida some ten years earlier had opened an alligator-hunting season, allowing people with spears and gigs to kill them. He said, "The alligators have become a lot less aggressive. When they see a boat, they go into the grass and hide."

More oranges were floating by, roughly at the rate of one orange per shad. You might have thought you were fishing in the Indian River. It occurred to me that someone reading this might think we were indeed on the Indian River, the two bodies of water being so nearly parallel and close. Deservedly celebrated for the high-sugar oranges that grow near it and eventually bear its name on their skins, the Indian River reaches a hundred and twenty miles from Turnbull Hummock above Cape Canaveral to St. Lucie Inlet near Palm Beach, and is in no sense a river. It is a tidal lagoon—a saltwater bay behind a barrier beach. Sam was outwitting another leaping buck. By now, we were down in the prime of Shad Alley, its principal thoroughfare—a mile and more with a very gentle bend, populated by half a dozen shad fishermen, who were all trolling in long oval loops, counterclockwise. We had caught the rhythm, and had joined them, catching fish. It was like group skating in a rink. The Alley was six or seven feet deep, with holes eight or ten. The shad were just downstream from sandbars. Now and again we cast, but mostly settled into the trolling mode—both ways getting bumps, hits, and shad galore, losing many as well. Going round and round—upriver, down—we became familiar with the people in the other boats. They were of many ages, all male. One called out, in the universal jargon of piscine lust, "Are you killin' 'em?"

My fly rod and fly line were particularly effective as trolling devices, a setup Sam regarded as funny until he noticed that the fly rod more often was bent over than straight. The shad were surely hitting in the brightest light, which would not be the case in the north. I remembered reading a piece by Robert Elman in *Fly Fishing Quarterly* and have since looked it up. He said, "Slightly turbid water is ideal; very clear or muddy will curtail strikes. An odd fact, which I can't explain, is that shad in Southern rivers hit well in bright sunlight, yet their Northern relatives hit best on overcast days, in light rain, early in the morning, or just before sunset." With their extreme sensitivity to light, shad in Canada relish the turbidity of the Bay of Fundy. In Florida, evidently, they are protected and contented by the dark-hued water, as any shad would be in a river of Coca-Cola.

In scientific papers Fred Cross had given us, I had read that anglers on the St. Johns in the previous season spent four thousand seven hundred and sixty-four hours catching five thousand four hundred and thirty-four shad. Two-thirds came from the Shad Alley. The anglers released eighty-nine per cent, and kept about six hundred shad. One season in the nineteen-fifties, when the U.S. Fish and Wildlife Service initiated a creel census on the St. Johns, they discovered that sport fishermen caught sixty-five thousand two hundred and forty-six shad. There had once been a large commercial harvest. In Palatka, in 1875, a single gill net caught eleven thousand shad. The peak period was 1888 to 1908. The peak year was 1908, with two million eight hundred and thirty-three thousand netted shad. They were not sold locally. Most were shipped to New York's Fulton Fish Market. Gill nets were eventually banned, but not until the nineteen-nineties.

In all, we hooked up with three dozen shad in Shad Alley. We also fished in what Fred Cross had called the Puzzle Lake stretch, fifteen miles upstream from Shad Alley, where flats skiffs were not available. We unstrapped Sam's old Grumman canoe, started off from a boat launch beside a bridge, and paddled south into a scene as broad, spare, and open as the Shad Alley had been lush and confined. This was savannah on a far-reaching scale, wide-floodplain river in Florida's expression of the term—a view, even from canoe level, two miles in one direction across panic grasses and bullwhips to cattle under hardwoods on enlofted ground, and in the other direction a mile to the nearest tree. The river was all but lost in its own channels, islands, meanders, and braids. In all that open space, we had to hunt to find it—to choose channel over dead water, mainstream over slough, sometimes guessing the difference. Exactly like the migrating shad, we were trying above all to sense current, which in places was easy to do but in others was baffling, and we lacked their neural equipment. The speed of the current was less than a mile an hour. Eel grass helped, bent along the bottom, pointing. This vast, serene world just enveloped the canoe and sent us into a separate existence. We came to a fence line that Fred Cross had pencilled in on our map, and to the "real popular area" opposite, where the current curled against a strip of hard ground. Lacking an anchor, we tied up to some cattails at its downstream end.

Sam lost a somersaulting buck. Failing to land hooked shad may be a norm of shad fishing but Sam and I seemed to be particularly good at it. I netted two, but lost two more. I caught a largemouth bass, a crappie, and a blueback herring—all on small shad darts. I used the fly rod more than the spinning rod. I lost another shad right at the boat.

Losing a few fish was hardly in a league with what we lost now. The weekend had come, and, with it, squadrons of jet skis. They came up the river in echelons—four, now five, now six—and bore down on us like Hornets, like F-18s strafing. We paddled hard for cover. They were harmless, of course, just "personal watercraft" flashing metallic colors, flown by sitting wetsuits. Materially, they changed nothing but the water in a temporary way, but in their sustained burst of decibels they deleted all serenity.

Then airboats came and outdecibeled the jet skis. Even from a mile away, off in the dead-water sloughs, the airboats—with their five-hundred-horsepower automotive engines, their fenced-in propellers whirling at supersonic speeds—made a blitzkrieg of the whole savannah, the spoken word inaudible from bow to stern in a canoe. From the Everglades northward, the airboat is the Florida state amphibian, its little brother the jet ski. It is said that when rain is plentiful, and water high, airboats coming down from Jacksonville could cross the north-south divide between St. Johns Marsh and Lake Kissimmee, and then continue to Key West. The peninsula emerged in the Pleistocene, when so much water was locked up as ice on the continents that sea level dropped a hundred fathoms. The sea has come back up a good way, but the glaciation in no small quantity remains on Greenland and Antarctica. When that melts, Florida is going back where it came from. On this eruptive day in the floodplain savannah, there was something to be said for global warming.

Later on, we moved downstream a mile or so to some firm ground close to the current. We beached the canoe. In knee-high boots, we walked along, casting from the bank. Jet skis in front of us, airboats behind us, we would make these casts and call it a day. A roe shad responded. She was no shadeen. She weighed about three and a half pounds.

Toward the end of afternoon, paddling north, we were passed by returning jet skiers, and, overhead, by crows on their way to roost—a ribbon galaxy of crows, three miles long. At the boat launch, the crowd was considerable. Up from the river we carried the canoe through a jam of pickups, SUVs, and boat trailers. After we set it down, a man with a Bronco, addressing me, asked, "How did you do?" It may be hard to say that without a smile, but it came across with a certain cumulus rumble. At first, nonetheless, I thought he was a fisherman. I said, "Fine. And how did you do?" Then I looked beside the Bronco and saw his jet ski. He had changed out of his wetsuit. Back there on the river, I may have seemed to have been signalling him with a part of one hand. He snarled: "I had fun."

# EIGHT

# THE FOUNDING FISH

The Schuylkill rises northwest of Reading and flows about a hundred miles before it bends right to run closely parallel to the Delaware River, framing the old city of Philadelphia—Independence Hall, the tree streets, etcetera—in a mesopotamian isthmus. At Long Ford on the Schuylkill, near Valley Forge, settlers in the early seventeen-hundreds fenced the river in various ways to intercept the spring migration of American shad. They constructed rock dams, V-shaped weirs of piled stones, and fish racks. A rack was an underwater picket fence with gaps narrow enough to stop shad and wide enough to accommodate the current. Shad piled up against the racks like driftwood. Shad that got past the racks were driven back into them by men on horseback beating the water with bushes. Weir, rack, or fish dam, the methods were so effective that farmers upstream complained. Fresh shad in spring and salt shad the rest of the year were basics in a farm's economy. In 1724 and 1730, the colonial legislature passed acts forbidding such obstructions and calling for removal of the ones that existed. The fishermen of Long Ford ignored these laws. Meanwhile, the settlements upriver had even greater cause for grievance than deprivation of fish. Coming downstream in loaded canoes heading for the markets of Philadelphia, they were swept into the weirs, racks, and dams. Here are some examples just from 1732. Isaac Smally and partner, with a hundred and forty bushels of wheat in their canoe,

"stroke fast on a Rack Dam and in order to save ye Load from being all lost, he was much against his mind obliged to leap into ye
River, the water being to his Chin frequently dashed into his
mouth, where between whiles he breathed, and both he and his
partner held ye Canoe with great labour: whiles a young man there
present ran above a mile to call help to gett off." Marcus Huling
"striking on a fish dam . . . took in a great deal of water into ye
wheat, by means whereof his wheat was much damnified." In the
"Extream Cold" of February, Jonas Jones "stroke fast on a fish
Dam, and to save his Load of wheat was obliged to leap into ye
River to ye middle of his body and with all his Labour and Skill
could not get off in less than half an hour, afterwards proceeding
on his journey with ye said wet cloaths they were frozen stiff on his
back."

Across the seventeen-thirties, similar things happened to
the freight-laden canoes of Jacob Warren, Walter Campbell, Jonas
Yeokam, Richard Dunklin, George Boone, James Boone, John
Boone, Joseph Boone, and Samuel Boone. All lived upriver from
Long Ford. All crashed into racks and dams. Official law enforce-
ment was ineffectual-to-nil. So on April 20, 1738, upstream farmers came downriver in a fleet of canoes to enforce the law
themselves. They deracinated fish racks and destroyed dams
and weirs, but failed to get away before downriver settlers in
their own fleet of canoes came out on the river and counterat-
tacked. Big swinging "clubbs" broke a bone here, bashed a head
there, and left John Wainwright "as Dead with his Body on the
Shoar & his ffeet in the River." The fish-dam defenders were superior in numbers and they dispersed and chased the upstream canoes, and wrecked them beyond repair after they were beached
and abandoned.

All those Boones on the losing side were siblings or close relatives of three-year-old Daniel Boone, whose Quaker parents, Sarah
Morgan and Squire Boone, had settled in 1731 in what became

Exeter Township. A story from Daniel Boone's later childhood, for which I am indebted to the biographer John Mack Faragher, shows that the fishing war was not a total loss for Boone's family and neighbors. In what must have been the early seventeen-forties, Sarah Morgan was cleaning newly caught shad at the edge of the Schuylkill one warm spring afternoon while her idle son Daniel lay on his back with his hat across his eyes. Two girls came along, picked up a bucket of shad guts and overturned it onto Daniel. He got up and smacked both of them, bloodying their noses. They ran off crying, and came back with their mother, who heaped scorn on Mrs. Boone as well as her son. Sarah looked inquiringly at Daniel. He said, "They are not girls. Girls would not have done such a dirty trick. They are rowdies." Mrs. Boone then said to the rowdies' mother, "If thee has not brought up thy daughters to better behavior, it was high time they were taught good manners. They got no more than they deserved."

The Schuylkill was to become the most storied river in the American history of American shad. This honor could have gone to almost any river of the eastern continent, so relatively abundant were the shad runs of the eighteenth century, but in the winter of 1777–78 George Washington elected to bivouac his army on the right bank of the Schuylkill.

It was the spring shad run in the Schuylkill that saved George Washington's army from starvation at Valley Forge.

The local shad run on the Schuylkill came as a godsend.

Then, dramatically, the famine completely ended. Countless thousands of fat shad, swimming up the Schuylkill to spawn, filled the river. Sullivan's men, accustomed to treading out fresh-water mussels in the stream, were astonished to see the water almost boiling with the struggling fish. Soldiers thronged the river bank. Then, at the advice of Pennsylvanians accustomed to the yearly fishing, the cavalry was ordered into the river bed. Carrying huge bushes, broken tree boughs, and long sticks, the horsemen rode upstream, noisily shouting and beating the water, driving the shad before them into nets spread across the Schuylkill at Pawling's ford, where the Perkiomen flows into the river. So thick were the shad that, when the fish were cornered in the nets, a pole could not be thrust into the water without striking fish. Thousands of the tasty, rich shad were netted at each haul. The netting was continued day after day, with more than a hundred horsemen continually beating the water, until the army was thoroughly stuffed with fish and in addition hundreds of barrels of shad were salted down for future use. The lavish fish feast was a dramatic close to a long period of privation.

In article upon article and book after book, a shad fisherman given to riffling pages will be drawn to the Schuylkill River in the fourth spring of the American Revolution. The random quotations above are, respectively, from Mary Anne Hines, Gordon Marshall, and William Woys Weaver's "The Larder Invaded: Reflections on Three Centuries of Philadelphia Food and Drink" (The Library Company of Philadelphia and the Historical Society of Pennsylvania, Philadelphia, 1987), David G. Martin's "The Philadelphia Campaign: June 1777–July 1778" (Combined Books, Conshohocken, Pennsylvania, 1993), and Harry Emerson Wildes' "Valley Forge" (Macmillan, New York, 1938).

With respect to George Washington, it would not have been a leap of the imagination for him to anticipate the spring shad run and choose a campsite accordingly. He was a commercial shad fisherman. Moreover, he did not require Daniel Boone to tell him that the Schuylkill was a prime fishery. While another river might be half a mile wide, this one was small enough to string a net across and by 1777 had long been synonymous with shad. Not to mention other species. Even in 1704, there was an established "fishing Damm" in Lower Merion Township. The best Schuylkill fishing spots were before long in such demand that stiff fees were charged for one cast with a hoop net. In the *Pennsylvania Gazette*, notices like this one (February 27, 1766) were not uncommon: "TO BE LETT, a SHAD and Herring Fishery, near the mouth of Schuylkill." In 1767, to ease farmers' tensions during the spring migration and give the fish themselves half a chance to complete their mission, the legislature decreed that fishermen on opposite banks had to fish on alternate days and, right bank or left bank, could use only one seine per twenty-four hours per pool. In 1771, fishing was banned in the Schuylkill from Saturday sunset to Monday sunrise.

The boats in use in fishing and freighting were pine, cedar, and chestnut canoes. William Penn observed a canoe hewn from a single poplar and carrying four tons of bricks. There were shallops piled high with hay, arks piled high with produce, and long anguilliform multipart rafts with steering oars bow and stern. These vessels, as noted, tended to "stroke" and disintegrate in the very places where shad congregate—the river's shelving rapids. Rounding the great bend at Spring Mill (now known in Schuylkill Expressway traffic reports as the Conshohocken curve), boatmen moving downstream came into view of rapids they called falls, the beginnings of a twenty-four-foot drop in six miles—Spring Mill Fall, Rummel Fall, Mount Ararat Fall, and Great Falls, more commonly known as the Falls of Schuylkill, which have been drowned for nearly two centuries in a dammed pool in the city of Philadelphia. The *Pennsylvania Gazette*, March 28, 1771:

> TO BE LETT, and entered upon the 15th day of April, THAT large and convenient TAVERN, where Mrs. CUMMINS now lives. The situation is one of the most pleasant in the neighbourhood of Philadelphia, and being only five miles distant, and a good road, it has long been noted for a resort of the best company, when the weather would permit. It has the advantage of a Shad fishery at the door.

The *Pennsylvania Gazette* was owned and edited by Benjamin Franklin, who knew a clean river when he drank from one. He first saw Philadelphia as it came into view from a boat on the Delaware he helped to row—on Sunday morning, October 6, 1723. He landed hungry and walked into town. He was seventeen years old. On Second Street, he bought three oversized rolls from a baker. He put one under each arm, and began to eat the other. It seems to have made him thirsty. "Then I turn'd and went down Chestnut Street and part of Walnut Street, eating my Roll all the Way, and coming round found myself again at Market Street Wharf, near the Boat I came in, to which I went for a Draught of the River Water." In the mid-twentieth century, a pollution block at Philadelphia—actually, a thirty-mile anoxic sag—would stop absolutely the springtime runs of American shad. But this was not the twentieth century. The river bottom was clearly visible even fifteen feet down. And shad in uncountable numbers ran up the Delaware and the tributary Schuylkill.

In July, 1748, a notice in the *Pennsylvania Gazette* said that Preserve Brown was selling pickled shad by the barrel at the upper end of Water Street. On Second Street, Preserve's son Preserve sold "Good Four penny Beer." Both Preserves were buyers of oats.

By 1748, when you sat down to high tea in Philadelphia you could almost count on being offered a plate of pickled shad. October 17, 1765:

> Some time in September last, was left at the House of George Gilbert, at the Sign of the Crooked Billet, near the Slip, in Vine Street, a Barrel of Salt Shad, branded on the Head Reuben Hains. The owner is desired to come and pay the Charges, and take the fish.

John Kaighn, of Second Street, took an ad on October 31, 1771, to say that he was selling "silver watches, neat fowling pieces, and fine and coarse three thread laid seine twine. Also pickled shad."

Isaac Melcher, of Second Street, June 9, 1773:

> Genuine Madeira, Lisbon and Teneriffe WINE, by the Pipe or Quarter Cask; West India and Philadelphia RUM; best French Brandy; Holland Geneva; German Scythes, Cutting knives, Grass hooks and Whetstones; best Oil flints, genuine French Indigo; choice Bohea Tea; Burlington Pork; and Fresh Shad, in barrels.

September 14, 1774:

> Choice Shad, in Barrels and Half Barrels are to be SOLD by William Milnor, in Water-street . . . They are exceeding fat, and are warranted sound and well cured; the great inconvenience that farmers and others, at a great distance from rivers, labour under in getting their supply of fish in the season, appearing obvious to the subscriber, he, in order to remedy this, erected a fishery on Patowmack river,

in Maryland, where the shad are taken in cool clear water, three hundred miles from the sea, and salted down immediately out of the water, which renders them much better than when they are carried a great distance before they are cured . . . Country store-keepers taking ten barrels, or upwards, shall have a proper abatement.

The *Pennsylvania Gazette* of January 4, 1775, reported "An Act to Prevent Frauds in the Packing and Preserving Shad." The standard barrel volume was defined as thirty-one and a half gallons, "well packed and well secured, with a proper Quantity of Salt and Pickle, in tight Casks, made of good, sound, well seasoned White Oak Timber."

I am much indebted to the Library Company of Philadelphia for the use of its electronic archive of the *Pennsylvania Gazette*, also the bound volumes. Now at 1314 Locust Street, the Library Company of Philadelphia was the first public library in America. It was founded—as who would ever guess?—by Benjamin Franklin.

William Penn visited his colony twice, for two years each time—1682–84, 1699–1701. Soon after his first arrival, he held a council with the Lenape and asked for fishing rights on the Schuylkill—so obvious was the abundance and importance of the fishery. In a pamphlet about Pennsylvania that Penn wrote in England in 1685 is a section called "Of the Produce of our Waters," the produce of greatest importance being whales, sturgeon, and shad.

Alloes, as they call them in France, the Jews Allice, and our Ignorants, Shads, are excellent Fish and of the Bigness of our largest Carp: They are so Plentiful, that Captain Smyth's Overseer at the Skulkil, drew 600 and odd at one Draught; 300 is no wonder; 100 familiarly. They are excellent Pickled or Smokt'd, as well as boyld fresh: They are caught by nets only.

Penn's daughter Margaret fished in the Delaware, and wrote home to a brother asking him to "buy for me a four joynted strong fishing Rod and Real with strong good Lines," but shad would not have been her quarry. Shad fishing did not attract anglers in large numbers until well into the twentieth century. In 1776, a sport-fishing tackle shop did exist in Philadelphia, as this advertisement in *Dunlap's Pennsylvania Packet* attests:

FISHING TACKLE of all sorts, for use of either SEA or RIVER, made and sold by EDWARD POLE In Market-street.

The suspiciously surnamed Pole mentioned "Red cedar, hazel, dogwood fishing rods for fly, trolling and bottom fishing . . . pocket reels . . . best green or white hair, silk, hardest hempen, flaxen and cotton lines . . . artificial flies, moths, and hackles . . . the best kinds of fish hooks, of various sizes, made at Philadelphia." All that notwithstanding, if you were specifically interested in shad, Edward Pole would sell you "seines ready made."

There was, to be sure, a sport-fishing aspect in small ready-made seines. For example, from 1732 onward the recreational gentlemen of the Colony in Schuylkill—a fishing-and-hunting club—caught shad in seines. Early on, they put them back, preferring, as food, salmon, perch, and rock fish (striped bass). Shad were only beginning to rise in status from the tables of the poor, and the members of the Colony in Schuylkill were not impecunious. They were golden flakes of the upper crust. They thought of themselves as a distinct political entity, the fourteenth-ranking colony, or possibly the first. Twenty-seven men in all, they cooked together and ate together what they killed and caught. They fished in rowboats, which they called frigates. Their collective frigates were their "Navy." They had their own Assembly, Governor, Sheriff, Coroner. They sometimes fished with rods twenty-five feet long. They used worms. The site of their first seat of government is beside Interstate 76 on the right bank of the Schuylkill in central Philadelphia. Before long they moved upstream to Lower Merion Township and the prime fishery of the Falls of Schuylkill. They pan-fried their perch, boiled their stripers and salmon, and eventually planked their shad. According to their first official history (published in 1889), they invented planked shad. On one of the Colony's outings in the seventeen-sixties—one of their "Publick fishing days"—the club member who had been designated Caterer of the Day came in with an eight-pound shad. The Coroner said it had not died in a sporting way. He said he had seen the Caterer buy it at the corner of Front and Market. Moreover, the vendor who sold him the fish accused the Caterer of trying to pass off a pewter two-shilling piece. The Caterer instructed an Apprentice to cook the shad on live coals. Instead, the eye of the inventive Apprentice fell on an "old oaken rudder" hanging on a wall and he removed it and nailed the split shad to it, skin side down. He slathered the fish with oil and wine, added salt and pepper, and propped up the rudder at an angle near the fire. As in a reflector oven, the shad baked in radiant heat, its juices migrating this way and that as the rudder was inverted. The result was so savory and aromatic that word spread and people combed the city for rudders and centerboards on which to plank shad, all but dismantling the ships at the Delaware wharves. That is the official story. In the twenty-first century, every shad festival from the Rappahannock to the Connecticut still features planked shad, propped before beds of live coals. As a registered curmudgeon, I broil my daily shad for fifteen minutes and thirty seconds under gas, and never go to festivals.

In the Connecticut River valley, shad were once known as Gill pork. It was a mean thing to say. It meant that people of Gill, Massachusetts, were so poor that they could not afford salt pork. They lacked "a competency"—that is, in Webster's words, "property or means sufficient for the necessaries and conveniences of life: sufficiency without excess." Gill is near Greenfield and Turners Falls, not far from New Hampshire, and the prejudice about shad seems to have faded north of Gill. But rifely downriver, in Connecticut and Massachusetts frontier towns, a sense of shame was set on the table with shad. In Hadley, near the present site of Holyoke Dam, a family about to sit down to dinner heard a knocking on the door and, before seeing who was there, hid a platter of shad under a bed. Churches had a practice called dignifying pews. The socially higher-ranking families got the better seats. Shad were plentiful, cost little or nothing, and were eaten by the poor. If you were known to eat shad, you got a bad pew. In his "History of Hadley, Including the Early History of Hatfield, South Hadley, Amherst and Granby, Massachusetts," Sylvester Judd wrote, "It was discreditable for those who had a competency to eat shad; and it was disreputable to be destitute of salt pork, and the eating of shad implied a deficiency of pork." Judd also said, "The story which has been handed down, that in former days, the fishermen took the salmon from the net, and often restored the shad to the stream, is not a fable." The fact that Indians were known to eat shad further deepened the taint, not to mention the humble employment given shad by the parvenu whites of Plymouth. December 11, 1621, less than a year after the Plymouth landing, Edward Winslow wrote in a letter: "We set the last spring some twenty acres of Indian corn, and sowed some six acres of barley and peas; and, according to the manner of the Indians, we manured our ground with herrings, or rather shads, which we have in great abundance." And in "New English Canaan, or New Canaan," 1637, the trader Thomas Morton reported that shad were "taken in such multitudes in every river . . . that the inhabitants dung their ground with them."

Even in Philadelphia, in William Penn's time, expensive places like the Blue Anchor, the Pewter Platter, and the State House Tavern served oceangoing turtles and migrating sturgeons, ignoring shad. Slowly, though, a change was taking place in the colonies, as the culinary appeal of the American shad overcame the inegalitarian attitudes of the American people. In 1683 in Massachusetts, the sawyer John Pynchon, a man of means, bartered a fishnet for packed shad that he could ship to market, and fifty additional shad for his family. Commercial seine-haul fisheries burgeoned not only in the Schuylkill, but the Delaware, the Susquehanna, the Hudson—and even in New Jersey's Raritan River. There was a realty selling point in the spring migration. In the *Pennsylvania Gazette* for October 30, 1729, a New Jersey land tract of a thousand acres was presented for sale, eight miles upstream from Perth Amboy, about where the New Jersey Turnpike now crosses the river, "a good Landing . . . excellent for taking of Shad at the Time of Year when they are in Season." By 1736, barrelled Connecticut River shad were being advertised in Boston. In 1743, in the Connecticut River town of Northampton, Deacon Ebenezer Hunt recorded in an account book the fish's ultimate breakthrough in respectability: "Shad are very good, whether one has pork or not." Fishermen tied rowboats to the rocks below the falls at South Hadley, and went after shad with scoop nets. They filled the boats to the tipping point, rowed them ashore, and rowed back to the rocks below the falls, their oar blades hitting shad. It was not uncommon, in a single day, for one man with a rowboat to bring back three thousand shad. As yet, almost no one cared for shad roe. The roe sacs were discarded. Or they were fed to pigs. Or they were given to the poor.

More than two hundred miles up the Delaware, in the early

seventeen-fifties, fishermen trapped shad with brush seines made of saplings that had leafed out. The saplings were tied together with pliant twigs, probably of willow. The brush seines were long enough to span the river.

At the mouth of the Hudson, netting was of course more advanced. The *Pennsylvania Gazette* printed this item in 1756 under the dateline New York, April 19: "The same day 5751 Shad were caught at one Draught, on the West Side of Long Island."

New York *Journal*, April 26, 1770:

> Last week a remarkable number of shad fish was taken at the Narrows, on Long Island. One of the seines, as it was drawn toward the shore, was so filled with fish, that the weight pressed it to the ground, whereby great numbers escaped. A second seine was then thrown out around the fish, a third around the second, and a fourth around the third . . . The number of shad that were taken by the first net was three thousand; by the second, three thousand; by the third, four thousand; and by the fourth, fifteen hundred; in all, eleven thousand five hundred!

On August 4, 1773, a farm was offered for rent in the *Pennsylvania Gazette*:

> . . . very pleasantly situated on Patowmack River, about five miles below Alexandria, and contains about 200 acres of cleared land, very good for grain of every kind, and tobacco; as also one of the largest and best springs on this side the Blue Ridge, within twenty yards of the door; it has a front upon the river of near a mile and an half, affording several good fishing landings; one of which only rented last spring, during the shad and herring season, for Twenty-five Pounds; to this belongs a well accustomed

Ferry, upon the most direct road leading from Annapolis through Colchester, Dumfries, and Fredericksburg to Williamsburg; on the premises are a dwelling house, with two brick chimnies and seven rooms, a kitchen, smoke-house, &c.

In block letters, the notice was signed, "WASHINGTON."

Was George Washington, in 1773, so well known in Philadelphia that all he had to supply was his surname? Evidently so. To be sure, he was a member of Virginia's House of Burgesses. But, reader, can you name any state legislator who lives in your own county, let alone a Congressman from the Eighth District of Virginia? Washington had become essentially a farmer. After returning from the French and Indian Wars, aged twenty-six, he had resigned his commission in the army, had been married soon thereafter, and had dedicated his energy to the success of his plantation, about a hundred miles up the Potomac River from its mouth on the Chesapeake Bay. The plantation, Mount Vernon, was his principal occupation for the sixteen years that preceded the American Revolution. One of his biographers, the novelist Owen Wister, describes this period in Washington's life as "the longest parenthesis in the rush of his public existence." To Washington, those years must have seemed less a parenthesis than a career.

He grew wheat and ground it in his mill. He grew corn. His cattle brand was GW. He rented his tobacco lands. His contiguous farms amounted to something more than eight thousand acres. He made boots and shoes. He wove wool plaid, barricum, striped silk, jump stripe, calico, broadcloth, and dimity. By 1769, his wheat milling was up to six thousand two hundred and forty-one bushels. He once said, in all modesty, that his flour was "equal, I believe, in quality to any made in this country." His coopers made the barrels in which the flour was packed and shipped. The barrels were stencilled "George Washington, Mount Vernon." Much of it went out in his own schooner, which he built in 1765. He shipped shad to Antigua and elsewhere, presumably with his name on the barrels. The Mount Vernon distillery did not come along until his second term as President, when he signed an excise law that made the whiskey business particularly attractive. Meanwhile, through the pre-war years, he augmented the profits of Mount Vernon's imperfect farmland by exploiting its river fishery. In 1771, for example, he caught seven thousand seven hundred and sixty American shad and six hundred and seventy-nine thousand smaller herring. He dunged his ground with them.

He also marketed them, mainly in Alexandria, averaging, over the years, ten shillings per hundred shad. "This river . . . is well supplied with various kinds of fish at all seasons of the year," he wrote, "and, in the spring, with the greatest profusion of shad, herrings, bass, carp, perch, sturgeon, &c. Several valuable fisheries appertain to the estate; the whole shore, in short, is one entire fishery." In his diary he noted that "the white fish [i.e., shad] ran plentifully at my Sein landing having catch'd abt. 300 in one Hawl." Always, he said, from the first catches of the spring migration he set aside "a sufficiency of fish for the use of my own people." Evidently, his people desired more. They borrowed seines from him. Sunday, April 13, 1760: "My Negroes asked the lent of a Sein today, but caught little or no Fish." The Potomac is a mile wide at Mount Vernon and the longest seines were drawn in circles far out on the river by boats, then hauled ashore either by hand or with a windlass turned by horses.

The American shad at Mount Vernon were passing through, or, in any case, intending to. Their spawning grounds were between Alexandria and Great Falls, inside and a little outside the modern Beltway. It was toward the end of the shad run of 1608 that Captain John Smith and fourteen others discovered the Potomac River. Sailing out of Jamestown, scouting the tidewater country in what Smith described as "an open barge neare three tuns burthen," they evidently got up at least as far as the site of Chain Bridge, which connects Arlington and the District of Columbia. The idea that "pristine" rivers teemed with life—that pre-contact American rivers were so thick with fish that you could almost walk like Jesus Christ on their backs—is sometimes thought of as gross exaggeration, but Smith described fish "lying so thick with their heads aboue the water, as for want of nets (our barge driuing amongst them) we attempted to catch them with a frying pan: but we found it a bad instrument to catch fish with: neither better fish, more plenty, nor more variety for smal fish, had any of vs euer seene in any place so swimming in the water." When the frying pan failed him, Captain Smith leaned over the side and went after fish with another form of tackle. He wrote: "I amused myself by nailing them to the ground with my sword."

Washington was a sport fisherman, too, but with a great deal less passion than he exhibited for hunting. He "went a dragging for Sturgeon" now and again. When he was in Philadelphia for the Constitutional Convention, in mid-summer 1787, he went up the Schuylkill in a phaeton for a reminiscent day at Valley Forge, and fished there for trout. Three days later, he was up the Delaware, casting again. August 3, 1787: "I went up to Trenton on another Fishing party . . . In the Evening fished, not very successfully." August 4: "Fished again with more success (for perch) than yesterday." As President, recuperating from an illness in 1790, when New York City was the capital of the United States, he went after striped bass and blackfish at Sandy Hook and caught plenty. But back in the pre-war Mount Vernon years, most of his journal entries that have to do with sport begin "Went a hunting . . . Went a hunting . . . Went a foxhunting." July 25, 1772: "Went a fishing and dined at the Fish House at the Ferry Plantation." December 3, 1772: "Went a Fox hunting . . . and killd it after 3 hours chase." In October 1770, on a canoe trip on the Ohio River, he used trotlines to catch catfish. They were modest for the Ohio but in comparison with the Potomac were "of the size of our largest River Cats." Back at Mount Vernon, though, fishing was business. April 10, 1771: "Began to Haul the Sein, tho few fish were catchd, and those of the Shad kind, owing to the coolness of the Weather."

The champion of inland navigation was not without a countervailing sense of an owner's riparian rights. In "Life of George Washington" (1856), Washington Irving tells a story of a

vagabond who infested the creeks and inlets which bordered the estate, lurking in a canoe among the reeds and bushes, and making great havoc among the canvas-back ducks. He had been warned off repeatedly, but without effect. As Washington was one day riding about the estate he heard the report of a gun from the margin of the river. Spurring in that direction he dashed through the bushes and came upon the culprit just as he was pushing his canoe from shore. The latter raised his gun with a menacing look; but Washington rode into the stream, seized the painter of the canoe, drew it to shore, sprang from his horse, wrested the gun from the hands of the astonished delinquent and inflicted on him a lesson in "Lynch law" that effectually cured him of all inclination to trespass again on these forbidden shores.

Of Mount Vernon's daily bill of fare, Washington once wrote: "A glass of wine and a bit of mutton are always ready . . . those who expect more will be disappointed." There was a garbage pit just outside the main kitchen. It is known to zooarchaeologists as the South Grove midden. Mount Vernon's slaves lived in a building called the House for Families, and their midden was below them in a small cellar. Boxes of bones from these middens are in the laboratories of the Department of Archaeological Research at Colonial Williamsburg. Joanne Bowen is the curator of zooarchaeology there. When I called on her one autumn day and asked about the Mount Vernon middens, she said, "They must have stunk to high heaven." Broadening the topic, she spoke of "the apparent disregard of odor on the part of colonial people." She said, "They were not above putting trash in cellars in New England. If a ravine was outside the door, trash went into it."

The House for Families at Mount Vernon was torn down in 1793 and replaced by new living quarters on another site, ending definitively a stratum in time for the contents of the old cellar midden. Wildlife bones are forty per cent of what was found there when the cellar was excavated in the nineteen-eighties, including fish and venison, wild mammals, wild birds, and turtles. Bones from the main house, excavated in the nineteen-nineties, are only 10.3 per cent wild. They include one—1—shad bone. There is a whole boxful of shad bones from the House for Families. Of George Washington's consumption of American shad, Bowen remarked, "Archaeologically, I would have to say, it was a minimal part of his diet."

Her field is known in Europe as archaeozoology, because in Europe the biological aspects are emphasized. "Zooarchaeology" is North American, where anthropological aspects are emphasized. On both sides of the Atlantic, the discipline is young. In earlier excavations, at Mount Vernon as elsewhere, interest in bones was low. Joanne Bowen's doctoral dissertation for Brown University was on the diets of two Connecticut River families in the eighteenth century. "You can tell diets better from bones than documents," she remarked to me in Williamsburg. In her lab she had material from more than eighty sites, and she was working on bones from a trash pit in Jamestown in use in 1610, 1611, and 1612. She had analyzed bones from Harpers Ferry, from the African Meeting House in Boston, from the Henry Tucker House in St. George's, Bermuda. Other archaeologists bring bones to her from their digs, or send her their data. From Annapolis, the table scraps of Charles Calvert, 3rd Baron Baltimore, were 1.7 per cent fish. Bones excavated at the Brush-Everard House, in Williamsburg, reflect a typical Williamsburg diet of 1700, she said—ninety-five per cent beef, pork, and mutton, plus "dribbles of chicken, fish, turtles, and birds."

She said, "It is a common tale about colonial days that fish were so plentiful they jumped into the boat. The bones tell you another side of the story. The bones have forced us to rethink. They're a wake-up call for how we think about the past. The essential message is that fish were not *the* major contribution to the colonial diet, not by a long stretch. They were never eating as much fish as we thought they should have been. Fish would not have been more than fifteen per cent."

Herding, animal husbandry, arrived with the first Virginia settlers, she continued. "Very quickly they established a diet that was not unlike what they had in England." By 1620, herds were established to the point that beef was the predominant meat. Shad bones are characteristic of slave foods. The "English" didn't eat fish.

After she presented these discoveries at a Smithsonian Institution seminar in Washington, one participant was so disbelieving—so certain that the facts were subversively false—that he asked in a ringing voice, "Who is that woman?"

Joanne Vickie Bowen has brown hair, a shy look, a darting sense of humor always at the ready. She has been at Colonial Williamsburg since the early nineteen-eighties and worked previously at the American Indian Archaeological Institute, in Washington, Connecticut. She grew up in the District of Columbia, went to public high school, and on to Beloit College, in Wisconsin, and then to graduate school in Providence. For the stove in her apartment there, she bought fish all over Rhode Island and as far away as Gloucester, Massachusetts—every kind of fish she could find— and for obvious reasons cooked them whole. The bones of those fish are on laboratory trays in Williamsburg. If you need an example of the trend to the finicky in American culinary taste, Bowen is ready to give one. She says that in the late eighteenth century students at what is now Brown University complained to the administration because at table they were not getting their fish whole. Whole meant with the guts in.

Her father, Murray Bowen, was a psychiatrist at the Menninger Clinic who went on to do pioneering work in family therapy at the National Institute of Mental Health. Her paternal grandfather owned a combined funeral home and store that sold furniture, hardware, carpets, and appliances in Waverly, Tennessee. On a visit to Waverly many years ago, Joanne told her grandfather how astonished she had been to learn that early Americans ate the jaws of pigs. He said to her: "Child, don't you know the best cut of meat?"

In Williamsburg, she has given bone-chewing parties at which the table settings include spittoons. She describes the bone-chewers as "students, volunteers, and professors." They show up with a lot to learn. Dog-chewed bones and human-chewed bones look alike, she says. It's a basic problem in taphonomy. Robert L. Bates and Julia A. Jackson's "Glossary of Geology" defines taphonomy as "the branch of paleoecology concerned with all processes occurring after the death of an organism until its discovery." Bowen told me that a whole subgroup in her field focuses on wolf-chewing and dog-chewing. Documents from medieval England contain edicts forbidding the populace to chew bones. Africans, though, have been chewing bones since Lilith, Eve, and Adam. This fact has caused me to think of myself as John McAfrican. Routinely, I chew up and swallow the cancellous ends of pressure-cooked pork spareribs. Cancellous bone is porous and, according to Webster, is "made up of intersecting plates and bars which form small cavities or cells . . . found near the ends of the long bones and elsewhere where both rigidity and lightness are essential."

Bowen said, "It has been claimed that the incidence of arthritis is less where bones are eaten," and she added, incidentally, that cuts of meat become smaller as you go forward through the American diet for three hundred years. In the eighteenth century, bones were chopped. In the nineteenth century, they were sawed. The saw cuts, she said, do not "follow the natural lines," and she does not like working on them. "You could cut bones with a kitchen cleaver. It's a talent we've lost. We've done butchery studies—gotten our axes and cleavers and gone out and used them. In the eighteenth century, heads and feet were well received. Heads and feet were delicacies, not to be tossed. It didn't matter how wealthy you were. You ate 'em. Peyton Randolph. George Washington. They all ate those pieces. Heads and feet. The total picture is truly compelling. How different our world is from theirs."

In 1988, Catherine C. Carlson, of the Department of Anthropology of the University of Massachusetts, published a paper she called " 'Where's the Salmon?' A Reevaluation of the Role of Anadromous Fisheries in Aboriginal New England." She quoted Anthony Netboy [*sic*], author of "The Salmon: Their Fight for Survival" (Houghton Mifflin, 1974):

> New England salmon provided food for the Indians, who taught the colonists how to fish for them and prepare them in their fashion . . . The fishes, which were sometimes so thick in the rivers that they overturned small boats, were probably as vital to the aborigines as the wild

turkey that has received so much publicity. To an extraordinary extent salmon served the Indians as the staple of their diet.

Carlson begged to differ:

The ultimate goal here is to explain why the evidence for aboriginal salmon exploitation in New England is almost totally nonexistent, while questioning the entrenched notion that salmon in New England was as important as salmon on the Northwest Coast . . . critically examining one of the numerous myths that have become ingrained in the environmental archaeological literature . . . All available evidence indicates that salmon was an extremely minor component of the prehistoric resource base . . . even at "classic" fishing locales, such as the falls at Riverside on the Connecticut River . . . The generally disappointing results of the modern salmon enhancement programs in New England may be due more to the fact that salmon is not naturally abundant in these waters than to historical and modern dams and pollution . . . Some accounts describing salmon actually may be referring to shad . . . Are shad, alewives, and/or sturgeon *combined* the "salmon" of prehistoric New England? Unequivocally, these three species are evident in the archaeological faunal record.

From various New England Indian middens, she recited the faunal record. At a site on Sebago Lake, in Maine, dating from Middle Archaic times, a hundred and sixty-two identifiable bone fragments were discovered. Twenty-one per cent were deer bones, 9.3 per cent were from small mammals, 6.2 per cent from reptiles and amphibians, 3.1 per cent from birds, and 58.6 per cent from turtles. Only 1.8 per cent were fish bones. Among them, only one deteriorated fragment may have been from a salmon.

From a three-square-metre midden on the Connecticut River near the present locations of Turners Falls and Gill, Massachusetts, five hundred and ninety fish-bone fragments were removed—all bones of shad or alewives.

The moon of the peak migration was known as the Spearfish Moon—the Algonquian April moon. According to the historian Charles Hardy, "the Lenape called the month of March Chwame Gischuch, which translates as the month of the shad." The Micmacs—another Algonquian tribe, centered in Nova Scotia and New Brunswick—mythologized the shad, finding its origins in its myriad bones. The shad was once a discontented porcupine. The discontented porcupine asked the Great Manitou to change it into something else. The Great Manitou "seized the animal, turned it inside out, and tossed it into the river to begin a new existence as a shad."

When George Washington thought to join the navy, in 1746, his mother was not in any way happy about it. He was fourteen. His brother Lawrence had helped him obtain a midshipman's commission. So far so true. Owen Wister takes up the narrative:

> The boy's kit had been carried aboard, and he was himself
> on the point of following it, when a messenger from his
> mother overtook him, and brought him her final word.

Her final word seems to have been, "Get off the ship." Had she been lenient, Washington might have been somewhere on the high seas—who knows in what uniform?—rather than at Valley Forge in the winter of 1777–78. Wister:

In the next order for supplies that his mother sent to England, she asked for a "good pen-knife." This, when it came, she gave to the boy in token of his recent signal submission to her, adding, "Always obey your superiors." He carried the token all his life, and to some of his intimates he from time to time explained its significance. One day at Valley Forge, when the more than half-naked men had eaten no meat for many days, and when Congress had failed once more to provide, or even to suggest any way for getting, food and clothes, the ebb was reached, and Washington wrote his resignation as commander-in-chief of the army. Among the generals sitting in council, Henry Knox spoke out, reminding him of the pen-knife, and upon Washington's asking what that had to do with it, he said: "You were always to obey your superiors. You were commanded to lead this army. No one has commanded you to cease leading it." Washington paused, and then answered, "There is something in that. I will think it over." Half an hour later, he tore his resignation to pieces.

In that account, fact and fiction are so conflatedly spiral that they resemble an electric barber pole when the shop is open. Just as Wister went on to say, the knife—pearl-handled, single-bladed, three inches long—is in the museum of the Ancient Free and Accepted Masons' Alexandria-Washington Lodge No. 22, in Virginia. George Washington was the first Worshipful Master of that lodge. (http://gwmemorial.org/Collections/george_washingtons_penknife.htm.) The knife was given to the museum in 1812 by George Steptoe Washington, the late President's nephew and executor. It presumably crossed the Delaware in the general's pocket on December 25, 1776. It presumably rode through the triumphs at Trenton and Princeton and on to the disappointments at the Brandywine and Germantown before the march up the Schuylkill in the third week of December, 1777, to the winter campsite at Valley Forge. Washington had been there three days when he wrote to the Continental Congress, in York, Pennsylvania:

> I do not know from what cause this alarming deficiency, or rather total failure of supplies, arises; but, unless more vigorous exertions and better regulations take place in that line immediately, this army must starve, dissolve, or disperse.

On February 12, one general at Valley Forge (James Varnum) wrote this memorandum to another general at Valley Forge (Nathanael Greene):

> The country in the vicinity of the camp is exhausted. There cannot be a moral certainty of bettering our circumstances, while we continue here . . . I have from the beginning viewed this situation with horror! It is unparalleled in the history of mankind to establish winter-quarters in a country wasted and without a single magazine . . . There is no alternative, but immediately to remove the army to places where they can be supplied, unless effectual remedies can be applied on the spot.

On February 16, General Washington wrote from Valley Forge to Governor George Clinton, of New York:

> For some days past, there has been little less than a famine in camp. A part of the army has been a week without any kind of flesh, and the rest three or four days. Naked and starving as they are, we cannot enough admire the incomparable patience and fidelity of the soldiery, that they have not been ere this excited by their suffering to a

general mutiny and dispersion. Strong symptoms, however, of discontent have appeared in particular instances.

The symptoms had begun to appear within days of the army's
arrival. As officers moved about the camp, hut doors would open a
crack and the voices of troops would call from within, "No bread,
no soldier."

Washington to Clinton, continued:

Our present sufferings are not all. There is no foundation
laid for any adequate relief hereafter. All the magazines
provided in the States of New Jersey, Pennsylvania,
Delaware, and Maryland, and all the immediate additional
supplies they seem capable of affording, will not be sufficient to support the army . . . When the before-mentioned
supplies are exhausted, what a terrible crisis must ensue,
unless all the energy of the continent shall be exerted to
provide a timely remedy!

Numbers varied across the months, but something like twelve
thousand men were encamped there—about three-fourths of the
entire Continental army. They could eat a drove of cattle in minutes. They required, but were not receiving, a hundred barrels of
flour a day. Typical Fahrenheit temperatures in late December and
well into the new year ranged from six to thirty-six.

The scene was set for the spring migration of 1778, the run of
the savior shad from Delaware Bay through Philadelphia and on
up the Schuylkill to Valley Forge, the deliverance of embryonic
America, the finest hour of the founding fish. The British certainly
sensed as much. Specifically to cut off the shad run, they stretched
a barrier seine across the Schuylkill near Philadelphia. Whatever
color your coat was, for anybody on an eastern river there was ample precedent for high expectation. In the winter of 1773, for ex-

ample, a settlement called Wyoming, on the North Branch of the Susquehanna River, was all but famished out of existence. The "History of Wyoming, In a Series of Letters from Charles Miner to his son William Penn Miner, Esq." reports the outcome:

> Never was an opening spring, or the coming of the shad, looked for with more anxiety, or hailed with more cordial delight. The fishing season, of course, dissipated all fears, and the dim eye was soon exchanged for the glance of joy and the sparkle of pleasure, and the dry, sunken cheek of want assumed the plump appearance of health and plenty.

Barrelled salt shad had been a common provision for American troops. In May, 1776, Lieutenant Samuel Hunter wrote from Fort Augusta, on the West Branch of the Susquehanna: "I have ordered some People that lives nigh the Great Island to preserve shad and barrel them up for the use of the Militia that will be stationed there this summer." According to A. J. McClane's "The Encyclopedia of Fish Cookery," "thousands of barrels of shad fed colonial troops in White Plains in 1776." Sylvester Judd notes that "some thousands of barrels of shad were put up in Connecticut for the troops." Harry Emerson Wildes writes in "Valley Forge":

> So hungry were the soldiers that when supplies trickled into camp the men pounced upon the food without waiting to cook it. "I found a barrel of shad," wrote one hungry militiaman, "and voraciously fell to eating them raw and I thought them the best I had ever eaten."

From the War Office, in York, on March 24, 1778, General Horatio Gates wrote to commissary Colonel Henry Hollingsworth a letter that included this sentence:

The Board are pleased to hear of your success with dried herring but have been informed dried shad are better.

The famine of Valley Forge, in 1778, was not alleviated by 1777 shad arriving in barrels. Nor, in fact, did it end as a result of the 1778 spring migration. When you read the narrative as it is commonly presented—"then, dramatically, the famine completely ended; countless thousands of fat shad . . ."—you are reading what the historian Wayne Bodle has called "the providentialist canard." The hunger crisis at Valley Forge reached its nadir in the last two weeks of February and the first days of March, when the shad were at Cape May, waiting for things to warm up. In Valley Forge, nothing was warming up. It was intensely cold and snowy in late February. In Philadelphia, a temperature reading on March 4th was seven degrees. On March 5th at Valley Forge, the river was frozen over. In days that followed, supplies arrived, the men were fed, the crisis passed. The emotive account of the nation-saving shad is a tale recommended by everything but sources.

Bodle, a professor of American History at Indiana University of Pennsylvania, is the author of "The Valley Forge Winter: Civilians and Soldiers in War" (Penn State Press, 2002). Easygoing and giftedly verbal, he is now in his middle fifties. His name is pronounced like "modal." His Valley Forge book evolved from his doctoral dissertation for the University of Pennsylvania, which in turn evolved from research he did for the federal government. In the nineteen-seventies, after the National Park Service took over from the State of Pennsylvania the site of the 1777–78 winter encampment, they hired Wayne Bodle and Jacqueline Thibaut, who were then graduate students, to write a Valley Forge Historical Research Report, which was completed in 1980. It is three volumes long. When I first got in touch with Bodle, in 1998, he said that fresh shad in all likelihood were consumed by soldiers at Valley Forge in the weeks before they broke camp in June, but that "the large and providentially early run is a legend not supported by a single document." There is no record of shad in the river during the "discrete periods of intense starvation," or, for that matter, throughout the easier days of spring, albeit if shad were there the soldiers would almost certainly have eaten them, and shad would have been "an invisible part of the substratum of the nutritional comfort in April and May."

John Joseph Stoudt's "Ordeal at Valley Forge" (University of Pennsylvania Press, 1963) gives a day-by-day chronicle of the weather. On the 6th of March, floating ice is in the river. On the 7th, the channel flows between shelves of ice coming out from the two sides. March 12th is "hot." On March 13th, "verdure" appears. March 14th and 15th are "very warm . . . uncommonly warm." That kind of warmth will drive shad upstream, but not so far so fast. On March 21st, "the false spring is over." On March 22nd, there is "ice an inch thick."

Washington's headquarters at Valley Forge were in a fieldstone house near a creek where it entered the river. He could look down a short modest slope and see the flowing Schuylkill. What was he thinking—this commercial shad fisherman who in one season had netted nearly eight thousand shad? He could not have helped but imagine and anticipate the shad run. Or so it seems. In that small stone house—twenty-five by thirty feet—Washington spent an hour each morning over breakfast with his wife in one of three upstairs bedrooms, then went downstairs to his desk next to the Officers' Workroom, where twenty subordinates, crammed around several tables, helped produce a lot of letters. The subordinates wrote drafts. Washington revised the drafts. They were copied with quill pens. Then he signed them. Among his drafters was Alexander Hamilton. In the months of March and April, Washington wrote in this manner upwards of thirty thousand epistolary words, including many an eloquent diatribe against the dearth of food and supplies. (Visiting the headquarters with me one winter day in 2001, Wayne Bodle said, "The Continental army is the first bureaucratic entity in America and they use a lot of paper. Washington is ready to deal with the devil, if he has to, in order to keep the food flying.") Nowhere in those thirty thousand words does the general mention the Schuylkill River shad run.

On March 26th, in British Philadelphia, a British army surgeon named Charles Blagden ended a newsy letter to a friend in London, saying, "The shad is just beginning to appear in the rivers here." Blagden seems to be the best source, and possibly the only source, on the military relevance of shad in the Schuylkill in 1778. I learned of Blagden's correspondence as a result of reading "Valley Forge: Pinnacle of Courage," by John W. Jackson (Thomas Publications, Gettysburg, 1992). "A bonanza that eased the food supply for the troops in the spring of 1778 was the large quantity of shad that was taken from the Schuylkill River," the author said. I wrote to him and asked his source, which was not given in the book. His widow replied, "In the Valley Forge book, information came from New York Public Library—Letters of Charles Blagden, April 20, 1778." The April 20th letter includes the fact that the British in Philadelphia did what they could to impede the shad run, but if Dr. Blagden ever described the extent to which the effort was successful the description is not preserved. The seine goes across the river. Extrapolation begins there, but not on the part of Blagden, who says nothing else about the 1778 migration, and seems a little more interested in the natural history than the wartime history of the fish:

> During this month a pretty large species of Clupea, called a shad, runs up the Rivers Delaware & Schuylkill in prodigious numbers. It has already proved a very seasonable relief to the inhabitants of this town. However, lest our enemies should receive as much if not more advantage from this benefit of nature, we have passed a seine across the

Schuylkill, to prevent the fish from getting up that river, upon the banks of which Mr. Washington's army is encamped. I will take some pains to learn how far this precaution is found effectual. It is nearly as good a fish as the Severn shad, & very much resembles it; but having lost that part of my System of Nature, I cannot say whether it be the true Alosa or not; however, I hope to send or bring you a specimen, & very much wish it may be the latter.

At Valley Forge on April 9, 1778, the air was raw and cold. April 13th was "sultry." April 20th was "rather cold." Washington remained full of complaint. On April 21st, he wrote to John Banister, Delegate in Congress: "No history now extant can furnish an instance of an army's suffering such uncommon hardships as ours has done . . . without clothes . . . without blankets . . . without shoes . . . without provisions . . . marching through the frost and snow." By May 6th—"a brilliantly clear, warm day"—the spawning season seems to have arrived for good. Whether the shad arrived with it is a matter of supposition. Surely the British net would not have stopped them all. As Wayne Bodle conjectures, shad almost certainly were consumed to some extent by the Continental army, for the army was there beside the Schuylkill during the entire migration period. Dr. Blagden, in Philadelphia, notes on May 22nd that "the run of shad has considerably lessened, & will soon cease entirely." But there is no documentation of the shad that reached Valley Forge, let alone of their numbers. There is nothing but the history books.

David G. Martin, "The Philadelphia Campaign: June 1777–July 1778":

The meat shortage did not begin to ease up until spring, and was not eliminated until the local shad run on the Schuylkill came as a godsend in April.

Donald Barr Chidsey, "Valley Forge" (Crown, New York, 1959):

The river ran shallow, and it was possible for cavalrymen to ride right up the middle of it, almost knee-to-knee. Each carried a cut bush with which he beat the water. At the narrowest point, Pawling's Ford, just outside of camp a little north of headquarters, where the Perkiomen Creek emptied into the Schuylkill, nets had been spread. The fish swam in, got caught by the gills, and couldn't get back. There were thousands of them, more and more coming all day, every day, all night too, for weeks . . . For almost a month the whole camp stank, and men's fingers were oily. In addition, barrels had been held in readiness, and hundreds of these were filled with salted shad for future consumption.

John W. Jackson, "Valley Forge: Pinnacle of Courage":

Inhabitants for miles around gathered on the banks of the river with branches of bushes, stakes and a variety of tools to march abreast upstream driving the hapless shad before them. Others on horseback cornered them in a fenced enclosure embedded in the river bed.

Of the innumerable newspaper and magazine pieces that have picked up the theme one from the other, here are just two examples.

Pat Camuso, *The River Reporter*, Narrowsburg, New York:

Washington's army was saved (and perhaps the great American Revolution as well) by the Susquehanna River's spring shad run after winter starvation nearly killed his troops and the American Revolution with them.

Steve Quinn, *In-Fisherman* magazine:

Rations dwindled and soldiers were driven to scavenge . . .
Morale ebbed . . . Provisions were nearly gone by the end
of March, with little hope of finding food . . . Huge schools
of migrating shad suddenly appeared, to feed the men and
rekindle the revolutionary fire in their hearts. Although
the soldiers reportedly grew weary of their shad diet, their
assault on Philadelphia forced the British to evacuate in
June 1778, and the tide of the war swung in favor of the
Revolutionaries.

On Presidents' Day, 2002, television's History Channel presented "Save Our History: Valley Forge." Scenes of buildings in
present disrepair. Scenes of archaeologists meticulously digging. A
happy scene far into the film showing actors, dressed as Valley
Forge troops, wolfing down food. "The American army's luck was
changing for the better now, in significant ways," the narrator said.
"Just months earlier, they had almost been starving. Now, huge
amounts of food came to them, almost like in a Biblical miracle."
The film then cut to a head-and-shoulders shot of Roger Mc-
Grath—"Author/Historian"—who said, "Late in the winter, early
in the spring, of 1778, was a tremendous run of shad up the
Schuylkill River that was intercepted with nets by the troops, and
tens of thousands of fish headed upstream; and they feasted on
these fish for a month. It almost seemed a sign of God's omnipo-
tence, something of Biblical proportions."

On Presidents' Day, 2002, those archaeological digs in
progress among the cabin sites of Valley Forge were in the second
of several projected years. In offal and garbage pits, a great many
food remains had been uncovered. Bones of cattle and pigs,
mainly. No deer bones. No rabbit bones. No fish bones.

In 2000, Wayne Bodle sent me an article from a recent issue of *Pennsylvania History: A Journal of Mid-Atlantic Studies*. Called "Fish or Foul: A History of the Delaware River Basin Through the Perspective of the American Shad, 1682 to the Present," the article was by Charles Hardy III, of West Chester University, near Philadelphia. Hardy's piece was thoroughly researched, with a huge bibliography. It was attractively written, and represented, at the very least, many months of work. Nonetheless, he did write:

Confronted by famine and starvation in the early years of settlement, the colonists, as the Indians before them, learned to preserve and husband food sources for the long winters. For human purposes anadromous species such as salmon and shad are by far the most important finfish. A migratory fish run concentrates a huge biological mass from the vast expanse of an ocean into a narrow geographical zone. Arriving in late March or early April, shad were one of the first food sources to relieve the shortages of the preceding winter. Indeed, Nathan Hale asserted that it was an uncommonly early run of the shad in the spring of 1778 that saved Washington and his troops camped in Valley Forge!

Some years before, Hardy had produced a public-radio documentary called "The Return of the Shad," in which the narrator said, "It was the early appearance of the shad in the spring of 1779 [*sic*] that may well have saved our nation in its most trying hour." At which point the apparent source, Max Hezelguesser—a dyed-in-the-wool-shirt Delaware River shad fisherman, a member of the Delaware River Shad Fishermen's Association, and, it goes without saying, a reader whose eye had often been caught by anything at all about shad—came on and said:

In the time of the Revolutionary War the troops were very depressed in the winter of whatever at Valley Forge. They were starving and they were hungry and they were beaten down, ready to go home, and that would have been the end of it. The shad run for some reason started three weeks early in the Schuylkill River . . . The word got to the troops. They took horses. They pulled trees into the shallow water and really scooped them together and they filled barrels and barrels and barrels of shad. They filled their stomachs. They felt good. They had the strength and the power to keep going. And this was in a letter that Nathan Hale wrote to somebody. And you know, be it at all true, that ought to be the American fish.

In a note accompanying the piece from *Pennsylvania History*, Wayne Bodle said, "The providentialist canard from Valley Forge pops up again, I suppose inevitably. I have come across it in a variety of versions over the years, although never in one quite this bizarre. Hale, of course, died on Long Island in September of 1776."

Restored to publication toward the end of the Revolution, the *Pennsylvania Gazette*, even in its shorter notices, was resonant with a couple of new terms, as on May 24, 1780:

WAS stolen from the fishery, near the mouth of Tyhukan Creek, on the Delaware, in the night of the 13th instant May, seven barrels salt SHAD, the property of the United States; the barrels are made of Black Oak Staves. Any person giving information . . . shall receive FIVE HUNDRED DOLLARS reward.

In 1782, a few months after the British surrender at Yorktown, the old fishing-and-hunting club called the Colony in Schuylkill changed its name to the State in Schuylkill and went on fishing and hunting. Colloquially, it would become known as the Fish House. Only two people among the twenty-seven were loyal to the king, and several signed the Declaration of Independence. The new State firmly retained the Colony's order of April 23, 1760, "that they may drink out of the Government Bowl of Punch as often as they like, and fill it again as often as they drink it out." Samuel Morris Jr., their Governor from 1766 to 1812, is credited with the invention of Fish House Punch (lemon juice, sugar, rum, and brandy), a drink as American as Betsy Ross. The guiding agendum of their assemblies to this day, it is ladled from an elegant Government Bowl.

In 1789, Peter Cortelyou caught nearly sixteen thousand shad in the Narrows off New Utrecht—the present-day Bay Ridge, Brooklyn. He used fyke nets, balloonlike, held open with hoops. In the same place in the six seasons 1790–95, he caught about a hundred thousand shad. By the eighteen-twenties, according to his ledgers, his catch was down ninety-six per cent, the result of over-fishing. By 1838, New York was buying shad from other rivers. On January 17, 1807, the *New York Commercial Advertiser* reported: "A shad weighing five pounds was caught this morning at the Narrows, and sold in our market for one dollar and twelve sents!" The exclamation point may have had something to do with the price but more with the date. It was even earlier than Philadelphia's harbinger shad of 1793, pulled out of the Delaware on January 20th, pronounced a "fine shad" by the *Pennsylvania Gazette*, and served that evening in the White Horse Tavern, on Market Street.

A fisherman in South Hadley, Massachusetts, "sold thousands of shad after the Revolution for three coppers each," according to Sylvester Judd, and found it "much more difficult to sell salmon than shad." The fish came from below the Connecticut River falls, where Holyoke Dam would before long be. Judd's writing fills in the scene as if it were a Flemish populated canvas.

> Shad seasons brought to the falls, on both sides of the river, multitudes of people . . . All came on horses with bags to carry shad, except a very few who had carts . . . For some years there were only two licensed inn-keepers at the falls—Daniel Lamb and widow Mary Pomeroy, but every house on both sides of the river was full . . . A great number of the men brought victuals with them; many cooked shad, and others bought food at the houses . . . Where there were so many men, and rum was plenty, there was of course much noise, bustle and confusion. The greater part were industrious farmers, and after leaving the falls, they wound over the hills and plains with bags of shad, in every direction. They were plainly dressed, according to their business. There was another class at these gatherings, composed of the idle, the intemperate and the dissipated. They came to drink and frolic, and some to buy shad if their money held out.

Under the impression that the Wyoming Valley of the Susquehanna River was a chartered part of Connecticut, people from Connecticut began settling there in the seventeen-sixties. This resulted in the two Yankee-Pennamite Wars (1769–71, 1784) between Pennsylvania and Connecticut, not to mention the British-allied Mohawk attacks that included a massacre of Connecticut forces in 1778. The Connecticut settlers raised flax, spun it, made twine, and knit seines. They fished in the Susquehanna for shad. To a significant extent, they came to depend on shad after crops and livestock were destroyed in the hostilities. As much or more than anywhere in America, the spring migration in the

Susquehanna became, and remained, a major event in the subsistence year. In 1798, when "uncounted thousands" of shad were caught at Nanticoke alone, the *Wilkesbarre Gazette* lost control of its metaphorical perspective. "Bonaparte and all his army was captured!" the newspaper reported, in acclaim of the fishermen's triumph. Napoleon had recently overrun northern Italy.

Gilbert Fowler, born in 1792 in Briar Creek Township, on the right bank of the river, recalled as an old man the spring migrations of his childhood. His words appear in a group of memoirs collected by the Wyoming Historical and Genealogical Society in 1881. "The Susquehanna shad constituted the principal food for all the inhabitants," Fowler said. "No farmer or man with a family was without his barrel or barrels of shad the whole year round. Besides furnishing food for the immediate inhabitants, people from Mahantango, Blue Mountains, and, in fact, for fifty miles around, would bring salt in tight barrels and trade it for shad. They would clean and salt the shad on the river shore, put them in barrels, and return home." Mary Coates: "The people had shad from spring to spring." Jameson Harvey: "We used to have shad until shad came again." C. Dorrance: "It was my business as a lad every evening, after school, to be with horse and wagon to receive our share of shad." In the lunch baskets that children carried to school were corn bread and shad.

Here Fowler describes the fishery of Samuel Webb, about four miles upstream of Bloomsburg:

This was an immense shad fishery. From the banks of the river at this fishery could be seen great schools of shad coming up the river when they were a quarter of a mile distant. They came in such immense numbers and so compact as to cause or produce a wave or rising of the water in the middle of the river, extending from shore to shore.

Near the Old Red Tavern, in Hanover, fishermen reported nine thousand nine hundred and ninety-nine shad taken in one haul. In the annals of prevarication, this may be the most modest extant example of fishermen's well-known tendency to exaggerate. A Mr. Duane was among those hauling the net. Duane admitted in later years that the count was actually nine thousand nine hundred and ninety-seven, but he and the other fishermen added two so the digits would all be nines.

In Simsbury, Connecticut, in 1995, I happened into a book on my in-laws' shelves that was three and a half inches thick and weighed almost four pounds. It looked like dimension stone. Attracted by its arresting title—"United States Commission of Fish and Fisheries, Part IX, Report of the Commissioner for 1881"—I looked through its twelve hundred pages, and with an expanding sense of discovery found these memoirs about shad on the Susquehanna, to which nothing compared—that I knew of—from any other river. I felt as if I had found in my own attic the lost letters of Georges D'Anthes. Since then, I have come upon the Susquehanna stories from the 1881 report in at least a dozen books, in numerous articles in historical quarterlies and general magazines, and in the newspaper pieces that appear routinely with the spring migration. So much for Scoopnose the Scholar.

A shad fishery on the Susquehanna would typically include about ten men—the number it took to haul the net. Shareholders each owned "so many yards of the net, and each one receiving his share of fish according to the number of yards owned." The fish usually weighed from three to nine pounds. Major John Fassett said he saw the weighing of a twelve-pound shad. Jennison Harvey said, "I saw one weighed, on a wager, which turned the scales at thirteen pounds!" There were several dozen shad fisheries in the Wyoming Valley, and at the end of the eighteenth century they were each averaging from ten to twenty thousand shad in a season. Circa 1790—no one seemed to recall the exact year—ten thousand were caught in one haul at the Stewart fishery, midway between Wilkes-Barre and Plymouth. They were caught on the first Sunday of the shad season. After the 1778 massacre, there were so many widows and orphans in the valley that a custom developed of giving one haul per fishery per season to them, always on that first Sunday. It was known as the "Widows' Haul." At roughly thirty cents apiece, the ten thousand shad from the Stewart fishery were worth about three thousand dollars.

The fishermen did their fishing after dark. They drank "old rye." Customers bartered with them, paying whiskey for shad. They were also paid with leather, iron, cider, maple sugar ("one good shad was worth a pound of sugar"), and cider royal (cider + whiskey). A bushel of salt bought a hundred shad. Walter Green, of Black Walnut Bottom, "gave twenty barrels of shad for a good Durham cow."

By the eighteen-twenties, several shad floats appeared annually near the mouth of the Susquehanna—great rafts, river-borne factories, as much as a hundred feet wide and three hundred feet long. On each raft was a bunkhouse, a mess hall, an office.

Thomas Jefferson, of Virginia, was born in Shadwell in 1743. His grandfather had settled there. The young Jefferson hauled seine for shad. Shadwell is about four miles east of Monticello, on the Rivanna, a tributary of the James. Jefferson was always mindful of the spring migration, mentioning it in letters and in his Garden Books and Memorandum Books. In 1798, he wrote from Philadelphia to Marie Jefferson Eppes: "Mar. 16. the 1st. shad here. 28. the weeping willow begins to shew green leaves." March 17, 1800: "First shad at market." April 9, 1801: "Paid $1.25 for three shad." May 8, 1809: "Paid $1.75 for six shad." In July, 1809, he wrote to Gordon, Trokes & Co., in Richmond, placing an order for, among other things, "Cod's tongues and sounds. 1 keg" and "salted white shads. 1. barrel of best quality." According to the historian Helen D. Bullock, "Jefferson retained his fondness for such native staples as sweet potatoes, corn, black-eyed peas, turnip greens, shad, Virginia ham, venison, wild swan, crab, scuppernong wine and grapes, throughout his life." A 1993 news release from Virginia's Department of Game and Inland Fisheries informed the public that "Jefferson once noted that shad in the Rivanna near his Monticello home were thick enough to walk across"—a remembrance unknown to Jefferson scholars. Shad-roe soufflé has been associated with his table, apparently in error. Jefferson liked his fresh shad laid open, broiled, and addressed with pepper, salt, and butter, and is not known to have eaten shad cooked another way. In 1812, he made a fish pond at Monticello, intent to fill it with carp. He sent a boatman down the Rivanna with a letter to his friend John Ashlin.

> I shall be obliged to you if you can aid him in getting them at as reasonable a price as you can. I presume they will not be higher than what is paid for shad, as they are by no means as good a fish. If through your interest he can be admitted to join in hauling the seyne & come in for a share of shad so as to bring us some, I will thank you, as well as for any other aid you may give him towards his object . . .

Thomas Mifflin, of Pennsylvania, had a mansion at the Falls of Schuylkill where he gave shad dinners for his founding friends. Mifflin was Quartermaster General of the Continental army, President of the Continental Congress (1783–84), delegate to the federal Constitutional Convention, and Governor of Pennsylvania throughout the seventeen-nineties, when the national capital was Philadelphia. Mifflin might be governor of Pennsylvania but not of the State in Schuylkill, in which he was just a citizen, as the members have been called since 1782. He knew better than to depend

on club fellow-citizens for fish, so he bought his shad from Godfrey Shronk. The Schuylkill's pre-dam shad fisheries were numerous, and involved such people as Woolery Meng, Melchior Meng,
Conrad Krickbaum, and Titus Yerkes. Titus Yerkes owned the
General Wayne tavern at Mary Walters Ford. When going for bass,
perch, and bullheads, the fishing citizens of the State in Schuylkill
used trot lines. They called them layout lines. On March 27, 1789,
Citizen Benjamin Scull, godson of Benjamin Franklin, caught a
fifteen-inch trout on his layout line.

In 1809, you could get three acres of riverfront land in Lower
Merion for three hundred dollars, yet a timberless and agricultur-
ally barren three-acre island in the Schuylkill River was worth
twice as much, because of its fisheries. In 1811, inmates of the
poorhouse of Montgomery County, in which Lower Merion is a
township, complained of being fed too much salt shad. Among the
populace at large, though, shad had risen a long way in their level
of acceptance. In that same decade, Pennsylvania Germans were
stuffing shad with oysters, baking them in parchment, and drench-
ing them in rich walnut sauce. In Philadelphia in the eighteen-
twenties, Joseph Head's Mansion House Hotel was looked upon as
the most elegant restaurant in town, where you ate stuffed baked
shad under a caper sauce, grilled shad with sorrel, and, for breakfast, shad roe with oranges.

Samuel Lane owned the Bull Tavern, near Phoenixville. According to Samuel Pennypacker's history of the town, Lane "had
an arrangement with the fishermen at the mouth of the Pickering,
that he was to furnish them each morning with a quart of whiskey,
and they were to give him in return a shad weighing eight
pounds." Pickering Creek flows into the Schuylkill a few miles
above Valley Forge. The fishermen filled their side of the contract
for a time, but the aggregate pressure of the fisheries was such that
the size of shad declined. The stomach of Sam Lane's last shad was
stuffed with pebbles.

The dams started coming in 1822, and the State in Schuylkill moved downriver to Rambo's Rock, a left-bank site in South Philadelphia, and on May 5th, in the spring migration, betokened its arrival with a dinner of planked shad. Three years later, M.J.P.Y.R.G. du Motier, Marquis de Lafayette, spent a day as a "stranger" at the club. He had been twenty years old when he arrived in Philadelphia in 1777. Martha Washington referred to him as "the French boy." Now he was sixty-seven and touring the nation he had helped create. His son George Washington Motier was with him, and successfully fished in the river. The marquis helped with the cooking. Of his visit he remarked, "It completes my tour of all the States in the Union."

In a dusty old cellar under the Historical Society of Pennsylvania, at 1300 Locust Street, are ten metal caskets numbered with gold paint. Inside the caskets are the suede-bound ledgers of the Colony in Schuylkill and the State in Schuylkill. Robert Peck, a citizen of the State who spends the rest of his time as a naturalist at the Philadelphia Academy of Natural Sciences, is the one person in Pennsylvania or anywhere else who has a key that unshelves those caskets. In his generosity, Peck has opened the caskets, and stayed there with me in the more than amply heated basement, hunting through the ledgers. I am as indebted to him as to the State in Schuylkill's two official histories.

In the eighteen-thirties, this first angling club in America acquired its own worm digger, Martin Lush. In 1832, on its hundredth anniversary, a hundred people (members and guests) sat down to a dinner that featured eleven pounds of food for each eater, and included, overall, forty-nine pounds of shad. They ate a hundred and seven pounds of beef, four pigs, thirty pounds of tongue, forty pounds of oysters, and twelve lobsters averaging 3.3 pounds. Filling it again as often as they drank it out, they drank on average of alcoholic drink some thirty-four ounces each—that is, was, seventeen gallons of rum and brandy, some of it mixed, and eleven gallons of wine, nearly all of it fortified.

Attracted to the table in 1849 were the "strangers" George Gordon Meade, of the West Point class of '35, and John Clifford Pemberton, West Point '37. On July 3, 1863, Meade defeated Robert E. Lee at Gettysburg. On the following day, Pemberton surrendered to Ulysses S. Grant at Vicksburg.

On October 31, 1920, when Prohibition was one year old, General of the Armies John J. Pershing wore an apron, peeled potatoes, and ladled Fish House Punch at the State in Schuylkill. Later, he recalled the visit, saying, "I don't know what particular State it was, but I was in a dreadful state when they got through with me. Still, the amusing part of it was that I didn't realize until the next day what a good time I had had." During his good time, the commander in chief of the American Expeditionary Force in the First World War—recipient of the Distinguished Service Cross, the Distinguished Service Medal, the Legion of Honor, the Grand Cross of the Order of the Bath, the Grand Cross of the Order of St. Marizio e Lazzaro, the Grand Cordon of the Order of Leopold, the Grand Cross of Commander of the Order of the White Lion, the Order of the Star of Karageorge with Swords of the First Class, the Order of Mihai Bravul, the Polonia Restituta, and the Order of the Rising Sun—was made an honorary citizen of the State in Schuylkill, and he wrote in a club ledger: "No honor has ever quite equaled this."

# NINE

# THE PORTABLE ROCK

In the Delaware basin today, sixty-five thousand people fish for American shad. I have no idea how the state surveys arrived at this officially concocted figure, but I find it hard to believe. While personally spending nine hundred and twenty-two hours on or in the river in many different places fishing for shad, I have developed a distinct impression that at least a hundred thousand people have crowded ahead of me into positions superior to mine. In 1965, I interviewed a citrus king in Florida, whose route to success he outlined in this manner: "When I was a small boy playing marbles, I learned that the most important thing is position. If you get in the right position, you can clear up some marbles out of the ring."

Starting out as a shad fisherman, I relied on the instincts of George Hackl, which was the first of many mistakes. As a consultant, Hackl has received stupefying fees. His expertise in the international licensing of pharmaceuticals would obviously qualify him as an authority on the whereabouts of shad. On our first day as shad fishermen, we went to a sporting-goods store, bought shad darts and two shad nets with their long handles and oversized hoops, drove to Roebling, New Jersey, and addressed ourselves in chest waders to the Delaware's tidal flats. The rationale was simple in every sense, but we would be slow to give it up: If half a million shad were in the river, half a million shad would pass Roebling—or any place in the lower regions of the river. Roebling is fifteen miles below the fall line at Trenton. We waded out from shore a good distance, and, in water to our waists, began to cast darts. You would not need an aerial photograph to sense the futility of this scene. A thousand feet beyond our casting range, oceangoing ships were passing by. They were in the river channel. We might as well have been fishing for ships. The shad were out there in the channel, too. For three hours, we flailed the barren flats.

Above Washington Crossing that spring, we crawled through a storm sewer under Route 29 in order to gain exclusive access to a broad shallow stretch of featureless river, which we also flailed without result. We fished the quiet current at a friend's house in Stockton, on the right bank of the river. We did as well as we would have done on the right bank of the Po. True, all shad in the migration go by any given point below the waters where they spawn, but when they are on the move the odds against a dart intersecting one are long to an extreme. Shad congregate below bridge piers, rapids, riffles, and islands, and fishermen do, too. Even a big boulder is enough to make shad stop, bunch up, and think. They collect in deep pools in the evening, and go up through rapids after dawn. Where white water flattens out, becoming slick and black on the surface of a pool, eddies tend to form on the sides. There is a distinctive seam where the southbound current and a north-drifting eddy touch. Shad cluster beside the seam, which is known as the eddy wall. After you cast crosscurrent and the dart swings, you connect with your shad at the eddy wall. You could make a long list of exceptions, but that in the main is where the fish are, and where the wading fishermen are, too— standing in the eddy, casting into the current across the eddy wall.

Four or eight or even sixteen of them are standing shoulder to shoulder like bears in a river in Alaska. Sometimes their casts overlap and intertwine. This puts to the test the renowned politeness of shad fishermen. Ed Cervone tells a story about dropping his wallet near the Lambertville launch. He went home, realized what had happened, and returned with a flashlight. No wallet. Home again, there was a message on his tape from a young shad fisherman in North Philadelphia who had found the wallet. Cervone: "Only a shad fisherman would do that. If you were at a polo match, they wouldn't do that. These are not just people catching fish. They're a breed apart, all to themselves." That's true, Doc, they will give you your wallet back. But they will not give an inch of position.

In a crowded situation, Buddy Grucela has seen a shad fisherman "k.o. a guy into the bushes," and then go back to his position.

Below the fast water at Byram, on the lower river, boats line up in echelon, anchored and still. The fishermen hold their darts in the river. When the fish are not there, which is most of the time, there is no movement in the boats. Against a backdrop bend in a stretch of river of amazing beauty, the scene is so peaceful it appears to be on stretched canvas. Then came a day of roiling high water when one of the boatmen nearly capsized and drowned. His anchor fouled, he needed to cut the rope, he had no knife, his life was in danger. No one moved to help him. To move meant to sacrifice position.

One Memorial Day weekend at nine in the morning, I was fishing in a pool far upriver when a canoe overturned in rapids above me. A boy about seven years old, his father, two paddles, a cooler, a thermos, and other buoyant cargo spilled into the river. The boy was wearing a life jacket with a wide collar that reached above his head like a coif. He bobbed upright in the swirling currents, screaming, "Daddy! Daddy! Save me! Save me! Daddy, save me!" His father struggled to move toward him. Slowly, though, like an opening flower, the boy, the father, the paddles, the thermos, and the cooler were being spread farther apart as they were swept downstream. The father, helpless, could not swim across the current. The little boy's jacket was doing its job, but he kept on screaming. "Daddy! Daddy! I'm going to die!" Standing about fifty yards from him in my neoprene space suit and my cleated heavy boots, I was helpless, too, as were other wading fishermen. Walking down to the river that day, I happened to glimpse a canoe stashed behind someone's cabin. To leave the river, climb a bluff to the cabin, locate a paddle, and return with the canoe would take so long that the effort seemed pointless, but I started wading toward the bank anyway. Then I noticed that the boy was being swept toward an anchored boat. Two shad fishermen were in it with four rods. The boy was fast approaching them, still screaming, "Daddy! I'm going to die!" They would end his panic. They would pull up their anchor and go into mid-stream to intercept him. As he went by them, they watched, and did not stir.

I continued wading to the bank, and was halfway up the bluff when I saw a canoe appear out of nowhere at a bend in the river. The two people in it had capsized earlier and must have been drying out. They picked up the boy.

A submerged boulder can offer great position to a wading fisherman who is able to reach it and climb aboard. A guy on a boulder dropped his dart box in the river one day. He stuck his arm down in the water and tried to retrieve the box with his long-handled shad net but failed. The pool was deep, the current strong, and the box with its numerous darts was too far down. After observing all this, another shad fisherman stripped to his undershorts, went underwater kicking hard, came up with the box, and handed it to the flabbergasted guy on the boulder. Cervone is essentially correct: Shad fishermen are fraternal and are not customarily greedy, mean, belligerent, or coldly indifferent. Still, the topic we have at hand here is the importance of position in cleaning up marbles out of the ring, and consists of significant if isolated fragments.

I have been crowded by a woman spin-casting in a bathing suit. I have edged close to a woman with piled red hair whose soft and nonchalant backhand cast came up with a lot of shad. She competed with the guy next to her, to whom, it turned out, she was married. One day, when I had asked him a question, she said, "Keep him talking, I'm catching up."

From time to time, I have encountered a small, slight shad fisherman from Philadelphia whose eyes are oscillating beads. If, arriving on the scene, he sees you with a fish on your line, he will wade straight to you and all but climb your back to see if he can cast from your shoulders. In my fishing diaries, he is called Snopes.

> May 13, P.M.: While I have a four-pound roe on the line, two men enter the river and stand virtually between me and my fish. One is Snopes McShad, an annoying and aggressive little ferret who fishes with a very light rod. I net the shad, and cast again. Snopes and his friend are so far out in the river below me that I am crowded and inhibited. As my dart swings toward them, I think it might snag them in the waders, a development that would in no way dismay me.

The first time my nephew Angus ever fished for shad, he arrived at the river, walked down the bank, observed all the fishermen lined up in an eddy, and waded into fast water far above them. He had never even seen a shad. Alone there—looking, maybe, foolish—he began to strip out line and send false casts in drapefolds over the river. His name is Angus Burton. At the time, he was president of Trout Unlimited in Baltimore. Who knows what fly he finally laid on the river, but it swung down into the eddy-sided pool and he had a shad on the line. It ran up and down and jumped twice. Angus's reactions were louder than the river. You could hear him redefining his sense of unlimited. When the fish was at his side in the water, he flicked out the hook and cast again. Downstream, Snopes McShad had pulled out of the line-up.

After splashing ashore, he ran upriver, reentered the water, and was soon within inches of Angus's casting hand. Angus is nothing if not polite, but you could see him wondering. This, after all, was not his game. He cast. He connected with another shad.

May 16, P.M.: Snopes showed up with a friend in a red hat. Red Hat caught a shad within ten minutes, and put it on a string. It swam like a dog on a leash. After an hour, he let it go—almost surely to die. He just walked away. When Red Hat got the fish on the line, Snopes moved to his side, like iron to a magnet. Detestable.

Once, when Hackl and I were hitting into fish, Snopes waded into the river eleven inches upstream. He said, somewhat testily, "I know where the school is." As if we were hiding it. I caught a buck shad, which I intended to eat, and I turned to set it on the bank. Snopes said, "Don't worry too much. I'm not going to take your place."

I looked around at him and slowly asked, "What did you say?"

He said, "I know where the school is."

Suddenly, the shad stopped hitting. Activity ceased as abruptly as it had begun. Hackl and I went on casting, but we were just throwing darts into an empty river. Five fishermen spread out below us were also catching nothing. Snopes vanished.

Snopes reappears far downstream, a speck in the river, and he instantly connects with shad. He may be the greediest, most aggrandizing, highly skilled fisherman in Pennsylvania. He knows where the school is. We know where the pool is.

A late afternoon in our second year, I stood in the river until dusk while a northwest wind blew my darts off course in the air.

Others around me were catching fish, and I was not. They caught fish after fish. I did not feel so much as a bump. The embarrassment was becoming an inflammation. I was standing on an underwater boulder, but evidently not a well-chosen boulder, and also not a very large boulder. A little after four, I slipped. I slid down the rock into the river. The water was cold coming into my waders, and when I stood up the wind felt colder. After sloshing ashore, I drained the waders, turned them inside out, and hung them on a bush to dry. In my undershorts, I went back to the fishing, and went on catching nothing while surrounded by success. I did not feel a strike that day. Slowly, my two-digit I.Q. wrapped itself around a conclusion: I was in the wrong place at the right time. The ring was full of marbles but I was not close to the ring. Position is everything. I could use a canoe. A canoe would be a portable rock.

I drove down the river three hours home to New Jersey. I spent two days chipping at a living. And then, from a rack in the back of the garage, I took down my sixteen-foot Mad River Malecite, my ash-gunwaled, cane-seated, Kevlar-covered chocolate canoe, a boat so responsive to the touch that a single stroke could cross a river. Or so it had always felt. I put it on the car and went back to the upper river with a formulated plan. I would drive down the railroad on the New York side. With my extensive jetsam, not all of which was flotsam—my rod tubes, vests, rain gear, pack basket, tackle bag, hoop net, anchor, fillet board, hand scale, Rapala knife, carrot juice, paddle, extra paddle, and uneaten lunch—I was better off going up a flat glide to a pool below white water than I would be heading downstream through rapids. If I spilled all that gear in the river, just the thought of the money it had cost might cause me to yell louder than a child in fear for his life. Some days before, I had driven along the edge of the railroad, on ballast the size of grapefruit. It was a little more than bumpy but the vehicle survived. And now, at the end of the journey north with the canoe, I went down into the river gorge to the grade crossing and began to turn onto the railroad's right-of-way. Beside the tracks, a pennant-shaped steel barricade, bright lemon chrome, had been erected by the railroad during the two days I had been gone.

I laid on the horn in sheer frustration. The point on the river that I wanted to reach was half a mile away, no more, but the portage was uninviting, and would surely require repeating twice to transport all that gear—not to mention a whole lot of time. The day was waning. I was primed to fish. There was only one thing to do. I went straight down to the river, parked the car, put the canoe in the water, filled it to the gunwales with all my gear, rigged up the anchor, and shoved off. The water level was a little high but that was all right, there might be more cushion over the rocks. Almost like a sled dog, the canoe seemed to sense where it was going and to leap forward toward the rapids, even while they were still out of sight around a bend. Their sound came first. And then all quickly we were right on top of them and sliding through a boulder field of chutes and souse holes, haystacks and swirling eddies. I did not do a whole lot with the paddle. The canoe seemed o.k. by itself. I looked down at the rod tubes, the vests, the rain gear, the pack basket, the tackle bag, the hoop net, etcetera, and marvelled at what had possessed me not even to tie them down. At the foot of the rapids, head of the pool, I saw fishermen on the Pennsylvania side. I peeled off the opposite way and into the New York eddy. You would not see a wader in the New York eddy. It was too broad, too deep. No wader could get out far enough to fish. It bordered the deep main current. I let the canoe get sucked up close to the white water, beside the eddy wall, where I lowered the anchor from its sprit on the stern. I turned and knelt against the center thwart, the river channel on my right. It was an awkward position for a right-handed caster, but I did not have that handicap. I picked up a rod. On the second cast, I caught a roe shad. I caught three more roes and two bucks with an attentive audience on the Pennsylvania side. As dusk came on, I hid the canoe in a sea of ferns.

I returned to the river soon after dawn and already three men were fishing. There was mist over the river and developing rain. What on earth did those fishermen think, at 5:45 A.M., when suddenly there slid out past them the low-freeboard dark-brown canoe? On the opposite side of the river, I went high up the eddy, and dropped the anchor. Roe. Buck. Roe. Roe. Buck. Roe. They leaped. They ran in wide circles and would not be turned. The line passed through curtains of mist. They stayed on for ten and fifteen minutes. One rose straight up like a rocket off a pad—the tail well clear of the water, the head three feet in the air. It leaped five times. It ran into the shallows and back into the channel. It swung the rod through ninety degrees. When it came into the net, the dart fell from its outer lip. My hands were cold and I warmed them in the river. Last night and this morning, I had thirteen shad on the line. Soaked in steady rain, I carried the canoe back to the car.

Now, years later, I fish in a canoe about half the time. Not all conditions are right. But it opens up the river—lets you drift down upon any rock or riffle, however inaccessible the banks might otherwise be. In the hundred and thirty-five river miles from Hancock to Foul Rift—from the start of the main-stem river to its preëminent rapid—there are at least five hundred riffles and rapids distinctive enough to stop migrating shad. The drop at Foul Rift is twenty-two feet in nine hundred yards—enough to shake the confidence of a muskellunge. You don't need a Foul Rift to find a shad. Any good riffle will do, not to mention other obstructions.

I was fishing one year on a cool spring day a short distance up from a sweeper. A big roe shad straightened and stiffened the line. There was no doubt about her gender. She turned sideways in the fastest water and engaged in a relentless tug-of-war. She was as big a roe as I would encounter all spring. I didn't have to see her to know that. I worried that something would snap, but I took my time and just held on. Unfortunately, the anchor was not also holding on. It bumped across the riverbed rocks, held, and moved again. Entering the equation between anchor and current, the roe shad was changing the balance. She was pulling the canoe downstream, ever closer to the sweeper. What to do? On brooks in New Jersey, as in the Brooks Range, in Alaska, I have been capsized by sweepers lying in wait for canoes. A sweeper is a toppled tree that looks like a broom in fast river current. A sweeper draws in a vessel, holds it broadside to the current, and inexorably rolls it over. Now, with this shad hauling me downriver, was I going to break off or not break off the line? The finest fish of the year versus almost certain disaster. I was locked stiff with indecision. This was the situation Jack Benny was in when the holdup man put the gun to Benny in his savings vault and said, "Your money or your life." Benny fell silent, unable to make a choice. The sweeper was now about fifteen feet away. I was unable to act. Suddenly the shad sounded, and then bolted crossriver. The leader broke. She was gone. I picked up the paddle, had time for one stroke, and barely missed the sweeper. The shad had tried to kill me. The shad had saved my life.

Sometimes, I have forgotten to take an extra paddle, a mistake that can become precarious if you are dumb enough to rest the paddle you do have across the gunwales while you fish. Once in early May on cold water I watched a lone paddle slide down a gun-wale and away in the current. What to do? I pulled up the anchor and tried to paddle with the shad net, which was like trying to eat soup with a ring that blows bubbles. To extend the shad net's length, I had fitted it up with a broom handle. I paddled furiously, and broke the broom handle. I went on whisking with the shorter version, and, some distance downstream, finally reached the bank. The lost paddle was a lifetime favorite—an old one of light spruce. I borrowed another paddle somewhere, went back to the canoe, took off downriver hugging the edge, and found the spruce paddle in an eddy.

That sort of thing does not happen every year, or even every decade, and my canoe is so involved with the angling endeavor that I would never abandon it in fear of more mistakes. Some-times, wearing knee-high boots and not waders, I look for a sub-merged, flat-topped rock, and get out of the canoe so I can cast standing up. In breeze or current, the anchored canoe will swing on its rope, and before long move upstream in the eddy below the rock. It bumps gently against my leg. It bumps again. Too much of that and I give it a shove, to put it out of my way. I cast, concen-trate. At the end of the swing, I bring in the line and cast again. The canoe has returned, and is nuzzling my leg.

One afternoon, I was fishing in this manner from a big rock covered with not much water and situated almost in the middle of the river—in effect a small submerged island. Deciding to leave and fish elsewhere, I pulled up the anchor and set it in the canoe. I had meant to change lures before leaving, and had forgotten to do so before lifting the anchor, so I sat down on the bow seat with my feet on the rock in the water. I removed a shad fly from the leader, and tied on a $\frac{1}{32}$-ounce dart. I stood up with the fly rod to try out the dart, and forgot all about the anchor. Slowly, while I cast, the canoe turned and drifted away. I was too late when I real-ized what was happening. The shad net fell off the canoe and stood upright under water, buoyed by the air trapped in its hoop. The canoe drifted past the shad net and on toward Cape Henlopen. What to do? I was marooned on a mid-river rock, in fifteen-inch rubber boots with deep fast water around me. This was embarrassment on a new scale. The dart on the fly rod was extremely small. I cast it into the canoe and made a slow retrieve. The dart maddeningly slid over everything—over the tackle bag, over the life vest, over the paddles, over the stern painter. It somehow missed a tote bag and even a large wire fish basket, as it climbed each thwart and dropped on the other side and made its way through the whole canoe. Coming over the gunwale, it fell into the river. I cast again. The dart missed the canoe. I cast again. The dart landed in the bow. Gingerly as I stripped it in, it hopped, skipped, slid over everything, and went back into the river. The canoe was gaining momentum and was almost out of range. I cast again, landed where I hoped to, but failed to connect. How can fishhooks get hung up on every twig and pant leg while this one intersected nothing? There might be space and time for one more cast, and that would be all she wrote, hoss. I stripped out more line, backcast twice, and sent the dart on its way. It landed in the canoe. As it made its way toward the stern, its barb lodged in the coiled painter. The painter came over the side of the canoe and steadily straightened. A great deal of tension developed against that tiny dart but I couldn't just stand there, I had to pull. Ever so slowly, the canoe began to move upstream, and a little less slowly when at last it felt the draw of the eddy. In the end, it bumped against my leg. On the way downstream, I picked up the shad net with the blade of a paddle.

Since the main-stem Delaware, in its full three hundred and thirty miles of flowing natural river, presents more range and variety of shad fishing than exist anywhere else, the fact that two out of three Delaware River shad fishermen are in boats is less significant than the fact that the other third are on the banks. Imagine casting a shad dart at the 79th Street Boat Basin. Imagine casting a shad dart in the Tappan Zee. The Hudson River, for all its historic commercial shad fisheries, is even less generous than the Connecticut to the lone angler. From New York City to Troy, its average width approximates a mile. Shad fishermen do not line the banks of this river, notwithstanding the success of Richard St. Pierre on the ferry dock opposite Catskill. Bank fishing is possible mainly where the Hudson's principal current—meandering like the jet stream—comes close to shore, as at North Germantown, Barrytown, Cheviot, and Coxsackie. For that matter, you need a lot of local knowledge to fish with success from a boat. There is a mid-river shoal about a hundred miles up, known as the Kingston Flats. It parallels the banks. The middle of the river may be two feet deep and the flanking channels seven fathoms. The shad go low under flowing tides and rise toward the shallows when the water is slack. Boats are waiting by the shoal.

One April Sunday in my fourth year of shad fishing, I called Ed Cervone, at his home in Pennington, New Jersey, to explore the possibilities for the coming Tuesday. As we talked, Cervone's absorption with the subject went into crescendo and we left for the river as we hung up the phones.

> Eighteen boats below the Lambertville–New Hope bridge. A light breeze and balmy sun. At no moment that I can remember was there not at least one shad on a line from a boat on the river. More often two or three. Rising from the boats, the rods were throbbing. The fishers were all men and their stiff rods were pulsating at the tips. I now understood the physics of shad. So intent is the man with filament engaged that you could cut off his foot and

he would not stop fishing. Cervone hit into six. I was using the same size and color dart, same split shot, same jigging motions. I never had a strike, not a nudge. This is proof: there is a God—a God who knows what He is looking at and enjoys making decisions.

In the territorial tensions that rarely but surely arise on the river, the aforementioned physics can't help but be involved. Off New Hope another time, Cervone and I had scarce anchored and made our first casts when a fisherman near us reeled in his line, found a strange dart caught on it, and waved the dart at me angrily, shouting, "You're fishing under my boat." This was most unshadly. It was also corrupted fact. The thing he was waving was not my dart.

Five days later, we were back in the same place and Cervone soon had a fish.

He loses it near the boat, because his knot untied. Cervone is furious with Cervone. Klutz is not his concept of Haut Cervone. Frustrated by my own failure to hook into anything, I begin to cast across current and swing the dart in an arc. The strategy seems to work. I hook into something very big: the boat next to us. My dart is embedded in its anchor rope. I yank and pull and cannot break my line. I carry the rod to the far end of our skiff, and yank and pull as hard as I can. At last the line comes free. The dart is still on it. The hook is bent out straight. If nothing else—and nothing else is the term I am searching for—I am the knot-tier in this boat. Cervone has a fish on the line. He lands a roe shad. Cervone has a fish on the line. He lands a buck shad. That is the last fish that Cervone is ever going to catch on this blue earth unless my rod bends. The Lares and Penates of Ed Cervone hear this declaration. My rod bends. It bends for ten minutes over a racing fish, a sounding fish, an unleaping unrelenting deepwater fish, a netted fish, a buck shad.

In New Hope one day in our sixth season, I got a fish on the line downstream right. It ran back and forth for a while, and then moved upstream until it was directly to my left, halfway to another boat. A man in the other boat had a bending rod, too. Our lines grew tighter and tighter, and eventually were aimed at each other. We were catching the same fish.

He yelled, "Let your line go slack."

"My line?" I called, incredulous.

"Yes."

I let my line go slack. He netted the fish. He unhooked my dart and returned it to the river.

I said, "Thank you."

He said, "Thank *you!*"

Cervone thought it was my fish. When I related the story to the editor C. Patrick Crow, Crow told me that what the man meant was "Thank you, sucker."

Crow was in a position to know.

May 24: In my canoe, I have a shad on the line. Crow, wading opposite, casts over my line. His fly slides down to the fish. He hooks into it, tries to hang on to it, and the fish breaks off. Crow accuses me of interfering with his fish.

After seven or eight years, I at last developed enough moxie to fill a reel with four-pound test. Its advantage is that it sinks rapidly and gets down to where the shad most often are. Its disadvantage lies in trying to bring in a fish known to break line twice as strong. The elemental requirements are experience and finesse. I caught a buck shad on the four-pound test. Next I got a big roe on the same line, and maneuvered it for fifteen minutes. There was a sense of expansion under my vest. I was thinking, Herewith I graduate to the subtleties of four-pound test. It's more difficult to use. It will catch more fish. I am turning pro. Gradually, I drew the roe shad closer and closer to the canoe. When it finally saw the boat, it power-dived. Explosively, the line broke in my face.

It took about ten seasons for me to shed enough humility to appear—even in a diary addressed to myself—insufferably pedagogical:

May 23: A lightly jigged swing, a quick retrieve, a new cast flowing right out of the retrieve: your dart is back in the water, where it belongs. The variables count, surely, but there is nothing variable about the fact that shad do not swim in air. A dart in the air will not catch a fish. When your dart is in the water, show it. Give it the twitch. You're trying to irritate a fish. Which is not hard to do if you're in the right place at the right time. A shad could not care less about your dart, and will not go looking for it. Show it to the shad. Uninterested in food, the fish will snap at it only if it's in its face. And where in the river is the face? That's for you to guess. With a few exceptions, you are not fishing to visible fish.

May 26: In the A.M., I fish in relative discouragement, netting two fish while a man from Reading with a thin alchemical mustache gets fish on his line in more than half his casts. Fish after fish after fish after fish he hooks into while the rest of us—four or five, on either side of him and opposite him—helplessly watch. One guy leaves, because he is so disheartened. Hackl, on the other hand, the eternal academic, apprentices himself to the Reading Rifle, and learns at the master's hip. He learns that he is using four-pound line with a six-pound leader. He is using a black-and-orange dart with a plastic tail. Of bucktail, he says, "Shad are not interested in that stuff." He points his long flexible rod low over the water in exact conjunction with the swing of the dart—leaning forward intently, sighting down his line, a subtle lifting every few seconds, the ghost of a jig. He is not taking in line. A finger is on the filament, lightly touching its tension, like the curling fingers of a cellist. He tells Hackl that the shad were so thick near Foul Rift a week ago that he could feel the line go over their backs, could feel the line go over one fish while another came up for the dart. Hackl later compares him to a safecracker, and says that very few people can feel the tumblers fall. The man from Reading reels in another. He is an adroit horser but a horser nevertheless. He nets a fish in two minutes. Hackl asks him if it is a roe or a buck. He has no idea. Moreover, he would never eat such an orthopedic mess. He says he tried shad roe once. And how was that? Awful, he says, reeling in another shad. He says he has no idea why he always catches a great many more fish than do the people around him. He says that shad take lures into their mouths and back away from them in the same instant. All you need to do is sense the crucial moment and lift the dart. As hours pass, no one present catches much of anything, except the Reading Rifle, who is rarely without a fish on the line. The weather has turned cold. The temperature of the river is dropping. The fish are becoming hypothermic. The superstar does not return in the evening. Fools return in the evening. Old fools, cold fools. This one feels nothing in two hours.

Jim Merritt watches shad going past a given rock and goes upstream to cast back to the rock. Merritt is an almost pure fly fisherman. He eats his fish sometimes, and uses bait in the ocean. Tall and very trim, he can shoot a fly line seventy feet with a motion so slow it looks lazy. We are friends, neighbors, colleagues in New Jersey, and fish together on the upper river. Author of "Trout Dreams" and other books, he writes for many publications, including *Field & Stream*. Merritt, I should pause to say with unlimited appreciation, is my ichthyotherapist. In addition, he has watched over this book with brotherly concern. He has made fly rods for me and tied flies to go with them. Merritt knows the zip codes of fish. If he is bored and shadless, he goes up the river and fishes for trout. He says he knows where they like to hang. He returned one afternoon with a two-pound rainbow caught on a weighted size 4 black girdle bug. He had damaged the trout, so he kept it. Merritt is not a serious shad fisherman. Imagine taking off up a river to make twenty-metre casts to rainbow trout when you could be fishing for shad. He spends no more than two days a year getting what he calls his annual "shad fix." He got it up in Equinunk one season, fishing around a boulder to a school of shad he could see. He said he noticed "that instant when the dart was inside the plane of the open mouth." That was the moment when a fisherman should strike. The books say that shad hook themselves, and this does not contradict either Merritt or the Reading Rifle. The fish's movement up, down, or sideways may, with luck, do the trick. Knowing or feeling the key moment, though, will greatly increase the percentage of hookings, and, even when fishing blind (as most shad fishermen routinely do) the superstars seem to be aware of the moment. How? Merritt says they would not really know. That sixth sense is something they just have—an innate or experiential talent—and in all likelihood a person with such a gift will not be able to articulate what it is that is felt. This I know for sure: I do not have it. In the lower river, people in anchored boats set their lines in the river and don't even hold onto the rods. They wait for the fish to do it all. I'm afraid that's analogous to what I do with rod in hand upriver. I jig randomly. I'm waiting for the fish to act. A superstar reacts to every swing, and knows what is where, and when.

June 4: Off to the river in waders on a Sunday morning, late. It is seven A.M., and the incomparable Erwin Dietz has been here catching fish since ten minutes after five. I haven't run into him in several years and have wondered what happened to him. The answer is "Nothing," as the shad could tell you. Erwin invites me to join him on his rock. I hesitate and move toward other water. Erwin insists, says he often fishes with his son, side by side on a rock. We cast, Erwin hooks into a shad. I watch him bring it in. We soon cast again. Erwin hooks into a shad. He says he can feel them bump the dart in the center of the current, bump it again, and then go for it. With a third fish on his line, Erwin tells me to move around behind him and keep casting, in case there's another where his was. I fire my dart. Shad! "Doubleheader," says Erwin. Fish netted, we are soon casting again. Another doubleheader. I am so high on adrenaline and vertically high on the rock that when the shad comes in and I scoop low with the net I poke it in the head and free the dart. "Quick release," Erwin says. For thirty minutes beside Erwin, I am matching him one for one, for two, for three, four shad. Five for five shad. Muggsy Bogues could just have hit me with a no-look bounce pass, setting me up for a back somersault while sinking an underhanded flip shot from downtown.

The citrus king I interviewed in 1965 was Ben Hill Griffin, of Frostproof, Florida. His beloved granddaughter, then seven years old, was Katherine Harris, who grew up to become Florida's Secretary of State, and to fulfill a crucial role in the disputed election of George W. Bush as President. Position counts. She cleared up some marbles out of the ring.

# TEN

# THE COMPENSATORY RESPONSE

When a river sorts out its sediment load—its boulders, cobbles, gravels, sands, and silts—the lighter things are carried farthest and the heavy stuff stays high, like placer gold in the first riffle of a sluice box. The upper Delaware is a big freestone stream, and some of the stones are the size of cabins. Many are not a whole lot bigger than armchairs. Wading on and among them can be difficult, especially where the currents are shoving you at ten thousand pounds per square inch. It helps that the water is clear. Except after long heavy rain, the water is clear. This is the Delaware River going past you at fifteen hundred cubic feet per second, and you can look down into it and read the label on your boots.

You could also read the Clean Water Act of 1972, whose effect is everywhere in the big free-flowing river. As it passes cities, of course, the narrative intensifies and in Philadelphia becomes one of the signal chapters in the ongoing chronicle of the environmental movement. The twentieth century was not a great one for anadromous fish, lord knows, and before it was half over the spring shad runs in the Delaware River had been stopped all but cold by municipal and industrial pollution. Unnatural sludges were three metres thick, the edge of the river a film of refinery waste. From mines above Reading on the Schuylkill came acidic coal silts by the tens of millions of tons. Added in were the effluents of paint-and-dye works, tanneries, chemical factories, paper mills, and slaughterhouses, and the flushed raw product of human bodies. A clean, green shad coming in from the ocean had about as much chance of getting past Philadelphia as it would have had surviving in a septic tank. Bacteria in the river consumed the water's dissolved oxygen. A thirty-mile reach from a little above Philadelphia to well below Chester was anoxic to the point of notoriety and acquired a litany of names: the black water, the pollution barrier, the pollution block, the Philadelphia sag, the d.o. sag. Ferries crossing the Delaware between Camden and Philadelphia plowed through dead fish. If shad made it past the barrier to go on upriver and spawn, their offspring faced the barrier coming down. In the summers of those years, shad schools in the Bay of Fundy commensurately declined.

The first fillip of environmental action came in the nineteenthirties when the Interstate Commission on the Delaware River went to court. The industrial prerogatives of the Second World War undid the effort. In the late nineteen-forties, the federal Water Pollution Control Act somewhat lightened the sag, but commercial shad harvests that had reached many thousands of tons at the turn of the century were now under forty thousand pounds. In Lambertville, Fred Lewis netted about four thousand shad in 1939, about two hundred in 1945, and zero in 1953. Curiously, the resurgence of the shad run in the Delaware River was stimulated by environmental action that had nothing to do with people or legislation. In August, 1955, came two hurricanes so close together that their eyes were almost like double yolks. Called Connie and Diane, they attacked and flooded eastern America. Far upriver, where I read the labels on those boots in water going fifteen hundred cubic feet per second, local gauges, as a result of Connie and Diane, produced readings of a hundred and thirty thousand cubic feet per second. Exponentially gaining momentum on the way downstream, the waters plucked millions of pumpkins off the floodplains and spewed them like birdshot far into the Atlantic.

When these same waters reached the filth and deep sludges of the pollution barrier at Philadelphia, they scoured them out like a blown nose.

In 1963, in Lambertville, Fred Lewis seined six thousand shad. Meanwhile, a vanished figure—the recreational shad fisherman—had returned to the river. According to Dennis Scholl, a past president of the Delaware River Shad Fishermen's Association, the spring shad run first came back significantly in 1960, and by 1962 the river was laced with anglers. Joe Kasper, a fishing guide in the Trenton region, has described the sixties revival as "a marginal reappearance," however. Enough remained of the pollution block to keep the runs modest, and another natural event—a prolonged drought—lowered the volume of the river and with it the levels of dissolved oxygen. After 1972, the enduring effectiveness of the Clean Water Act ever widened the way to the large migrations of the last quarter of the century, and to descriptions like this one by Anthony Brandt in *American Heritage* (April, 1994). ". . . the rocky bottom of the river is visible at depths of up to eight feet. You can also see the trout, which are plentiful, poised among the stones, and the pods of shad, twenty, fifty, one hundred fish moving upstream." The shad were counted at first by extrapolation from the results of tagging programs, and later by hydroacoustical instrumentation attached to the pier of a bridge. In the eighties and nineties, according to the instruments, there were spring migrations in the Delaware exceeding seven hundred thousand shad. In summers in the Bay of Fundy, the schools commensurately increased.

Nature being in so many ways cyclical, it is not surprising that the twenty-first century brought more alarm than confidence to the likes of me. Despite the official figures—the twenty-year averages of three hundred and fifty thousand shad in the Connecticut River, four hundred thousand in the Delaware—it seemed obvious to shad fishermen that runs were again diminishing. The evidence was in large part anecdotal. George Bernard, co-founder of the Shad Museum, in Higganum, Connecticut, said he knew a commercial fisherman in Nyack, on the Hudson River, who used to take his shad to the Fulton Fish Market in a tractor trailer and now used a pickup. The number of commercial shad fishermen on the Connecticut River had rapidly dropped from twenty-five to four. Sport fishermen were spending more time casting and less time reeling in fish. My own fishing diaries were showing a marked increase in time on the river versus shad in the net, but I didn't care.

Not only were the fish more scarce but also they were younger and smaller. In the Connecticut, which had known eleven-pound shad, a five-pound six-ounce roe had taken first place in the 1999 Shad Derby at South Hadley. In the Delaware, some roe shad were now in the two-pound range, and there were bucks of twenty-four ounces. The rogue roe shad I caught in Lambertville that took a hundred and fifty-five minutes to land was, as I have mentioned, only three years old, while the ages of virgin females coming in to spawn had long been four or five years. In that era (the early nineteen-nineties) the fact that she was three years old was even more unusual than her exceptional tenacity. She signalled what was to come. The number of three-year-old roes in the spring migration considerably increased in following years. "A population reduced in abundance needs to spawn earlier," Boyd Kynard explained. "It's a compensatory response to mortality. As populations decrease, they become sexually mature earlier. When populations do this, they're not just doing it for the hell of it. One of the first signs of an overfished or otherwise threatened population is when the average age goes down. Somewhere in the shad life cycle, abundance is being affected. All the populations that we know of on the East Coast show this decline in abundance. Our run in the Connecticut River is down fifty per cent. There's mortality happening somewhere."

Ask a shad fisherman where the mortality is and you'll get a strong, clear answer. Ask another shad fisherman, and you'll get a strong, clear, different answer. This is topic B on the river. When shad fishermen are not talking about the fish they have caught, they are talking about who caught the fish of which they have been deprived.

"Portuguese."

"There's Portuguese fishing boats out there in the ocean stealing shad."

"I don't know if they're Portuguese or Japanese, they're gill-netting shad in the ocean."

"They're Americans. They're commercial fishermen from the Chesapeake Bay who go out off the Virginia Capes and haul in shad for cat food."

"They call it the 'ocean intercept fishery.'"

"It's not them. It's sport fishermen who are really killing off the shad."

"Striped bass are what's really murdering shad. Stripers in the rivers in the fall eat millions of baby shad. Their bellies are bulging with juvenile shad."

"It's not the striped bass, it's the algae blooms that are killing off the shad."

The indictment of striped bass, also known as rockfish, might have been a little more airtight if people on the river had not been making the same complaint for a century: "The rock fish, in fact, comes into our rivers for the sole purpose of feeding upon the young shad," said Dr. J. Ernest Scott, of New Hope, Pennsylvania, in a paper called "Old Shad Fisheries on the Delaware River," read before the Bucks County Historical Society in 1908.

In 1998, the Shad and River Herring Management Board of the Atlantic States Marine Fisheries Commission decided to phase out the ocean-intercept fishery. The commercial interceptors were getting only five cents a pound for shad, but the fishery filled an important gap for them. "Shad carry fishermen through the early part of the year—the time of year when other fish are not present," said Jack Travelstead, Virginia's Chief of Fisheries. Implying that ocean catches were indeed the cause of the decline in population, he added: "The offshore fishery harvests the greatest number of shad harvested—the majority."

With regard to the diminished population, Boyd Kynard is not much moved by blooming algae, voracious bass, or floating interceptors from any nation: "There's a lot of us who believe it's not as simple as that, and what could be causing these decreases in abundance is not the traditional overharvest, because the data are in, and there's no large foreign fishing fleet or sport-fishing groups that are causing this massive decline in abundance out there. You have to look to more natural cycles, about which we know very little. We know that the climate is changing. We know that the sea temperatures are changing. We know that areas which were previously very warm in the North Atlantic are now very cold, and very unsuitable for Atlantic salmon. The same sorts of things may be going on with American shad—that is, areas in the ocean that were formerly good places to overwinter, good places to feed, may now be colder and not have those food resources that shad have evolved a genetic homing to. When they get to those places, there's very poor feed. This may be causing mortalities. There's also striped bass. I am one of the school that doesn't believe that striped bass are the sole contributing factor to the decline of abundance of shad on the East Coast. I certainly think they can be a factor. If you talk about the potential loss of feeding areas at sea and the increased predation by striped bass on a shad population, now you're talking about two factors that—acting together—could possibly be responsible for the large declines in American shad in rivers all up and down the East Coast."

I asked him if sport fishing could change the population.

He said, "Not unless the number gets way down. Then, any kind of mortality—sport fishing, problems with dams—gets to be a great deal more important."

The twentieth century's crenelated pattern of abundance and decline and then renewed abundance and recurring decline is generally taken as a textbook example of latter-day environmental stress—the world in its handbasket approaching its landing in hell. It is of interest, though, that in the nineteenth century this same anadromous species went through a crenelated pattern of abundance and decline and then renewed abundance and recurring decline—a result and example of environmental stress. The first dam in the Connecticut River was constructed, after all, in 1798. In 1822, Philadelphia blocked the Schuylkill, the city's need for reserved water taking automatic precedence over the free-flowing nature of the river. In 1830 and 1839, dams were completed on the Susquehanna that pushed back the spring migration to within forty-odd miles of the Chesapeake Bay. Meanwhile, the Connecticut had been blocked in all but its first fifty miles. As demand increased and supply dwindled, commercial fisheries prospered where rivers still flowed free. All through the nineteenth century there were commercial shad fisheries in many places on the Delaware River. They had names like modern music groups—New Shaven, Quick Step, Snapjaw, Wool Cap, Jug, Crab, Purgatory—and they lasted in large numbers a hundred years. Many a "water haul" was made—that is, the seine came in empty. At the fishery at Betley's Point one season, soon after the turn of the nineteenth century, thirteen consecutive water hauls were made. The fourteenth pass netted eighteen hundred shad. That—to a fare-thee-well—is shad fishing. One day in the eighteen-thirties, Dr. Samuel Ladd Howell's Fancy Hill Fishery, on the left bank across from Philadelphia, hauled in a net containing ten thousand eight hundred shad. In the *American Journal of Science and Arts* (July,

1837), Dr. Howell praised both God and shad for their abundance and availability: "They afford a striking illustration of the goodness and design of an all-wise Providence, in making it a law of their nature that they shall thus annually throw themselves within the reach of man."

In 1839, the Massachusetts Zoological and Botanical Survey reported: "The Concord shad have almost entirely disappeared, their ascent having been cut off by dams." Henry David Thoreau, two years out of college, was not unmindful of this development, least of all during the fortnight that summer when he travelled by dory with his brother, John, on the trip that resulted ten years later in "A Week on the Concord and Merrimack Rivers." Thoreau and the aquaculturist Seth Green were the nineteenth century's foremost defenders of American shad—Green the more practical, Thoreau the more passionate.

Thoreau was a sometime fisherman. He "caught white chivin of great size in the Aboljacknagasic, where it empties into the Penobscot, at the base of Mount Ktaadn." But his hands-on relationships with fish went far beyond the imagination of an ordinary angler. He actually said, "I have not yet met with the philosopher who could in a quite conclusive undoubtful way show me the . . . difference, between man and a fish." He could all but converse with river partridge, more commonly known as perch. In the evening at pond's edge, he would ripple the water with his fingers, and perch would come to his side. He understood the chain pickerel—"the swiftest, wariest, and most ravenous of fishes . . . stately, ruminant . . . lurking under the shadow of a pad at noon . . . still, circumspect . . . motionless as a jewel set in water," and then exploding forward like a barracuda to eat whatever might swim into range. Thoreau continues: "I have caught one which had swallowed a brother pickerel half as large as itself, with the tail still visible in its mouth. Sometimes a striped snake, bound to greener meadows across the stream, ends its undulatory progress in the same receptacle."

Wading in shallow water, he visited the nests of sunfishes.

I have thus stood over them half an hour at a time, and stroked them familiarly without frightening them, suffering them to nibble my fingers harmlessly, and seen them erect their dorsal fins in anger when my hand approached their ova, and have even taken them gently out of the water with my hand; though this cannot be accomplished by a sudden movement, however dexterous, for instant warning is conveyed to them through their denser element, but only by letting the fingers gradually close about them as they are poised over the palm, and with the utmost gentleness raising them slowly to the surface.

The thought of American shad in their thousands coming up against a new commercial dam—desperately trying to find a way to complete a reproductive journey their forebears had made since time immemorial—was just too much for Thoreau. It was in "A Week on the Concord and Merrimack Rivers" that he made his noted lament, "Poor shad! where is thy redress?" and pictured them approaching the continent to "inquire humbly at the mouths of rivers if man has perchance left them free for thee to enter."

He is radically and almost subversively anthropomorphic in his regard for the founding fish, asserting that American shad are "armed only with innocence and a just cause," and suggesting that the dams that impede them will ultimately crumble, the shads' "watery dream" will be fulfilled, and nature will take back her own, for these fish are "reserved for higher destinies." Meanwhile, he urges them, "Keep a stiff fin and stem all the tides thou mayst meet."

Thoreau was nostalgic about the "dim visions we still get of miraculous draughts of fishes, and heaps uncountable by the river-side, from the tales of our seniors sent on horse-back in their child-hood from the neighboring towns, perched on saddle-bags, with instructions to get the one bag filled with shad, the other with alewives." He described certain fishermen on the Connecticut River suspended in armchairs from a high steep rock face, scoop-ing shad with dip nets. One dipped shad, he reported, had a rat-tlesnake's head in its stomach.

Three years after the river trip, during the period when Thoreau was reorganizing his journal notes into the more tightly structured composition that was published in 1849, his brother, John, cut himself slightly when a razor he was stropping slipped in his hand. He developed tetanus, and died. The scholar Linck Johnson, author of "Thoreau's Complex Weave: The Writing of *A Week on the Concord and Merrimack Rivers*," noted Thoreau's predilection for shad among all familar species and pointed out the ways in which Thoreau associated them with his brother: "Like John, who was 'cheery still' when confronted by the seemingly cruel 'fates', the shad confront their 'stern Fates' with equanimity."

Thoreau mentions a revolutionary militia unit known as The Shad, which stood bravely at the bridge in the Battle of Concord, prepared in every way except training. A day had been scheduled for military drilling, and the militiamen had all showed up, but their captain's sense of duty had been overcome by his sense that shad were in the river. The captain went shad fishing. The soldiers learned nothing. The name Shad was applied to the unit, and later, according to Thoreau, to "all the irregular militia in Christendom."

George Edward Pickett, who was a cadet at the United States Military Academy when Thoreau was writing "A Week on the Con-cord and Merrimack Rivers," may never have read or heard of the Concord militia unit known as The Shad but he would live to cause an army to deserve the name. This was, of course, the Pickett of the charge—the Confederate general, fifty-ninth in his West Point class of fifty-nine, who helped end the Confederate invasion of Pennsylvania when he ordered his troops to scramble up Cemetery Ridge under heavy Union fire on July 3, 1863, at Gettysburg. Pickett followed the charge, while two thousand seven hundred of his soldiers fell. That was not, however, the scene reminiscent of the Concord militia. On April 1, 1865, in Virginia, Pickett was defending an intersection known as Five Forks, six miles south of the Appomattox River and a good bit closer to the Southside Railroad, the last remaining supply line to Richmond. While thirty thousand Union troops led by Little Phil Sheridan approached from the southeast, Pickett's twelve thousand, spread two miles wide behind fences and in ditches, braced to meet them. Pickett's supreme commander, Robert E. Lee, was headquartered ten miles away, near Petersburg. Should Pickett fall to Sheridan, Lee would be forced from Petersburg, the Federals would capture Richmond, and the Confederate cause would be lost. Someone mentioned shad. The spring spawning run was in full penetration of the continent. The fish were in the rivers. Tom Rosser, another Confederate general, had caught some, and on the morning of April 1st ordered them baked for his midday dinner, near Hatcher's Run, several miles from Five Forks. He invited Pickett and Major General Fitzhugh Lee, nephew of Robert E. Lee, to join him. Pickett readily accepted, and rode off from his battle station with Lee. The historian Shelby Foote continues the narrative ("The Civil War," vol. 3, p. 870): "Neither told any subordinate where he was going or why, perhaps to keep from dividing the succulent fish too many ways; with the result that when the attack exploded—damped from their hearing, as it was, by a heavy stand of pines along Hatcher's Run—no one knew where to find them. Pickett only made it back to his division after half its members had been shot or captured, a sad last act for a man who gave his name to the most famous charge in a war whose end was hastened by his three-hour absence at a shad bake."

Pickett's lust for American shad was not an eccentricity in his time, as John Graham could have told you. John Graham? Honored guest at a dinner at Buena Vista House, in Gloucester, New Jersey, April 17, 1864, at which the menu listed Shad *la Bordage*, Shad *Rôti sur le qril*, Shad *Rôti en entier*, Shad *Friture*, and more Shad *Rôti*. No other entrées were offered. Just Shad, Café, Pain, Beurre, Dessert. Bordage was ship's planking. The Shad *Rôti en entier* might have required a very large platter. Roe shad of more than thirteen pounds—exceeding by two and a half pounds the greatest specimens in modern angling records—were not uncommon in the Delaware in that era. With fish of such size in the river, it seems incongruous that "as thin as a shad" was a cliché in vogue at the time. True, when shad spawn out they do become thin to the point of rigor mortis. In any case, Abraham Lincoln knew the expression. One day, in the winter of 1862–63, he used it as a springboard for what his biographer David Herbert Donald called "an atrocious pun." It was, in fact, a pun so bad it was good. A light eater and not a drinker, Lincoln was consuming even less than usual in those grim, anxious days—an apple and a glass of milk for lunch, an analogously hearty dinner. He had become very thin— "cadaverous," according to Donald. Told that he looked "thin as a shad," he said he was worse off than that. He said he was "thin as a shadder."

Two years later, after John Wilkes Booth murdered President Lincoln on the fourteenth of April, Booth fled south, hiding in woods, looking for ways to cross the Potomac River and the Rappahannock River and fade into the former Confederacy. This was at the height of the 1865 spring migration. Booth was assisted at both rivers by shad fishermen. The Potomac was two miles wide where he crossed, in a twelve-foot flat-bottomed boat that had netted seventy shad some hours before starting out with Booth. The party lost its way at night on the wide river, but made it across on a second try.

On the Susquehanna, shad economics had caused the Great Safe Harbor Shad War (upriver interests versus downriver interests), which was fought in the eighteen-fifties. In a book on the fisheries of Hunterdon County in New Jersey, Phyllis B. D'Autrechy mentions a widow who inherited shad (1860), and another widow, who inherited even more shad (1866), and a doctor whose bill was paid with shad, and a tailor who sold a garment for four shad. In 1867, Thomas De Voe published "The Market Assistant, Containing a Brief Description of Every Article of Human Food Sold in the Public Markets of the Cities of New York, Boston, Philadelphia, and Brooklyn." Of American shad, De Voe said: "This well-known fish is a general favorite among all classes of persons, as its flesh is considered among the best, sweetest, the most delicate, as well as being the most plentiful when in season. Nothing but its numerous bones can be said against it."

In the eighteen-forties, a standard pork barrel held forty shad. By the end of the eighteen-sixties, the same size barrel held a hundred shad. In eastern American rivers, the species had seriously diminished not only in numbers but in size, as it would, cyclically, into and beyond the century to come. In Thomas Jefferson's era, one shad would feed one poor family. By 1870, one shad was too small, and—*la Bordage, Rôti en entier*—too expensive. As the fish's popularity had risen, ruthless and reckless harvesting had proceeded uncontrolled. While dams had shrunk the population so had widespread pollution. Across the years 1825 to 1875, the spring migrations of American shad declined by eighty per cent.

The natural way to deal with something like that is to set up a government agency. In 1871, Congress established the U.S. Commission of Fish and Fisheries. Various states had been establishing their own commissions as well. With respect to the American shad, which had become not only a domestic food of prime importance but also a major export, the cumulative result of the commissioners' deliberations was to pin their hopes on Seth Green.

For some years, Green had been having exceptional success in the artificial fertilization and subsequent hatching of the species. Where nature achieves one or two fry out of a hundred eggs, Green was hatching ninety-eight per cent. He stripped milt and eggs from living fish and combined them without first immersing them in water. The technique would become known as dry spawning. It has been described by the fisheries scientist and aquacultural historian Nick C. Parker as "the first significant contribution of Americans to the practice of fish culture." Green was in business as well as science. He had begun his career selling fish at his own stall in a market in Rochester. He gave lessons in pisciculture for ten dollars an hour. For fifteen years, he did what he could to keep his dry-spawning method a trade secret. It didn't help that his friend Thaddeus Norris pretty much spelled it all out in an article called "A Plea for the Shad" in the April, 1869, issue of *Lippincott's Magazine*. Green had first tried his technique in Holyoke, where—in Norris's words—he "expressed the spawn and milt from shad into tubs; and after stirring gently, and allowing the fecundated shad-seed to stand a while, has placed them in his hatching-boxes, which he anchored in the current. Placing ten thousand eggs in a box, so arranged as to keep them suspended and in motion by the action of the current passing through, his loss in hatching hardly averaged one egg in a thousand."

Green obtained a patent on the hatching boxes. Roughly a foot and a half square, they had wire-mesh bottoms and strips of wood fixed on a slant to the sides, affecting the flotation in such a way that the bottom screens were slightly tilted toward the current. This kept the eggs in constant motion, as they needed to be. In Holyoke, on the payroll of several New England states, he hatched forty million shad in a couple of weeks. As an upstate New Yorker and a New York fish commissioner, he went on to establish a large hatchery in the Hudson River at Coeymans, ten miles south of Albany. His boxes were in shallow water in rows of six. Forty-two of them show in a pen-and-ink sketch in *Harper's Weekly* for April 27, 1872. On the riverbank, Green had a wall tent that would have looked like home to General Pickett. It was from Coeymans that Green took shad fry to California on the two-year-old transcontinental railroad, initiating a West Coast shad fishery that has far outgrown the runs of eastern rivers. Pennsylvania wrote to him asking to rent some hatching boxes for three years. That will be two thousand dollars, Green replied. With New Jersey's help, Pennsylvania paid, and shad runs in the Delaware soon began to rise. Never again would he make the mistake he had made in New England, where he told commercial fishermen that his purpose was to make shad "cheap." He paid the same fishermen to collect fish for him to strip, and they readily pocketed the money, but— according to *Harper's Weekly*—they also enjoyed "flopping shad across Mr. Green's face, stumbling over the boat and upsetting the pans of impregnated spawn, or dropping the lantern into the water at a critical moment."

"Shad are following in the wake of salmon in consequence of American energy of destruction," Green and R. Barnwell Roosevelt wrote in 1879. Green on his own was routing the problem with his little boxes. "The fish for cultivation in American waters, the fish which nature has given us preeminently as one of its best gifts to man is the shad," he and Roosevelt declared, as Green's shadlings caused runs to burgeon and supply to outreach the highest demand. Restoring a diminished species, he was making it once again plentiful and cheap.

In the eighteen-nineties, Rand McNally published an anthology called "American Game Fishes," by twenty authors, including the preëminent American sport-fishing writers of the nineteenth century: Thomas Chalmers, Frank Forester (whose real name was Henry William Herbert), and Thaddeus Norris (known in the fishing world as Uncle Thad). "American Game Fishes" dealt sequentially with a great many species but not with shad. Although

Forester, Chalmers, and Norris had all described casting for shad with fly rods, those were isolated virtuoso performances and did not bespeak a national recreation. Henry William Herbert was at least a century ahead of his time. In 1849, in "Frank Forester's Fish and Fishing of the United States and British Provinces of North America," he said of American shad: "This delicious and well-known fish, which is by many persons esteemed the queen of all fishes on the table, has been, until very recently, regarded as one that could be taken only with the net, and therefore of no avail to the angler. It is, however, now clearly proved that . . . American shad will take a large gaudy fly freely, and being a strong, powerful, and active fish, affords a great play to the sportsman . . . The flesh of the shad is perhaps the most delicate of any existing fish; and, though it lacks the lusciousness, as well as the glutinous fin of the Turbot, it is preferred to that fish by many judicious epicures, notwithstanding the drawback occasioned by its innumerable and sharply-pointed bones." So literate was Herbert in his fishing pieces that he occasionally broke into sustained runs of untranslated French. His Swiss-born friend Louis Agassiz, discoverer of continental glaciation, was also a celebrated paleoichthyologist, and he contributed fish sketches to Forester's research. Forester was an early craftsman in liminal advertising, e.g., "I can assure the fly-fisher that he will find much sport in fishing for the Shad . . . with a powerful Trout-rod, a long line, and such flies as he will procure in perfection at Conroy's, in Fulton-street, New York."

Conroy, it seems safe to say, did not grow rich on shad flies. Almost fifty years later—in the eighteen-nineties—shad were still beyond the conversation of most sport fishermen, despite the magic spawnings of Seth Green and the replenishment of eastern rivers. State hatcheries had long since developed, and by 1896 commercial seiners were harvesting fifty million pounds of shad— "far and away the Atlantic Coast's most valuable finfishery," in the words of the historian Charles Hardy. So relevant was the shad to the economy of Connecticut that Johnny Flynn's Market, in Hartford, sent its first shad each spring to the Old State House, and the governor had it for breakfast. The premier river, however, was then—as it is now—the Delaware, which accounted for one-third of those fifty million pounds. Fresh Delaware shad were sold off carts in Chicago. The zoologist W. K. Brooks, of Johns Hopkins, called shad "the most remarkable of domesticated animals, for it is the only one which man has yet learned to rear and to send out into the ocean in great flocks and herds to pasture upon its abundance, and to come back again, fat and nutritious, to the place from which it was sent out. From this point of view the maintenance of the shad fishery by man is one of the most notable triumphs of human intelligence over nature." Or, as Hardy has amplified the thought, "shad ranged free in the great plains of the oceans just as cattle grazed freely on the great inland ocean of the Plains."

Yet, as equity markets routinely demonstrate, there can be too much of a good thing. Steam winches were hauling in the fish. On railway spurs, freight trains were waiting to carry them to market. Seines were two miles long, three miles long. Charles Hardy calls this "a final cashing in on a once renewable resource," and continues: "The shad renaissance . . . lasted perhaps forty years. After a peak harvest of more than sixteen million pounds at the turn of the century, landings in the Delaware plunged to only three million pounds in 1905. A resurgence to seven million pounds in 1906 was then followed by another plunge. In 1916, fishermen took the last million pound haul out of the river."

In the same year, in the "Transactions of the American Fisheries Society," Charles Minor Blackford, M.D., of Staunton, Virginia, reported: "In the Chesapeake Bay, the nets extend out, in some cases, to a distance of twelve miles from shore, and the only chance that the fish have to get to their spawning grounds is to keep within the ship channels which are kept clear by the federal authorities." Blackford suggested that in addition to all their other talents shad would do well to study federal navigation laws.

By 1925, the drop in shad populations in eastern rivers had become so drastic that Herbert C. Hoover, Secretary of Commerce, called a conference to discuss the emergency. Two million pounds of Seth Green's transplanted *Alosa sapidissima*, he pointed out, were being shipped east annually from California and sold as "fresh Atlantic shad."

# ELEVEN

# ABSENT WITHOUT LEAVE

In stocking waders and cleated boots, I am standing in a clump of bushes that spend most of the year far out of water. Not to mention the trees. The water comes up to my waist. If I were to step a wee bit farther out, cops would pick up the body in Trenton. The river here is only one or two hundred feet wide, and the number of cubic feet per second going by is six times normal. If you like, you could call it a flood, but the Delaware gorge in the Pocono-Catskill plateau is so confined that the water is not pooling out all over the countryside but is concentrated in a silt-laden flume of what appears to be hurtling cement. All the sane people have long since quit and gone home. Stick around. There's a challenge present. The fish are in the river, where else? They're just as unhappy as you are. Out from the water's edge, they can't go much farther than you can.

Toss into the river a twig or a leaf or anything else that floats. Watch it go. If there is some kind of eddy, it will find it. Cast a bright dart into the big current so that it swings into the seam of the eddy. Do not be discouraged by the fact that deer have been known to sleep where you are fishing. This situation is extremely marginal, and you will not have a banner day, but one fish caught under these conditions is worth sixteen in a low river with big schools. A guy in Hankins told me that high turbid water, within reason, "can even be good for shad"—from the angler's point of view. They hit the darts more readily, he claimed, than they do in low, clear water. A local newspaper described fishermen using weighted flies for shad near the edge of the swollen river. There are things to be said for catching fish in a forest. The dart swings out of the brown-and-white turbulence into the haven shallows. Suddenly the line sticks fast to a five-pound two-ounce roe.

> May 22: Was out on a rock in the afternoon, the river down and clear. The event of the day was a weird, deceptive snag. It felt like river-bottom monofilament—the lost fishing line, mine and others', that all of us so often get hung up on. It's like a bungee with your hook in it. Snags of one kind and another are routine in shad fishing, because you generally fish along the bottom. I tugged at this one, and dragged it a little, hoping not to snap my rod. The burden at the far end kept coming—a slow, elastic dead weight. Then the line came up like a blade through the water and the surface of the river burst open. A roe shad the size of a blimp jumped and soared two feet in the air. Simultaneously, the dart came free. That huge roe shad had been sulking on the hook the way salmon do. Indisputably, she was the biggest shad anywhere in the river. I am off the mark, of course, in comparing her to a blimp. She was more like the Hindenburg. Beware. Nine snags will be snags, but the tenth will have a caudal fin.

An AWOL is a shad absent without leave. AWOLs in shad fishing are numerous and inevitable and deserve to be in the statistics. They are shad that hook up and later get away—the ten-second shad, the ten-minute shad. Solidly, the fish hits the lure; and completely it gets away. How it gets away is the nature of the AWOL.

Many are the result of very light hookings, and most hookings are very light—nicks in the front of the mouth. After a time, the hook pulls loose, and that is routine shad fishing. That is what it's like. Fish on the line are by no means halfway home. Most of all, the shad you hook but don't land are a part of your season— the hooking being in some ways more significant than the netting. In one ten-year span, I hooked up with a little over a thousand shad, and lost two hundred and ninety-eight. Roughly one in three. Most that get away are no-fault AWOLs. For example, the planer AWOL. Far out on the line, the shad comes to the river surface lying on one side. This is no spent shad. It skitters like a surfboard on the top of the river. There is nothing you can do except watch in wonder. The planing sometimes sets the fish free, even more than tail-walking and aerial somersaults. Selected examples:

May 7: Around four-thirty, I hooked a shad that was on for three or four minutes before it shed the hook, jumping, and the dart flew back past my ear.

May 13: Four AWOLs—one near the boat after twelve minutes. No mistakes.

May 25: Spectacularly, a buck shad does three consecutive somersaults, high above the water, remaining on the line. Now comes somersault four. He ejects the dart in midair.

Draped over the tip of the jaw, the hook may have penetrated—as the hook often does—the thin soft tissue that the anatomist Willy Bemis calls "the membrane of the maxillary recess." After the hook has gradually widened the hole it makes in the membrane, the hook falls out.

June 10: She leaped, leaped again, tail-walked, all over the river. The line was high and taut and the dart securely tied when, after five or ten minutes, she was gone. She expanded the penetration. She got herself away.

When a shad goes AWOL, you often cannot tell if it's your fault. You may have put on too much pressure. You may have used too little pressure. You don't know. All you know is that the line is slack, the fish gone. The hookup may have been so tenuous that it had no chance of lasting. You don't know. It may have been adequate but you tugged too hard, assuming an even firmer connection. Some shad are so securely hooked that there is almost no way to lose them. Most are hooked in such a way that the dart easily falls out when the line goes limp, whether the fish is in the water or in the net. You must assume that any fish is scarcely hooked. Shad fishing is a shrewd trade-off between handling and manhandling. Too much—she's gone. Too little—she's gone. That is one of the many reasons why you squirt adrenaline when they tail-walk or do somersault leaps. When they go AWOL, a choice is yours: to blame, or not to blame, yourself.

There is a good deal less latitude when the cause is impatience or bumbling—faults of the failed fisherman. Me, for example. Such as the time I jabbed that incoming shad in the head with the net, dislodged the dart, and the fish vanished. Among AWOLs of embarrassment, humiliation, and shame, the lowest form is the unravelled AWOL. The line unties itself at the hook. This is even worse than the horse AWOL—a fish lost to impatience by being yanked in too fast. Little buck shad invite the horse AWOL. They are male and they lack character, dimension, determination, and eggs. For ever and eternity they are second class. They are not roe shad. So you see them in the water flipping out on the end of your line, and your tolerance contracts. You yank them up hard and they fly away. You are a bad fisherman.

May 17: Two of my AWOLs were bucks that I lost beside the canoe because I muscled them too hard. I probably did that because I could see that they were bucks and was showing disdain for their sex and size. Little white males. I denigrated them because they weren't females with roe. They deservedly escaped. I should be fined for contempt of shad.

May 31: One of my AWOLs was a horsed buck. I was so irritated by him that I lost him—annoyed that he had the temerity to get on the line and flip and flap and wash and leap and execute complete somersaults while the females were patiently waiting their turn.

Twice in one week in my chocolate canoe I pulled a buck shad straight up out of the water, and then in midair it shed the hook, and then—free as a basketball—it dropped into the net in my hand. Those two fish deserved something better than a slam dunk.

May 12: Two AWOLs—one from another unravelled knot. I caught five or six fish on the dart and did not trouble to retie it; I got what I deserved.

May 13: Two got away at the net, including a big roe. The dart fell out of her mouth as I leaned toward her and forgetfully released tension. Lefty, you've done it again.

May 14: This would be humiliating if it weren't inconceivable. Four fish were lost after long battles because the knots came untied! Knots are not one of my failings, or used not to be. Five other fish simply got away. Three hours, nine AWOLs, one shad.

May 15: After thinking about my lost fish for twenty-four hours, I remembered that I was using old line. Dried line is difficult to knot snugly and may slip. I bought new line.

May 23: At the end of an hour and a half, the last of several fish simply leaves as the dart unties—a complete-fault AWOL. Careless. Inspect the darts, jackass. Retie the darts.

May 25: In the net, the fish had nothing in its mouth, the dart was not tied to the line. The dart was hanging in the mesh of the net. Evidently, the knot untied in the moment that I netted the fish.

Things have become so bad that I have been to see a fishing shrink. This was after a record loss of nine out of ten hooked shad. I had of course consulted Merritt but I wanted a second opinion. The slippage in old dry line was surely the problem, the doctor said. Yes, I told him, but most fish I lose, I lose in other ways. He said that I probably hold the rod high and straight up and keep the line taut like everybody else, right? Right. That's what they all do. Whenever you see a shad fisherman with a shad on the line, the rod is high and he is working in a plane straight in front of his nose. That's not the way to deal with a fish. The fish is always upright and knows where he is and what he's doing. You want to control, confuse, and direct the fish. Hold the rod horizontally off your left hip. Firmly, not too firmly, direct the fish that way. Make it move that way. After a time, swing the rod over until it projects horizontally to the right. Lead the fish that way. Now lead him the first way. Now the other way. He will become so confused he will turn on his side and take orders.

I also told the shrink I had particular trouble with freshly hooked fish that came near the canoe and were too active to control at close quarters. A just-hooked fish that gets close to the fisherman has "freedom" written on every scale.

Do you know how to make a fish turn over on its back? he asked.

Not without shooting it, I said.

He was holding a rod in his hand. You do this, he said. And he plunged the rod straight down. You plunge the rod into the river as if you were a matador killing a bull.

Returning to the river, I hooked into only eight shad, but I landed them all, and each time I held the rod on the horizontal. I drew them to the left, then drew them to the right, switching from the one side to the other every half-minute or so, and more frequently as the fish came closer to the canoe. In the end, I was switching from left to right every five or ten seconds. The shad went schizophrenic. Even when they were fresh and only seconds on the line, they got so addled that they turned on their sides and frog-kicked. They were so cross-eyed they were not alarmed by the net. In close proximity to the canoe, one shad was a good deal more vigorous than the others had been. I plunged the rod tip straight down into the river. The shad turned belly up and backstroked into the net.

On a June morning, dawn to sunrise, Erwin Dietz—as usual—was catching shad as if he were eating potato chips. After I pulled anchor and got ready to depart, I paddled over to have a look at his equipment. He was using two lures: a dart, larger than a quarter ounce, and—three feet farther down the line—a flutter spoon. He said, "If you hit the daily double, it's a bitch."

All that rigging depresses me. I refuse to fish that way. In the words of the master, Merritt: "Don't do it if you don't like it. You fish on your own terms." Merritt uses two flies sometimes: a dropper and—a couple of feet farther out—a point fly. In Erwin's rig, the dart is the dropper and the flutter spoon is analogous to the point fly. Shad fishermen call it the stretcher. Maybe, after all, I should try doubling up just once. I tie on two darts, a couple of feet apart. On the second cast, two shad strike simultaneously. In the comedy that follows, one goes AWOL. After catching another fish or two on the double rig, I revert to the single mode. As Shane said to Joey: "One gun is all you need, if you can use it."

Two weeks later, with a small dart doing nothing on my fly line, my resolve weakens again, and I tack on a flutter-spoon stretcher. Fish hits, nice weight, slowly comes toward the canoe. Fish digs in, becomes heavier and tougher, dives. Line goes out against the drag. Ten minutes. No progress. Twenty. Every time I move the fish, I lose the ground I have gained. Thirty minutes. Two fishermen on the New York bank have stopped to watch. I cannot bring the fish upriver. Thirty-three minutes. I am saying to myself, "This is not going to end well. Before long I am going to feel the weight go off the line." I can see a fish at the surface, evidently exhausted, but the pull is too hard to shorten line. Something is going to break. Therefore, I reach around with one hand and weigh the anchor enough to get it off the bottom, and step on the rope to keep the anchor from dropping. The canoe drifts downriver, while I reel toward the fish. There's a roe shad on the shad dart. I lift it into the canoe. The line to the flutter spoon is still taut. What to do? I pull it in by hand, and lift into the boat a second big roe shad. Two on one cast. Thirty-four minutes. It's a bitch when you hit the daily double.

In the near darkness of an early morning, a towering mist was moving south across the surface of the water. Wading, I was spin casting and catching fish. After a time, the dawning sun made shafts in the mist, gilding the line when it was in the air, and shining on the dart as it fell to the river. The dart was a $3/16$-ounce chartreuse with a dark-green head, and for some reason I didn't lose it.

I lose at least a hundred darts a year to bottom snags; it's just routine. This dart had a charmed existence. In late afternoon, I anchored the canoe high in a New York eddy, and resumed catching fish with the same chartreuse dart. From time to time, I ran my fingers over the monofilament and felt so much abrasion made by fish dragging the line over rocks that I snipped the dart away, removed the weakened line, and tied the dart back on. As dusk settled down, I became anxious to preserve and retire this amazing dart. I cast it gingerly into the middle of the channel, jigged it lightly along, retrieved it early, but kept on catching shad. For the day, six roes, eleven bucks, and three AWOLs—twenty shad on a single dart. It's one that I keep at home, mounted on a small cedar shake.

I made that dart with the lead wrapping from the neck of a bottle of wine—a messy, inadvisable process with highly impure metal, but I could not resist the idea. You heat up the lead in an electric pot and pour it into a mold in which you have first set a No. 2 O'Shaughnessy hook. A machinist in rural Pennsylvania fashioned the mold in his basement. It makes only one dart at a time, but perfectly—the head guillotined flat. The painting takes me several weeks, because I've got other things to do, also because I want time to pass between coats—the white undercoat, the two color coats, and then a dip of the head in a differing color. In a fly-tying vise, you tie on the bucktail at the tip of the cone. You seal the tie with head cement.

Essentially all shad darts are homemade. If you don't make your own, you buy darts that someone made at home. Scattered tackle shops make them on the premises. Behind the cash register, waiting for customers, the owner kills his day wrapping bucktail. Most tackle shops get their darts from nearby residents. The quality of shad darts is therefore as varied as the quality of organic fruit. Some darts that look beautiful lose their paint on the first rock they hit. Most look as if they were painted by someone watching television. Darts are sufficiently idiosyncratic to be traceable to the zip code where they were sold. A friend of mine likes to swim in the river with fins and face mask, picking up lost darts. He hooks them into his T-shirt until it weighs so much he almost drowns. He throws away the shirt and keeps the darts. On this planet, there may be fewer languages than varieties of shad dart.

I would be unforthcoming if I did not tell you that my darts are terrific-looking darts. Their colors are bright and sharply defined. If my darts were for sale, I'd be cleaned out. Their durability is as high as their gloss. Yet for quality, consistency, appearance, and allure, it is an adventure in pretension even to allude to them on the way to further discussion of the shad darts of Armand Charest.

When he was a kid in Holyoke, Massachusetts, fishing off the Willimansett Bridge, shad darts were unknown to him. He used brass spoons, and spinner blades with beads. Hand over hand, he lifted the shad from the river and pulled them thrashing all the way up to the roadway, never mind that his line could have lifted a mako shark.

His forebears were French, Scottish, Micmac, and Malecite. His father was a loom fixer. Armand's grammar school was Precious Blood, his high school Holyoke Trade. He was trained as a linotype operator in an era when a linotype operator was soon to be as current as a tailor of chain mail. He became a wire-strander operator at a manufacturing plant in South Hadley, a job he held until an industrial accident led to his retirement at the age of thirty-five. He did not stop fishing.

He bought his first shad darts in a barbershop. He bought

them also in Ma's Bait Shop. He couldn't find a good one any-where. The paint was dull. The paint came off. The adhesion of the paint is fundamental: a shad dart relates to bedrock as a basketball relates to the floor. Charest therefore—in the middle nineteen-eighties—began to make his own darts. Selecting paints, he began with lacquers and was later drawn to "glo-in-the-dark" vinyls. That first year, he made four hundred darts and went shad fishing in the Connecticut River, leaving darts in a box on the bank behind him, with a sign: "3 for $1."

The following year, he made eleven hundred darts and sold them out of his tackle box in a single weekend. For the next sea-son, he made three thousand darts. Selling them, he moved around—from the South Hadley Cove to the dam tailrace to the rapids above the Willimansett Bridge to the Chicopee boat launch to the bottom of Granby Road. He stopped at the waterwheels of Holyoke—the industrial-power-canal outlets that attract fish. He sold darts at Gas House, Valley Paper, Crocker A-B. Across the river, at the South Hadley boat launch, he parked his Toyota with the tailgate open and a card table beside it displaying his wares. Naturally, the scene attracted police. They told him he needed a Massachusetts hawker-and-peddler's license. He got one, but gov-ernments were not through with him. Enter the Internal Revenue Service. If you sell fishing lures, you must have a federal tax ID. Did he have an ID number? No? Really? Had he been selling shad darts in the previous fiscal year? The year before that? For some time, he paid the IRS twenty-five dollars a week.

Charest's darts, with their shifting levels and colors, are like the stratigraphic miniatures of Paul Klee. I would have thought it took him hours to make just one, but visiting his house in South Hadley a couple of years ago I learned that he could give a coat of paint to sixteen hundred darts in ninety minutes. He had added di-mension to the term cottage industry. We ranged from second floor to basement in a house that was essentially a workshop.

Striper jigs were drying on the second floor among rods he was making and rods in for repair. The living-room couch was the workbench where he and his wife, Denise, would sit side by side in the evenings with racks of darts before them, tying their own blend of Flashabou and Polarflash in lieu of bucktail. In the basement, though, was the machine that had put this whole operation into a class by itself. Consisting of tricycle wheels, bicycle chains, hexagonal nuts, and threaded lengths of stiff wire, it would not have looked amiss beside an orrery. Functionally, it circulated in the way that an escalator does, with the difference that it not only revolved but also porpoised in and out of paint. Each wire was thirteen inches long and was threaded with enough hex nuts to make ten spaces where darts could hang wet and not fatally adhere to one another. The two ends of each wire intersected a bicycle chain, from which Charest had removed rivets so the wire would fit. When Charest turned the tricycle wheels, the whole rig moved. Rising, descending—into the paint or dripping above it—sixteen hundred darts were in simultaneous motion. At the time, his best-sellers were "hot pink and purple" and "hot pink with eyes." His personal favorite was "glo-yellow chartreuse and blaze." The red-and-white dart is still the classic of the craft—as enduring as the black hockey puck. Yellow-and-red is nearly as traditional. Charest makes darts in bewildering variegations of hue, saturation, and brilliance. ("It matters to the fisherman.")

I learned from George Bernard, at the Shad Museum, in Connecticut, that William C. Miles, a Pennsylvania patent lawyer, poured metal into a turkey quill in the nineteen-thirties, making his patented Quilby Minnow, from which shad darts evolved.

Charest makes them now in Inverness, Florida, in smaller volume and with simpler apparatus, delivering them to the post office. His retreat from the bank of the Connecticut River was less a matter of retirement than a matter of moral choice. He says he became more than disgusted by "the needless slaughter of the fish," and was made uncomfortable by the thought that he was contributing to the slaughter. "My presence there was more harm than good. If I wasn't there, maybe they wouldn't have did that." It gave him a sense of acute discomfort "to watch a person take what you made, catch a fish, and throw it in the bushes." He saw too many fishermen "from out of state" ignore the six-shad Massachusetts limit, fill up coolers, and go home to sell the fish. "Somebody's got to be a guardian," he once remarked to me. "People on the bank catch shad and kick them up into the trees. That's pathetic. It's not fair to the fish." One day, sitting in his van, he watched two guys in a boat catching shad. With a small baseball bat, they bashed the shad, and then returned them to the river. After a while, they came ashore to buy darts. Charest told them he had seen what they were doing. One of them shrugged, and said, "I've got to get them off my hook somehow." The guy was addressing the last person who was ever going to sell him another dart.

A dart that weighs a thirty-second of an ounce is so small that it can call to mind the dorsal hump of an ant. Thirty-second-ounce darts are in all respects like other darts, but Charest will tell you that some fishermen refer to them as "shad flies." The list would not include this fisherman. A shad fly is a furry, bead-eyed product, not a little drop of lead. Some fly fishermen—casting for shad— use tapered thirty-foot fly lines that are backed with monofilament. The thirty feet of fly line shoots through the rod guides and over the water like a javelin, with the monofilament hanging on behind. It is a way of crafting an extra-long cast—more, sometimes, than a hundred feet. When the fly descends toward the water, the line coming off the reel is the same kind of line that comes off a spinning reel. Shooting tapers, as they are called, come in a variety of sink rates, in order to give you an opportunity to buy three of them instead of one. A sinking fly line is an alternative to the shooting taper. In the Delaware, you might want a line of special density in the higher water of early spring. When the river quiets down and warms up, you will want a floating line with a sinking tip, a so-called wet tip. This requires enough reels and spools to fill a closet. Nelson Bryant, writing his fishing column in the *New York Times*, once pointed out candidly that fly fishermen trying for shad "cannot cast as far or as often" as spin fishermen can, and in high water have more than a little difficulty keeping the fly deep, even with full sinking lines. He went on to say, "Blind casting with a fly rod for hours is also hard work, particularly if one is standing waist-deep in cold water." To anyone hardy enough to ignore these truths, he suggested using a weighted fly with a five-foot (or shorter) leader and a one-foot tippet of ten- or twelve-pound test. The largest shad ever caught on a fly rod came out of the Feather River, in northern California, on a tippet of two-pound test—a seven-pound four-ounce roe shad, the foster progeny of Seth Green.

In *Fly Fishing Quarterly*, Robert Elman wrote that shad will hit "sparsely tied yellow, white, or orange streamers," also White Millers, Royal Coachmen, Parmachene Belles, White Marabous, Dark Edsen Tigers, and Silver Yanks. The Delaware River guide Michael Padua has caught shad on a size 14 green-body caddis—a dry fly, always an uncanny achievement with a fish that has no interest in food. Padua says "you can catch shad on just about anything" from Twister-tail jigs to No. 2 and No. 3 spinners. Above Callicoon, he once saw two shad fishermen using No. 6 bare gold hooks.

Jim Merritt, who ties dry flies and can lay one on a floating leaf far across a current, will attach to his leader, without the least loss of self-esteem, an ordinary small shad dart—even a not-so-small shad dart weighing an eighth of an ounce. He nevertheless insists that he is fly-fishing for shad. After all, he is surrounded by people with spinning rods, slinging, as the phrase goes, hardware. He may say that he is fly-fishing for shad, but I would say that he is shad fishing with a fly rod.

Now another June has arrived, and the river is low and therefore tight in the sense that fishermen on the two sides of the main current are not as far apart as they would be in times of high water. I am in my canoe, and across from me is the great Erwin Dietz, standing on a rock, catching nothing. This happens to him so infrequently that he shows bewilderment and annoyance. While his spinning gear sweeps the channel, I slip into the river a small yellow dart by Armand Charest. In my hand is a nine-foot fly rod that Merritt made for me with Winston blanks. It is strung with a six-weight sink-tip line, five feet of braided leader, four feet of lead-core leader, and a 3X tippet. In no time, the rod is an arc, and I am dealing with a roe shad. Soon, I am dealing with a second shad. A third shad. My routine is risible, but it works. I am not casting a green-body caddis. I am casting weight, and there is nothing feathery about the motion. I flick the dart behind me (there's plenty of room) and let the line load up on the water. I cast it forward a short way into the current, then backcast it farther into the eddy behind me, where it lands and reloads for the long shot across the river. The rig is so heavy the water helps. With so much weight, you cannot conventionally forward cast and backcast, forward cast and backcast, making flattish loops in the air until you are ready to let the whole enterprise go. You'd be cracking a lead-tipped whip. Finally, I bring the rod forward and let it all fly. The dart goes out maybe sixty feet. It connects with another shad.

Erwin shouts above the sound of the river: "Was you here yesterday? Yesterday I had eleven. Today I can't catch nothing."

I am shad fishing with a fly rod, not because of some holy reverence for the fly rod, but because sometimes in the milder currents it seems to work better than a spinning rod, somehow does a better job of finding the fish. Erwin shouts again: "I'm beating a dead horse."

Just for the sheer science of it, I first used a chartreuse dart with a green head, then a white-and-red dart, then yellow-and-red, then orange-and-black, then green-and-black, then gold with white bucktail, then pink-and-black, and now green-and-white with more sequins than Elvis Presley—a dart I made six years ago and have hitherto preferred not to use. All have provoked strikes.

"I can't pick my nose," Erwin shouts. He had his eleven yesterday, and will no doubt double that tomorrow. But this is today.

I have seen odder forms of fly fishing. Once, in a single week in July, I connected with two smallmouth bass in the Delaware River and two king salmon in the Gulkana River, in Alaska, in water restricted to "fly fishing only." On the Delaware, I was drifting, fly casting, and letting the canoe guide itself around rocks. The bass, which hit woolly buggers, came out from behind the rocks. Collectively, they weighed thirty ounces. The combined weight of the two salmon was around a hundred pounds. I imagine. I had walked several miles to the clear Gulkana, a tributary of the Copper River, which was opaque and swollen with glacial meltwater coming off the shoulders of stratovolcanoes twelve and sixteen thousand feet high. There were four of us, and we had come down from the University of Alaska, in Fairbanks. Frank Soos, a fiction-writing English professor, rigged up an authentic fly rod, but the rest of us conformed to the local interpretation of "fly fishing only." We used rods big enough for surf casting with large-diameter spinning reels. The current was so deep and heavy that a lot of weight was needed to take the fly down, and the regional idiosyncrasy in this respect was pencil-thick plumber's lead. You unrolled four, five, six inches of lead, cut it, and slipped one end into a tight-fitting sleeve of surgical tubing that was tied to the line. The fly was a pom-pomic wad of orange-and-black yarn around a hook that seemed large enough to hang beef. You heaved the rig a hundred yards. Or something near it. The long stick of lead bounced on the bottom. In seven hours, I had five or six hits and the two strikes. One salmon was on the line for about ten seconds, the other more briefly. The first, when I struck, came up, porpoised, and looked like a whale. I lifted the rod tip, and reeled in sinker and fly. The other salmon picked up the fly and immediately took off for the far side of the river. It felt like a dump truck. After it was gone, I retrieved the surgical tubing without the metal, the unravelled line without the fly. Hence there was some disgrace involved. Had those salmon stayed on the line and come to the riverbank, I would have smoked them, broiled them, and made gravlax. But they were not absent without leave. From time to time, all day, the running kings in the Gulkana broached and flashed their colors. Just the sight of them in their setting was catch enough.

In the Delaware one spring, I was fishing in waders in fast water when a big roe shad got on the line, and I walked her ashore, walked her out of the current into two inches of water, where she flipped, threw the dart, and went AWOL. Minutes later, I was out there casting again, and I felt something stop the dart, something that felt the way a large twig will feel if, in fast current, it intersects a dart. In shad fishing, from time to time, your dart hooks into a sort of inverse AWOL—a by-catch, a species other than *Alosa sapidissima*. After a time, I realized that what I thought was a small floating stick was actually something moving, slowly, lightly, in sinister undulation. Delicately, I reeled the thing in. When it was scarcely a rod's length away, it came up into view—a sea lamprey, with a shad dart in its mouth. I don't know if you have seen a lamprey's mouth—known to Willy Bemis as the oral hood—but it is probably the last thing in this life you would want to touch. Large, annular, cuplike, suctorial, it has several rings of conical teeth. On its tongue it has larger teeth. A lamprey's mouth would fit around your thumb. What to do? Three feet of cartilaginous snakebody were moving sinuously behind the dart, and there was no way in this universe that I was going to put a hand on either the body or the dart. I walked the lamprey ashore—out of the river and up the bank and onto a big flat sunbaked boulder, where the dart fell out of the mouth. I went back to the river. The lamprey never moved.

Under the sun, its skin darkened from greenish-brown to carbon black.

When you look up from the river, you see bald eagles waiting to feed on dying shad. You do not see the timber rattlesnakes up the bank. One afternoon, when I had finished fishing in the canoe, I paddled toward shore and saw a fresh green willow branch blocking the small landing place I had left two hours before. A fat beaver, its back toward me, was feeding on the branch. Silently, over the flat water, the canoe approached it like an arrow. When the canoe was within inches, the beaver turned, tail-slapped the river, and submerged. I saw it stretched out in the shallow water to my left, like a long-haired fish. It poked its head up, saw me, slapped, dived, and shot away for the deep river. Soon it was up again, head out, swimming back and forth, back and forth, its eyes on me. I held up the willow branch for it to see, and flung the branch in its direction.

In addition to rainbows and smallmouths, I've caught dace on shad darts, and chubs. One time, my friend Hackl, fishing in waders near two other shad fishermen and opposite me in my canoe, overheard this dialogue while my rod was bent and throbbing:

"That guy across the river is really catching 'em."

"What does he know that we don't know?"

This is what I knew that they did not know: the fish on my line was a sucker.

The strangest catch I have ever reeled in on a shad dart was a shad scale and a gypsy-moth caterpillar. For a couple of seconds, I felt a shad on the line in the middle of the river. Then the shad was gone. As the dart came in through the fast current, it felt odd—the smallest bit heavy. Up out of the water came the impaled shad scale, the caterpillar alive and clinging to it. The shad had been foul-hooked, nicked in the side. The hooked scale, coming toward me through the water, had been seized by the caterpillar, swimming in the river.

One morning around the end of May, I was fishing a bright-pink dart and quickly netted three roe shad. A fourth strike came, a succession of thumps on the line. It felt just like a shad, so I was really surprised when it came in close: a writhing American eel. American eels are not lampreys. Long narrow fish with gills, fins, backbones, air sacs, and ribs, they are delicious. Nevertheless, they look like snakes and have razor teeth. The hook was in firm and I had no inclination to remove it. After hoisting the eel into the canoe, I picked up a pair of scissors and snipped the line.

Eels are everywhere in the river, in and around the big rocks. A drop of blood will convene them. That evening, cleaning shad, I was sitting on a flat rock surrounded by flowing, shallow water. I had dropped the giblets into the water. Now, with the shad on a filleting board, I slid a knife blade along the backbone, slicing off a fillet. I leaned over, reached into the river, and began to wash the fillet. Like a flash of lightning, an eel came up and grabbed it, tore it right out of my hands, and started off with it. I picked up the filleting board, leaped off the boulder, and smacked the eel. The eel gave back the fillet.

# TWELVE

# THE SHAD CITY

My grandfather was a publisher in Philadelphia who bought his shad from a street vendor and took them home wrapped in the morning *Inquirer*. Some of the vendors were women who carried shad in osier baskets on their heads. Others had carts and wagons. As they moved along the city streets, they cried out, "Shad-e-o! Shad-e-o!" It was the Philadelphia yodel. This was before and after the start of the twentieth century. Shad skiffs, powered by oars and sails, worked the nets of the Delaware estuary, and sold their fish to lay boats, which took them to Philadelphia. Farmers in their wagons with teams of horses were among those who picked up fish at the river and carried them into town to sell. In New York City, vendors carrying tin horns sold Hudson River shad out of two-wheeled pushcarts. They would sound the horn three times and then yell, "Fresh shad!" De Voe's "Market Assistant" (1867) claimed that Connecticut River shad were "known by their superior size, length, square-shaped back, and a fatter fish." But appreciation in greater Philadelphia seemed to soar a little higher than it did anywhere else, with the result that the American shad related to Philadelphia as the cod did to Boston.

This was, after all, the city of Stewed Shad *à la Mode de Touraine*, of Shad *à la Soyer en Bordure*, of Shad *à la Sainte-Menehoulde*, of Shad Pittsburgh *Vert Pré*. In "The American Angler's Book," published in Philadelphia in 1864, Uncle Thad Norris

had noted that "the shad is held in greater estimation by the epicure than by the angler," and had gone on to say, "It is considered
by many . . . the most delicious fish that can be eaten. Fresh
Salmon, or a Spanish Mackerel, or a Pompano may possibly equal
it; but who can forget the delicate flavor and juicy sweetness of a
fresh shad, broiled or 'planked,' hot from the fire, opened, salted
and peppered, and spread lightly with fresh May butter?" He
might have added that an undershirt would taste good prepared in
that manner.

In 1901, Louis N. Megargee, author and publisher, wrote in
his Philadelphia periodical *Seen and Heard*, "A Philadelphian has a
right to talk about shad, because only in and near Philadelphia are
the delights of the fish appreciated, and only in and near Philadelphia is it ever properly prepared for gastronomic delight . . .
There's only one way to cook a shad. Take her squirming out of the
water, run with her to an open fire, clean her quickly, nail her on a
thick hickory board, stand her in front of a fierce blaze and continually baste her with the finest gilt-edge butter until she is of golden
brown color. That is the whole story; nothing remains but the
eating."

In his 1908 paper read before the Bucks County Historical Society, Dr. J. Ernest Scott said, "Do you ask why the shad of the upper Delaware are the best in the world? It is largely because this
stream has no mud. It is practically rock bottom from its source to
its mouth." Calling the Delaware's shad "a gastronomic luxury"
preëminent "in all those qualities that please the eye and tickle the
palate of the epicure," he described the feverish anticipation created by "the approaching spring campaign against the finny hosts
when the vernal sun shall have begun to take the chill from the waters of this fitful river."

In his December, 1916, article in the "Transactions of the
American Fisheries Society," Charles Minor Blackford of Virginia

reflected Uncle Thad Norris's theme minus the Philadelphia prejudice, praising the taste of red snapper, pompano, bluefish, weakfish, Spanish mackerel, hake, haddock, and cod, before saying, "Without disparaging these or the equally luscious fishes of the Great Lakes and the Pacific, it may be safely said that the veritable king of food fishes is a denizen of our waters, for there is probably no fish on earth that surpasses the shad in all the qualities that go to make up an ideal food fish."

By then my mother, who was born in 1897, was in college, and all those spring evenings when she had greeted her father coming in the door with his bundled shad were essentially in the past. In the future, though, were grandchildren, and more wrapped shad. My cousin Billy Russell hated shad. Grandfather said to Billy, "The density of thy ignorance is appalling, child. Don't worry about the bones. Forget them. The fish is good." Billy didn't forget them. But he liked shad roe with bacon, as we all did, I think. My grandparents had a son and four daughters, whose children grew up on shad roe and shad.

If I may digress for a few paragraphs, the inside of my grandparents' house can be said to have resembled the interior of a shad, with cattle horns protruding everywhere as if they were the curling tips of bones. If someone like Daniel Boone had come into my grandparents' house and hung up his powder horn, he would have had a very hard time finding it when he was ready to leave. Their place was a Philadelphia Victorian at the edge of the city, with a vestibule that led into a kind of atrium—a squarish hall, in part a sitting room, through which other rooms opened. You might not have noticed the ruby-glass window, the coal-burning fireplace, the grandfather clock, the stairway bending around the clock, because the furniture in that most trafficked part of the house—the American box settle, the library table, the sofa, the clothespole, and miscellaneous stools—had been lovingly hand-made with such a liberal use of cattle horns that the vestibule, atrium, and front parlor had the combined effect of a condensed stampede.

In a chair beside the arch to the dining room, my grandfather sat in the evening, reading the *Evening Bulletin.* The legs of the chair were cattle horns, tips down, touching the floor. There were no armrests, but behind his head and shoulders was an intricacy of multiple horns. Next to him was the library table, its two levels separated and supported by horns, its four legs concatenating so many horns that they looked like gill rakers. Across the back of the sofa in the front parlor were tier on tier of horns. In the vestibule was the American box settle with a mirror above the bench and protruding horns running up the two sides and across the top. You hung your hat, your scarf, your powder horn on the horns. A clothespole that had horns coming out of it like bones from a shad fillet was just inside the atrium door.

All these pieces were made by Joseph Palmer, a farmer at Doe Run, thirty-five miles west of the center of Philadelphia, whose daughter Laura was my mother's mother. His farm was all-purpose, self-sufficient, with horses and cows and cannable crops, a smokehouse, chickens. Doe Run was dammed to reserve the water that turned the wheel of the mill. Joseph Palmer was, among many things, an energetic woodworker in various genres. Who knows when he became interested in horn furniture, but it was at least by 1892, when he made that *Evening Bulletin* chair as a wedding present for his daughter Laura and her husband, John Williamson Ziegler, who gave me the John and was called Will. Whittling mahogany, Joseph Palmer made pointy tenons to reinforce the horns from inside. The horns were from Texas, long and short. He evidently had them shipped to him, and may have obtained others locally. He was working in a tradition that reached into the Middle Ages, had some modest popularity in Europe in the mid-nineteenth century, was shared by others in America in his time, and attracted no followers.

In the mill, Joseph Palmer also made bookboards—the hard parts of what are now called hardcover books. He sold them to Charles Ziegler, my great-uncle, who owned Franklin Bindery, and whose best customer was the John C. Winston Book and Bible Company, where my grandfather Will Ziegler was second in command. Winston published more Bibles than anyone else in the world, and at the other end of their list was my grandfather's specialty, the hardcover equivalent of the newspaper extra, now known as the quickie. In 1912, he published a book on the Titanic while the bubbles were still numerous and the ice had yet to melt.

He would have been sitting in his chair, supported below and behind by two dozen cattle horns, when he read that the great ship went down. Being a publisher, he naturally kept a pair of pearl-handled .44-calibre Colt Peacemakers in a velvet-lined box upstairs, but even they, in the persistence of memory, are no match for the horns—the functional horns, the decorative horns, the functional-decorative festoons of horns.

No wonder he did not mind a fish festooned with bones. Somewhere in the evolution of fish-eating in America there came a moment when the inconvenience of a mass of bones generally overcame the appeal of the flesh they supported. If I had to find the moment, I would look for it in the gap between my grandfather and Billy Russell—more or less the nineteen-thirties. Before then, there were plenty of jokes about the topic but people unfussily ate the shad. In an appendix to his book "Domesticated Trout" (1872), Livingston Stone reprinted an article called "A Dissertation on Shad." Its anonymous author not only called shad "nature's pin cushions" but also included this general statistic: "It is calculated that during the shad season a good shad-eater will get from ten to fifteen bushels of bones from what shad he eats. After the last shad is destroyed, he tears off his shirt, sandpapers off the ends of the bones which are sticking out through his skin, dons clean linen, and is himself again." And McClane's "The Encyclopedia of Fish Cookery" says of early American settlers: "It had been wryly observed that in spring people couldn't get their shirts off without help, because of the shad bones which stuck out of their skins like porcupine quills."

In 1588, an English traveller reported that he saw herrings in American rivers "some of the ordinary bignesse of ours in England, but the most part farre greater, of eighteene, twentie inches, and some two foote in length and better . . . and in best season were found to be most delicate and pleasant meate." He was describing *Alosa sapidissima*, the bones of which, evidently, were not considered offputting in 1588. If you take a shad out of a river and cut the fillets off the shad and presently broil or bake them, they will rise, aromatic and golden, like fresh bread. The spiny tips of the intermusculars emerge. You eat your way down the clear middles in the orchard of bones. Picking the bones is the time-consuming part of the process. In Washington County, Maine, and elsewhere, when people say "You've been eating shad," they mean "You're late."

Thomas Eakins of Philadelphia (1844–1916) was a photographer as well as a painter and sculptor, and he pursued photography not only as an end in itself but as a sketchbook phase in the evolution of a work on canvas. Independence Seaport Museum, in Philadelphia, has about four dozen Eakins photographs of commercial shad fishing, for the most part on the left bank of the Delaware opposite Philadelphia—hip-booted men, oared boats, haul seines flashing silver. While still in his thirties, he moved through the photographs into drawings and watercolors that culminated in oil-on-canvas as "Shad Fishing at Gloucester on the Delaware River," which is ranked—with his oarsmen in shells and his operating surgeons—on the highest level of his work. Eakins and family were very fond of planked shad.

The largest Gloucester seine boats were sixty feet long and twelve feet wide. With eighteen men rowing them, they looked like uniremes. Some of the fishermen, moonlighting in two senses, were farmers by day. When the moon itself was not working, there were lanterns in the bows. Down the broad reaches of the river below Philadelphia lantern lights extended for tens of miles. There were drift nets, and nets strung between driven stakes. Holding pens were constructed in the state of Delaware so that shad could be transferred into tanks in freight cars and hauled alive to Philadelphia. Alfred Rice, a shad captain in the early nineteen-hundreds, had a crew of thirty-six and a two-mile seine. His customers for the most part were in Pittsburgh. In spring, so many shad boats would be on the river that ocean liners bound for Philadelphia failed to avoid them. In *MotorBoat* magazine, May 25, 1911, C. G. Davis described "a big Italian steamer . . . sheering up the Delaware" through fleets of shad boats that could not tell which way to move. They stayed put. "The steamer came head on," caught a net in her screw, and pulled the boat attached to it stern-first up the river.

Annually in the eighteen-nineties, commercial fishermen took four million shad from the Delaware River. A "forty-cent shad" was the fattest and finest. In the Hudson River, shad were taken commercially from Troy to the sea—with drift nets down to Catskill, anchored nets to the Tappan Zee, and, on the New Jersey side opposite 125th Street, nets fastened to poles set in the bottom of the river. A similar sequence filled the Connecticut to Saybrook, where nets were fastened to poles set in the bottom of the river. A hundred years later, as the twentieth century ended, most shad marketed in the Northeast were being shipped from Georgia and the Carolinas. The number of commercial shad fishermen on the

Hudson and the Connecticut was down to a remnant few. On the Delaware, of the tens of dozens of commercial fisheries in the hundred and twenty miles between tidewater and Port Jervis, only the one in Lambertville survived. Richard Holcombe began it in 1771, on the small New Jersey island just north of the New Hope bridge. William Lewis took it over in 1888, and was on the island more than seventy years. His son, Fred Lewis, long in years, runs the fishery now. He remembers fishing fifty-two hours nonstop in one of the fishery's banner years. He calls it "the longest day I ever put in." The day started at midnight Sunday and finished on Wednesday at four A.M. When his crew today starts a typical haul, they walk up the riverbank some two thousand feet, lining a U.S. Army assault boat of the type that crossed the Rhine. They carry the net. A crewman stays ashore, holding one end, while the others row much of the way to Pennsylvania, and then drift downstream before rowing back to New Jersey, making inches per sweep. Two are at oars, a third is poling. They wear hip boots, sweatshirts, watch caps. Only the assault boat would look different to Thomas Eakins. And maybe Sue Meserve, pulling in the haul. She is Lewis's granddaughter-in-law. His grandson Steve Meserve is in the boat, too. Others in the crew are John Baker, who is Lewis's grandson-in-law; Anna May Windle, Lewis's niece, and John Isler, who is related to Lewis only in the sense that he has worked for him about forty years. Lewis lives where his father did—on the island, in a frame house whose relationship with the river is a good deal more intimate than it would be even on a floodplain. The front porch is eight feet above the water. The parlor windows are eight feet higher than the porch. The river from time to time has been higher than the windows.

To form a great C with the nine-hundred-foot net, the rowers and poler work harder than galley slaves. The guy at the starting point holding the upstream end of the net walks it down to close the loop. On shore, they and others lean into the haul, folding the net as it comes in, its pocket full of thrashing fish. By no means all of them are American shad. Many may be gizzard shad—a fish that likes vegetables and grinds them in a gizzard like a bird's. The net has brought in a muskellunge more than a metre long, striped bass, black bass, trout, catfish, walleyes, and quillback carpsuckers. Six-foot sturgeons have been seen in New Hope but not across the river in Lewis's net.

A footbridge connects the island to Lambertville, and, not infrequently, a hundred and fifty people might collect to watch the net come in. I have seen hauls bulging with American shad, and a haul in the dearth year 1999 that landed one buck shad and one roe shad. The fishery in itself is a record and recapitulation of two and a half centuries in the life of the species, richest in detail in the Lewis years. In its peaks and valleys, the fishery's success-and-failure chart resembles the stock market's, with booms near the ends of the centuries and epic busts in the middle. Not to mention the decline as the twenty-first century arrived. In 1896, the Lewis fishery caught ten thousand shad. In 1949, it caught three. In 1953, as noted earlier, the total catch was zero. In 1956, the total catch was zero. The largest catch for any year in that decade was ninety. Then larger runs returned.

Before the mid-century crash, Lewis would fish beyond midnight and then take his catch to the big-city market downriver. After the depressed, pollution-block years, he changed his practice when the shad came back, keeping only what local people and local stores and restaurants ordered in advance. He returns the surplus to the river. It's a biological decision, he says: "We figure the shad are better off going up the river than to Philadelphia."

The fact that the main-stem Delaware is free of dams is attributable in large part to its shad fisheries. In 1783, Pennsylvania and New Jersey formally agreed to prohibit the building of dams unless both states agreed to repeal the treaty. In "Shad Fishing on the Delaware River," a paper read in 1920 before the Bucks County

Historical Society, Horace Mann reported that shad-industry op-position had steadily prevented the construction of dams. Anglers everywhere on the main-stem river, who owe so much to that 1783 treaty, are indebted to the Lewis fishery in more than an histori-cal sense. The hotline of the Delaware River Shad Fishermen's Association is in daily touch with Lewis, whose lone commercial fishery—more consistent and reliable than any hydroacoustical survey—is the antenna of the spring migration.

If no two shad fishermen agree on much of anything, Lewis makes a fitting third. He has worked with the biologists—Canada's Mike Dadswell, New Jersey's Art Lupine and Mark Boriek—but he can deliver an observation that would make a biologist blink. He says, for example, "Shad go to the sunny side of the river." He should know. "I don't care what theory you develop on shad, the shad will prove you wrong," he concludes. "Dad always said, 'You don't know what's out there until you put your net in the water.'"

# THIRTEEN

# INSIDE THE CAVITY

In the evening after fishing, I carry my shad to a flat boulder at the edge of the river, lay them out, and sit down beside them, my legs in the water. The light has softened. The river comes down through one lyrical vista and goes off into another. The upper Delaware is rich in big flat boulders—rich, too, in scenes of beauty. Since I am left-handed, my fish lie on their left sides. You open a shad not along the axis of its belly but a short way up, because a shad has a keel that is hard as bone and is covered with scutes—sharp plates that can cut you open while you are opening the fish. You cut above the scutes from the pectoral fins to the anus. Professional shad fishermen use a T-shaped knife with a hooking blade. I use German scissors. I buy them in New York City from a surgical supply company on Lexington Avenue. Near the anus, you pick up the bowel and tug. With whatever comes out attached to it, you toss the bowel in the river. If this is a female, roe sacs crowd the cavity, self-contained like sausages. You put both hands in the cavity and work your fingers around the sacs, lifting them, breaking the thin and transparent membrane that holds them in place along the cavity walls. It breaks easily but I help it with the scissors, especially at the tail end, snipping the roe sacs free. My hands are covered with bright blood. A shad is an unusually bloody fish. Cradling the roe, I lower my hands into current, which carries the blood away.

Thus begins a process that is as much a part of the fishing as the anticipation, the casting, the hooking up, the maneuvers with the taut line, the netting, the eating, and the making of the dart. Only in part because I'm tired, I pause often to look up, down, or into the river. There's a break in the surface, a splashing flip, dark forms—blood-attracted eels.

Often, a shad's air sac—its swim bladder, a small linear balloon—peels away with the roe. Pulling all these pieces apart, which I have been doing in various kinds of fish since I was five years old, I used to lack a clear sense of their components, my vocabulary seldom rising much past "guts." Remembering indistinctly a description I had read, I once asked Boyd Kynard what it is that connects the swim bladder to something in a shad's head, contributing to its extraordinary sensory perception. Kynard, the fish behaviorist, said, "I don't know. You need Willy Bemis for that."

Before long, I was standing at a dissection table in a lab at the University of Massachusetts, opening a shad with an audience of one: the anatomist Willy Bemis. Willy, like Boyd, had led me in multiple ways through the chambers of natural history. Willy is not specifically a shad biologist, but if you live in Amherst, Massachusetts, and are known far and wide for your knowledge of fish anatomy, it would be hard to overlook the anadromous migrations in the nearby Connecticut River. When I met him, a couple of years before the turn of the century, he was scarcely forty—a dark-haired dark-eyed life-loving hedonist in sandals, always moving mountains of research, post-deadline, with the air of a distractable tactician. His lab had a snake in it, reagents in glass jars, lungfish dating from his doctoral dissertation, stereo microscopes, vacuum jars filled with scanning-electron-microscope specimens, print dryers, water stills, light tables, cameras, and more than enough clutter to represent the cutting edge of science. In more than a thousand square feet, there was no working surface that did not need to be cleared before working. In a fresh and modest clearing—muralled in petri dishes, books, bottles, and flasks—I did what I do at the river, and asked him to describe what I was doing, while Sony preserved his voice.

"John is starting his incision by moving aside a few of the scales below the right pectoral fin. He makes a small opening. He's above the level of the scutes, maybe half an inch. He inserts the blunt side of the scissors into the body cavity and cuts backwards, caudally, along the top edge of the scutes."

I roll the shad onto its back, so that gravity will create a space between the roe sacs and the cutting.

"His right index finger is in the incision, lifting, as he goes on with the slice. He continues the cut to the anal fin. The egg sacs are unbroken. Now he's stripping out the gut tube, and pulling it forward. It comes out nice and cleanly, with the pyloric caecae."

The pyloric caecae look like a clump of angel-hair pasta. In the digestive tract, they follow the stomach, and always break away with the gut tube.

"They're little blind-ended diverticula, off the intestine at the level of the pylorus, which is the bottom end of the stomach. Pyloric caecae in fish are a way to increase the surface area for digestion and absorption."

As I remove the roe, Willy narrates: "The next step is to pry open the body cavity a little bit further, and gently reach around behind the egg sacs to free them up from their mesentery connecting them to the wall of the body cavity there—and then gently, gently, free them up from the back. John is using his finger to free that up, and now a scissors cut in the mesentery that's carrying the egg sacs. He's cutting them free. Now a last couple of cuts, in the caudal end, and there they are—two lovely, lovely egg sacs."

I am slow, fastidious, and amateur. A commercial worker can remove the contents of three hundred shad in an hour, just reaching in and deftly scooping out everything at once, a guts-and-roe ensemble.

These roe sacs will, alas, not end up under bacon. Not under my bacon, in any case. We did not catch this specimen on a dart in the river but instead picked it up at the top of the elevators in Holyoke Dam, where Willy anesthetized it with methanesulfonate salt. Truth be told, we fished side by side without a strike for several hours on the left bank of the river, and then went into the dam, where we learned from a bulletin board beside the powerhouse door that the elevators were lifting shad at the rate of three thousand a day while we were catching nothing. Issued hard hats, we put them on and watched a car rise five stories jammed to the gills with American shad, not to mention other species. Near the top, a lamprey's tail stuck out and was guillotined. Behind the observation window—beheld by a decibel of schoolchildren—was a mass of woven silver, enough shad to rattle the glass. Well beyond the public area—after we went down and up a steel complex of stairs—we came to a vertical chamber, vaguely similar to a navigation lock, known to management as the Fish Trap. Doors open, shad swim in. The doors close. The floor of the trap rises, lifting shad. They start flopping as the water drains away. This is how Edgar Allan Poe fished.

Gene Lavoie, the bearded and barrelly lift manager, weighed the trapped shad and measured them, picking them up by pressing his fingers into spaces below and behind the eyes. "Luckily these fish come with a built-in handle," he said. After rubbing off some scales with an inverted knife blade, he gave four roe shad and two buck shad to Willy, who anesthetized them in buckets, and then put them into a big plastic bag. The anesthesia notwithstanding, the bag pulsated with contained shad. It sounded like heavy rain.

Now, in the university's Merrill Science Center, in Amherst, I open the shad's empty stomach, as I do routinely at the riverside, testing—always positively—the established thesis that shad do not eat on the spawning run, and finding only bits of vegetation or, more commonly, nothing, perhaps hoping for a rattlesnake's head to support Thoreau in his claim that a Connecticut River shad swallowed one. A study in the York River by John Walter and John Olney, of the Virginia Institute of Marine Science, showed that shad eat mysid shrimp and copepods while still in the estuary making the salt-fresh transition, and, rarely, eat water fleas upstream. Water fleas, like mysid shrimp and copepods, are plankton. George Bernard, of Wallingford, Connecticut, who is a hundred per cent shad fisherman and zero per cent biologist, is of the opinion that shad on the spawning run do feed. On a wall of his Shad Museum, in Higganum, is a photograph that would not shock a surgeon, but might startle almost anyone else. A shad's head has been largely severed, and swung out like a door on the remaining hinge so the camera can see into the sliced-open stomach, where a flutter spoon is hooked solid.

Willy encapsulates my next move: "John reaches around and pulls at the liver and the rest of the viscera in the anterior part of the body cavity—pulls those all out—and then uses his scissors to cut the esophagus. Now he breaks into the pericardial cavity and pulls out the heart. There you go. If this were not happening in a university building, an eel would be lucky enough to get that heart."

"Look around," I suggest.

After snipping the esophagus, I usually break open with my thumb the chamber in the front of the body that contains the heart. The heart pops out. Smooth and firm, it resembles a chicken's, but is without fat and curiously bloodless.

"With cold running water, he washes out the body cavity."

When the cavity is empty, one organ remains—isolated high behind the cavity's membrane—its soft, dark-mulberry material covering and concealing the backbone. All my fishing life, I've been scraping it out with my fingernails in sunfish, perch, pickerel, rock bass, trout—giving little thought to what the material might be. In a shad, the covering is too tough for fingernails and I use the surgical scissors. Sometimes the air sac clings to it, and I have to pull it off beforehand.

"Now he is using the scissors again to cut into the retroperitoneal space there, where the kidney is. It's called 'retro' because it's behind the peritoneum, the layer that lines the body cavity. First he peeled away the air sac, which adheres very tightly to that peritoneal membrane."

One season, after catching a remarkably undersized female, I asked Willy what would cause a young adult shad—a year, and even two, before its time—to leave the ocean and come into the river to spawn? He answered, "I don't know. For that you need Boyd Kynard." Now, in the lab as the air sac peels away, Willy is saying, "The air bladder of these clupeids is highly specialized. There are ducts which lead forward from the air bladder to the posterior part of the skull. They transmit vibrations of the swim-bladder wall directly to the inner ear of the fish. This is a way these fish have of detecting high-frequency sounds under water, or sounds that are far away. These swim-bladder-to-ear connections have evolved many times in different groups of fishes, and it's one of the specialized sensory devices that we see in many groups of teleosts."

Acoustical experiments at the University of Maryland have shown that American shad are sensitive to sound at very high frequencies (a hundred and eighty thousand hertz), far beyond the known range of any other fish. In seeking prey in the ocean, certain echolocating cetaceans (dolphins and porpoises) make clicking sounds at that level. Dolphins and porpoises prey on shad, which evidently hear the clicks and either cluster for protection or scatter for freedom. Videos made in College Park record the explosive scatteration when sounds in those frequencies pass through tanks full of shad. In the words of an e-mail from Arthur N. Popper, one of the Maryland biologists, "American shad can hear ultrasound, and, indeed, they probably have a wider hearing range than any other vertebrate."

The shad in Willy's lab, its cavity emptied from the lower right side, is now lying on the table as a shad does in a fish market when a professional with a knife is about to remove its scales, head, fins, and bones. Like other fish, shad are shipped intact—minus only their innards—to avoid deterioration. I remark to Willy that when people in fish markets see my fish—as they sometimes do when I shamelessly appear for help in removing the bones—they usually say, "You're left-handed."

"Ichthyologists always cut the right side of a fish to save the left side for illustrations," Willy notes. "Fish illustrations always show the left side. So you're obviously an ichthyologist."

I pause, and think it over. "If I'm an ichthyologist, how come I don't know what a teleost is?"

"The superorder of fishes to which American shad belong is the Teleostei," he says.

I to him: "Keep going."

"Well, they are bony fishes, Osteichthyes, and their subgroup is Actinopterygii, or ray-finned fishes. The shad's family is the Clupeidae, the genus is *Alosa*, and the species is *sapidissima*. Teleos means 'higher'; ostei, of course, refers to bone; so these are higher bony fishes. Anadromy is so widespread, it has evolved in fifty different groups of fishes. Anadromous fishes almost always have difficult interactions with people. We build dams on their rivers. We build cities on their rivers. Shad and their allies are really primitive teleosts. Worldwide, they include many species from sprats to alewives to the denticle herring of Cameroon."

Soon he is describing the walking catfish in southern Florida, which breathes air and sometimes walks on land. After anatomy, free association is Willy's subspecialty, and he flies on into an encyclopedic comparison of fishes. "There are two big evolutionary stories," he inserts. "Herring and their allies, and carp and their allies. You could add a third: the spiny-rayed fishes. Easily ten thousand species have spiny fins."

Willy informs me that he is going to Alabama a few weeks hence. There is a fishing tournament in the Gulf of Mexico that brings in a large variety of species. He will be dissecting them.

"Why don't you come to Alabama? It's a scene and a half. It's so cool. In a general way, you would learn a lot about fishes."

He doesn't need to say that twice.

# FOURTEEN

# CATCH-AND-DISSECT

The boats come in through Petit Bois Pass, make an arcuate turn in Mississippi Sound, and line up on final in the Aloe Bay Channel. The afternoon sun is behind them. The boats in the middle distance are indistinct, and the far ones are lost in summerhaze. They are like airliners coming in from the west, descending in an endless queue.

Willy Bemis is waiting at the dock. The judges' stand is behind him. In the fish bin there—on five tons of solid ice—are redfish, lookdowns, stargazers, amberjacks, and kings, not to mention congers, morays, spadefish, ladyfish, catfish, bonitas, barracudas, and guaguanches. In the sense that he means to pay nothing, Willy is begging fish. As the competitors tie up and reveal their entries in the Alabama Deep Sea Fishing Rodeo—twenty-seven hundred competitors, in eight hundred boats—Willy casts a selective eye on the catch. When he decides he wants something and makes a pitch for it, his line is so incongruous that most of the fishermen seem to grant him the benefit of the doubt. Dressed in shorts and sandals and a T-shirt covered with sharks and other fish, he tells them that he is a professor of ichthyology from the University of Massachusetts, and that his purpose in coming to the rodeo is to collect skeletons.

As American fishing tournaments go, this rodeo is, in various respects, at or near the No. 1: number of boats, number of fisherwomen, number of fishermen, number of species. The last is what attracts Willy. Most tournaments award prizes in one category, and some in four or five categories. These fish, though, are coming from the Fertile Crescent, the fishery piñata of the Gulf of Mexico, in forty-five thousand square miles of which the action takes place; the catch is brought here to Dauphin Island, at the mouth of Mobile Bay; the prizewinners are in thirty categories; and they will range in length from four inches to eight and a half feet.

In the manner of a major golf tournament, a large leader board keeps the crowd informed. Among the categorical leaders of the moment are Robert Groh, with a hundred-and-fifty-six-pound tuna; Creighton T. Parker, with a thirty-three-pound wahoo; Melvin Dunn, with a thirty-three-pound barracuda; John Holley, with a fifty-one-pound grouper; Michael Burgess, with a six-and-a-half-pound flounder; and Jeff Gaddy, with a gafftopsail catfish a hair under eight pounds. Competitors are out there in twelve-foot homemade johnboats fishing "inshore" for redfish, flounder, and speckled trout. Competitors are out there in big cruisers that carry four hundred and fifty gallons of gasoline and troll along the lip of the continental slope. With fourteen rods in rod holders, brass reels, the big boats, as they come in, bristle like porcupines. Ladders go up to their flying bridges, where other ladders go on up to tuna platforms. They have outriggers, gin poles, venturi windshields, and fighting chairs that would not attract attention in a barbershop. The occupants of these vessels tend to be wearing one-way sunglasses that flash carnival colors—red, green, orange, purple, and blue. When these fishermen are milling about the dock, it appears to be a disco. Other fishermen have big tattoos and no sunglasses.

Resting on the bridge of Willy's nose are two clear lenses, surrounded by gold circles. His hair falls long in all directions from a bald spot at the top. He is a professor with an inquiring mustache, and enough extra weight to make him seem trustworthy—enough to help him float. More, he is amiable, straightforward, and benign. He explains his way of working the fishermen. "I just stand here and see how badly they want their fish." After a moment, he adds, "We came to get tarpon, ladyfish, and sharks, but we'll take as much diversity as we can handle."

Now comes Steve McConnell, in Play 'N' Hookie, with a hammerhead shark. Play 'N' Hookie is powered by a two-hundred-and-twenty-five-horse Johnson outboard, and is twenty-one feet long. The shark is nearly nine feet long. Steve—compact, wiry, his hair close cut—presents his ticket to the Mobile Jaycees who officiate the tournament. A portable crane on a bright-red truck moves toward the dock. It lifts the hammerhead out of the boat and moves it to a fish rack, a wooden arch twelve feet tall—a gibbet. There the hammerhead is hung, ogled by the crowd, and weighed (a hundred and sixty-three pounds). It looks a little like a steer and a little more like nothing else in the world, this creature with a widespread rectangular cranium like the bar antenna on a spinning radar. Jerry Walden, the crane operator, has been coming here ten years and has picked up some heavy fish. He remembers a fisherman who came in with a three-hundred-pound shark longer than his boat.

And now a man in sandals with sharks on his shirt appears before McConnell mentioning marine science, mentioning the possibility that McConnell's great fish could find a home in Massachusetts. So far, McConnell's day has included getting out of bed at four A.M. and fighting a shark for two hours. He was thirty miles off Dauphin Island, using fifty-pound-test line, a fifteen-hundred-pound-test leader, and two hooks baited with a ten-pound bonita. The hammerhead hammered it. And when all was over, and the fish, exhausted, neared the boat, McConnell saw that a ling, or cobia, about twenty-five pounds, had come up with it, and a second shark was chasing the ling. McConnell's wife and two friends were with him. They went to the rail to see the second shark. Immediately, they all stepped back and clustered in the middle of the boat. The second hammer, as McConnell would describe it, was the largest shark he had seen in fifteen years of shark fishing—"a monster." Now, contemplatively, McConnell looks at Willy Bemis. "Massachusetts?" he says, and donates his fish. An Ohioan who was trained at Cornell, Michigan, Berkeley, and Chicago, Willy is a world-class ichthyologist—co-author, with Lance Grande, of a six-hundred-and-ninety-page book called "A Comprehensive Phylogenetic Study of Amiid Fishes (Amiidae) Based on Comparative Skeletal Anatomy"—but he is only in his second year at Dauphin Island, and this is his first hammer ever. The crane lowers the fish into Willy's pickup. The nose is near the cab and the tail is out the back. Willy says, "If I live to be a hundred, there's nothing like the first hammerhead you have as a specimen."

Willy adds other species—including a white sea trout and the gafftopsail catfish—and takes off for his lab. The dorsal fin of this catfish will rise so far and so acutely that it closely models the highest sail on the mainmast of a schooner. Otherwise, the cat looks like an ordinary bullhead, barbels and all. The fish ride three miles down a palm-lined boulevard to the old Army post around Fort Gaines, beside the mouth of Mobile Bay, where floating mines were ignored by David Farragut, in 1864, when he sailed through, saying, "Damn the torpedoes, full speed ahead!" People now pronounce the name of the island as if it were "dolphin," which, as it happens, is the primary meaning of *dauphin*. The Army post has become the Dauphin Island Sea Lab, marine-science laboratory of a consortium of Alabama colleges and universities. In a breezeway between two buildings, Willy has created a dissection room, with a floor of crushed shells, screen walls at the two ends, and a four-foot belt-driven fan. With the help of two assistants, he has dug two offal pits, found a darkroom sink and plumbed it himself, and set up an operating table with a surface area of twenty-four square feet.

The hammer is on the table, catercornered. Nonetheless, it overhangs. Willy picks up a Rapala filleting knife, its thin blade eight inches long—the same kind of knife I use at home to fillet shad that weigh five pounds. Also on the table are razor blades and a scalpel. Idly, he slides the palm of one hand away from the shark's head and along its flank; gingerly, he moves the hand in the other direction. "It's smooth one way, but like rose thorns and will tear your flesh the other way. This is caused by a shagreen of denticles. Placoid scales. The skin of the hammerhead was used like fine sandpaper at one time." The wallet in Willy's pocket is made of carp skin.

The hammerhead is male. It has two claspers—hard penislike pelvic appendages. "That is really, really, really fancy," Willy says admiringly. "They penetrate the female and shoot." Internal fertilization, standard for sharks, is not uncommon in other fishes, he remarks. The Phallostethidae, for example, are a family that includes *Gulaphallus falcifer*, whose females lay fertilized eggs, like chickens. Various families of fishes, including sharks, deliver live offspring. He slides his knife through the big shark as if he were cleaning a cod. "You're taking off a hundred pounds before you dry the skeleton." A large mass of muscle plops onto the table.

"Every few years, a guy makes a name for himself by claiming to find bone in a shark. The consensus is that there is no bone."

"So how can you be collecting the skeleton? What is the skeleton?"

"Calcified cartilage. The distinction between this type of cartilage and bone is somewhat subtle. True bone has bone cells, calcified cartilage does not. You would need a microscope." Another muscle mass falls off the fish, joining the first one on the table. The shark's vertebral column is becoming well exposed. "The hammerhead has negligible rib structure," he observes, and, with a heavy cut, he starts another blob on its way to the pits.

Ready for finer work, he picks up a large steel kitchen spoon and uses it as a scraper, working rapidly, removing berms of shark tartare. Hammerheads will kill people. Normally, they eat fish, squid. He drops the spoon and opens the mouth wide, demonstrating its great flexibility, displaying its dental coronet and the hyoid arch. "The hyoid arch is suspended from the jaw by the interhyal, which allows the hyoid arch to move independent of the jaw. It's the only joint that connects the hyoid arch to the rest of the skull." Snap. He goes back to work with the spoon. The Navy became very interested in sharks and shark repellents after the U.S.S. Indianapolis disaster, in the Second World War, he says, and much of what we know about the sensory biology of sharks—their brains, their nervous systems—we owe to Navy funding. Look at that weird head—leading the fish like the crossbar of the letter T—with eyes at the extremes, nearly half a metre apart. The hammerhead's vision is stereoscopic. The nostrils are long slits, also well separated, like leading-edge grooves near the tips of a wing, allowing three-point olfactory discrimination, receiving scents from great distances. All over the roof of the skull are the gray peppery speckles of the ampullae of Lorenzini, which detect electric fields, maybe including the earth's magnetic field. "These animals live in a very different sensory world than people do. They're detecting things we never detect. The lateral line—a distant sense of touch—senses movement in the water column by detecting changes in water pressure. The hammerhead has a very large brain, comparable to some mammals'. People think of sharks as 'swimming noses.' There's a lot about them they don't understand."

The thin tubes of lateral lines run along the sides of most fish. A submarine passing fifty fathoms below a ship will feel the pressure of the ship, and note it with instruments less sensitive than a hammerhead's lateral line. The Indianapolis was the heavy cruiser that delivered the fission bomb Little Boy to Tinian. After the ship left Tinian, alone, it was fatally torpedoed. Sailors were in the water for as much as five days. Of the eight hundred and eighty-three who died, a great many were killed by sharks.

Eric Hilton, who is completing his Ph.D. under Willy at U Mass, removes from the hammerhead a plug of flesh to be studied for its DNA. Hilton's rufous ponytail and pharisaical beard offset the barbered hairlessness of Willy's other assistant. Tall, bare to the waist, he is an undergraduate named Mark Grgurovic. Dangling from a chain around Mark's neck is a golden fish.

Willy opens the hammerhead's body cavity. The liver, brought out on the tabletop, is a large scale model of Oahu. Why so much of it?

"It contains a lot of lipid material, which is light. It is thought to help with the fact that sharks have no swim bladder. They are very agile in the water column. They have to be neutrally buoyant to be agile. The liver helps that happen."

Would Willy comment on the conventional wisdom and litigatory metaphor that sharks can never stop swimming, have to remain in motion as long as they live, because they have no air bladder?

"A lot of sharks stop swimming. A lot of sharks are bottom feeders."

The shark's stomach is now on the table, too, and it is such a gross and loaded bag that it could easily have inside it something I would prefer not to see. As Willy slices into it, I nearly look away. It contains large hunks of large fish—whole severed segments of twenty-pound, thirty-pound fish.

Opening a thick tube about fourteen inches long, he reveals the hammerhead's spiral-valve intestine, which corkscrews around a stringlike membrane in the axial center of the tube. "Food goes down the spiral, which has a tremendous surface area. It's a Slinky inside of a pipe."

Willy now opens the penetrating end of a clasper, the part analogous to the glans of a penis. He slices it the long way and spreads it out to show the range of its ability to expand. "Doesn't that look nasty," he comments. "Claspers go in the cloaca and then spread out."

The shark is so long that Willy and Eric break the skeleton into five pieces before putting them in a tub of alcohol for drying. The tub is half of a fifty-five-gallon drum—sliced the long way, like the clasper. The alcohol draws nearly all the water from the tissue, making a great stride in the skeleton's advance toward an exhibition cabinet—exactly what happens in a person who drinks like a fish.

The collection of fish skeletons at the American Museum of Natural History, in New York, is in many respects unrivalled, and can be compared only with skeletal collections in London, Paris, and Chicago. There are more than ten thousand fish skeletons in the American Museum, and about a quarter of them came from the Alabama Deep Sea Fishing Rodeo. Most of these specimens were dissected and prepared by Gareth Nelson, an American Museum ichthyologist, who, over the years, scraped and dried on Dauphin Island more than twenty-five hundred skeletons representing two hundred and fifty-three species. A year ago, on the verge of retirement, Nelson brought Willy Bemis with him and showed him how to work the rodeo. Then Nelson went off to Australia. The American Museum, in Willy's words, "is out of the fish-skeleton-collecting business now," and Willy has an obsessional dream. He sees in his mind's eye a Massachusetts Museum of Natural History. He has already sketched a logo for it. He has designed an M.M.N.H. green-and-gold flag, which is flapping even now on a pole within a few feet of the space in which he is dissecting. He knows just where on the U Mass campus, in Amherst, he intends the building to be. Already, he has raised $1.3 million. He needs twenty.

Sponsored fishing teams are in the rodeo. Young, photogenic pros, they go from tournament to tournament, representing boat makers, engine makers, or tackle companies. Appearing on the dock in essentially identical clothes, they look like assistant basketball coaches: Team Big Boy, in green and gold; Ranger Sportfishermen, in blue. Their boats are as showroom-fresh as they are.

Second afternoon, and Blue Monday ties up—a homemade boat flying two Confederate flags. She is skippered by a competitor who is also a commercial fisherman. He has shrimp stickers on his wheelhouse and trawl doors aft. Blue Monday, imperfectly fashioned from quarter-inch steel plate, is possibly a sister ship of the African Queen. The skipper's face is quizzical and darkly bronzed. His eyes seem to be narrowing on something they can't quite hit. He says he has asbestosis. He says he has been shot eleven times, mainly in Vietnam. He says he has had a heart attack and lung disease, and each day he lives for the day. His bluefish and red snappers are not going to appear on the leader board. He casts off resignedly, and leaves.

Ynot comes down the Aloe Bay Channel. Ynot is a Fountain, a thirty-one-foot open fisherman, with a fineness ratio (length to width) of such elegance that it seems to slice—rather than part— the quiet water. Watching it approach, Jerry Walden remarks that it's "a high-dollar boat." Two people are aboard: a man, at the wheel, and a smiling—not to say exuberant—young woman eyeing the dock. They are father and daughter. Five feet tall, wearing shorts, a T-shirt, and New Balance boat shoes, she is as trig and pretty as the boat—blond and fine-featured, with the shape of a gymnast. Ynot waits for an opening and then moves into a slip.

They got up at four, at their home, near Pascagoula, Mississippi, and at six were trolling off the Chandeleur Islands in thirty-five feet of water. Due south of Biloxi Bay, the Chandeleurs are seventy-five miles east of New Orleans. The skipper on this run was John Colle (*kolly*), and the fisherwoman Natalie Colle. With two drift lines and a third line on a downrigger, she was fishing for king mackerel. On each line she used a single hook and a treble hook and a hundred-pound-test metal leader. ("Mackerel have such sharp teeth.") The bait on each line was a ribbonfish, "which we call a silver eel, a skinny eel—the single hook goes through its mouth and nose and the treble hook goes on its back to make it seem to be swimming right, even though it's dead." The line itself was thirty-pound-test, appropriate for a king. Each rod was seven feet long—"a king/ling rod, a standard king-mackerel rod." The rods were held vertically in hardware rod holders.

Off the curving Chandeleurs, the Colles were following birds. ("Where there's birds, there's baitfish; where there's baitfish, there's fish.") They trolled around the feeding schools. ("It was real slick water, real calm. We could see the schools.") Suddenly, one of the drift lines moved. Natalie picked up the rod. For forty-five minutes, the fish on the line held her off. It felt sizable, and Natalie wondered how it might place among the tournament kings. When the fish came to the boat, though, it was a blacktip shark, about five feet long, with three sharksuckers riding on it. She released it, and rerigged the line.

Something hit heavily at noon. The rod was in a rod holder. The reel, on light drag, started "zinging."

"We had the clicker on. Tournament rules—you reel it in yourself. I went to the rod, put it in my rod belt. I'm thinking, It's a big king. A real big king. The prize king! Before long, it jumped. It shook in the air. It was a tarpon! Again, he jumped. He twisted in the air. We call it skyrocketing."

What Natalie had on her line was like this—described for all time by Thomas McGuane, in the collection he titled "An Outside Chance":

> The closest thing to a tarpon in the material world is the Steinway piano. The tarpon, of course, is a game fish that runs to extreme sizes, while the Steinway piano is merely an enormous musical instrument, largely wooden and manipulated by a series of keys. However, the tarpon when hooked and running reminds the angler of a piano sliding down a precipitous incline and while jumping makes cavities and explosions in the water not unlike a series of pianos falling from a great height. If the reader, then, can speculate in terms of pianos that herd and pursue mullet and are themselves shaped like exaggerated herrings, he will be a very long way toward seeing what kind of thing a tarpon is. Those who appreciate nature as we find her may rest in the knowledge that no amount of modification can substitute the man-made piano for the real thing—the tarpon. Where was I?

When her tarpon jumped, Natalie saw a spray of blood leaving the gills. This was neither the scene nor the fish she had imagined, and she felt an impulse to cut the line and let the tarpon go. Her father, John Colle, suggested that she stay with it. In all his years, he had never caught a tarpon. His father's dream had been to catch a tarpon. He never did. And now his father's granddaughter had a tarpon firmly hooked—a fish at least as big as she was. The tarpon, in a sense, was hanging by a thread. Her monofilament line was thirty-pound-test.

An hour passed as Natalie dealt with the tarpon. "He fought and fought. He would surface and jump. He stayed strong the whole time. I'd huff and puff and reel and get him in close, and he'd take off again. At least ten times he did that. I thought the rod was going to break. It was totally bending over. Then he would sound, and sit there like a dead weight. Every time he did surface, he would take my line back out and just sit there."

John Colle had shut off the engines. Now and again, the tarpon pulled the boat. This way. That way. Several times, Natalie walked completely around its periphery "trying to keep him clear."

After an hour and fifteen minutes, little had changed. "Was I exhausted? No, I'm in pretty good shape. I work out a lot. I do triathlons. I got, if anything, kind of bored. You have to keep the rod tip up the whole time. I'm kind of a hyper person. My attention span isn't real long. When he sat there, I could not reel him in. So I just sat there, too. Each time, he came up a little more slowly. He would make an arch and go down again. When he was making the arch, you could see the brilliance of his body shining off the water. I thought, This is a beautiful animal and he's fallen into a terrible trap. He came close to the boat four times, regained energy, and went off. After an hour and a half, we missed him twice with the gaff. The third time, my father and I hoisted him into the boat together. My first tarpon. My first time, for sure. I had no plans to catch that fish."

She decided to go in and enter the fish "before he loses a lot of weight"—fifty miles to Dauphin Island. As Ynot reached the sound and swung into the Aloe Bay Channel, she was, as she would later describe herself, "beaming with excitement." She was thinking, This is going to be great. Maybe I'll set a record. Maybe as a woman angler I've accomplished something. It all seems worthwhile—the heat, the sun, the effort.

Now Ynot, after waiting its turn, at last nudges the dock. A Jaycee says to Natalie, who is standing in the bow, "You have a kill permit—right?"

"A kill permit?" she repeats.

"A fifty-dollar tarpon kill permit. You can't enter the fish if you don't have one."

"But I didn't know I was going to catch it—I wasn't trying to catch it."

The Jaycee says he is sorry.

"We were not aware of it."

The Jaycee repeats that he is sorry.

Her great surprise is not as great as her palpable disappointment. Her triumph in vapor, she is struggling to deal with the psychological bends, and in this moment is confronted by a professor from Massachusetts saying, "Can we have your fish? We're marine scientists. We're going to do research."

She is bewildered but she gives him the tarpon. "All right," she says slowly. "You can have him. At least it's good for research." The tarpon is lifted by two men and carried in a trough to a large scale. Ninety pounds. The tarpon is driven off in an A.T.V.

Tarpon permits are a requirement of the State of Alabama. Over the years at the deep-sea rodeo, tarpon permits have not been required, because they have always been superseded by the "permit for scientific collecting" that pertained to the American Museum of Natural History. Because Gareth Nelson retired and the tournament was not sure that anyone would be here to replace him, the tarpon permit is mentioned on the competitors' tickets this year for the first time—mentioned, as Natalie Colle sees it, "in little-bitty writing."

The Colles might have won prizes for most beautiful boat, most beautiful competitor, most beautiful fish, but those are not categories in this tournament, and Ynot goes up the channel into the haze. She is heading back to Pascagoula, the largest deepwater port in Mississippi, where a tugboat named Natalie is one of seven vessels in the fleet of Colle Towing—"the place with the big American flag"—where her great-great-grandfather worked, and where she works now. What Natalie Colle doesn't know is that her tarpon's complete and bushy structure, mounted on mahogany, is destined for a wall at the Massachusetts Museum of Natural History.

"If we do a nice job with this fish, it's a major exhibit piece," Willy remarks at the dissecting table, knife in hand. "This is the largest living representative of a group that hasn't changed much in a hundred and twenty-five million years. They are the fishlike elopomorphs, and are generally thought to be closely related to eels. Eels and tarpon have similar larvae—leptocephali—so thin they're almost transparent. I mean big larvae, some of them like a foot long. As larvae metamorphose either into eels or into fishlike elopomorphs, they shrink. It's counterintuitive. Bonefish and ladyfish are elopomorphs. The group also has an interesting fossil history and is probably among the most primitive of the teleosts. We study them to get that insight."

In a day or two, Natalie will send her tarpon's measurements ("I'm sixty inches, he was nine inches longer") to J. T. Reese Taxidermy, Inc., in Fort Lauderdale, Florida, which will feed the data into a computer and reproduce the tarpon in glass and fiberglass, and send it to Pascagoula. Willy, meanwhile, at the dissecting table, begins to remove the tarpon's skin. With the knife, he is as slow and careful now as he was swift and casual in addressing the shark, because the tarpon has three thousand bones, including six sets of intermuscular bones, the tips of which touch the skin. Eventually, he holds up what appears to be a vest of chain mail. A single tarpon scale is nearly as large as a playing card, and the third of it that is not overlapped by other scales is covered with what appears to be silver plate. You can read the age of the tarpon in the rings of the scale. This one is thirteen years old. Like shad scales, tarpon scales are deciduous—lightly attached, easily removed—

and almost pure bone. People collect them as souvenirs and paint seascapes on them where they are shell white, above the silver.

The flesh looks wine red, but the red muscle is only a veneer over a white inner mass. When fish swim idly, routinely, steadily, Willy says, they are using red muscle, but when, for any reason, fish require great speed they use white muscle. The flesh of the tarpon, like the flesh of an orange, is divided into segments. In this tarpon, each segment is about half an inch wide. The intermuscular bones are ossified connective tissue between the flesh segments. The intermuscular bones are attached variously to ribs and to the vertebral column. They are so numerous that the skeleton, to a remarkable extent, will resemble the complete fish. With the filleting knife, Willy makes long slices between the intermusculars—angling with them toward the tail—and then begins scraping with the cooking spoon, driving shredded flesh along and off the bones as if he were cleaning a pitchfork.

Detaching the skull from the bony curve that is known as the pectoral girdle is not easy without an axe, but Willy patiently succeeds, commenting as he works: "Fishes have a loose pelvic girdle, just floating, whereas the pectoral girdle is attached to the back of the skull tightly—the reverse of land creatures like us, tight in the pelvis and loose in the shoulders."

Now he has the tarpon's head in his two hands and, with a little pressure, causes the mouth to open so wide that a small car could park inside it. Or so it seems. "The hyoid drops down, the top of the head comes up, then the two sides go out. What an incredible expansion! It flares the suspensorium!" Between the lower jaws is a bone called the gular, common in fossil fishes but rare in the modern world. Also evident, with steel connective wire, are Natalie Colle's hooks—one in the urohyal bone, ventral to the gill arches, and the other in connective tissue between the urohyal and the lower jaw.

Going into the tarpon's swim bladder, Willy removes a thick, spongy cord that resembles lung tissue. "These fish come up to the surface and gulp air," he comments. "It's because of this special tissue in the swim bladder. In the Florida Keys, tarpon come up, breathe air, and eat what tourists feed them."

With a wire brush, he scrubs the cavity of the tarpon along the bottom of the backbone, locus of the kidneys. You could knit a wool sweater with two tarpon ribs. Not long ago, Willy was diving in the Cayman Islands, and he went into a natural tunnel in a reef. The tunnel was full of tarpon. Hundreds of tarpon. "They are not skittish," he says. "They are so peaceful. They let you swim around them." Much like caribou.


Albert Reynolds, a Mobile stockbroker who is a former chairman of the rodeo, takes me out to the action in his twenty-two-foot single-engine Grady-White. Through early-morning air too thick to be haze, too thin to be fog, we go to the western tip of Dauphin Island and then run south about seven miles. Suddenly, in the cottony seascape, looms a great standing structure, more than two hundred yards long, in three parts joined by long aerial footbridges. Rising through fifty-seven feet of water and continuing on up ten stories, the Triple Rig, as the fishermen call it, is Chevron 864MO, largest of the numerous platforms that collectively produce a hundred million dollars' worth of natural gas in this area of the Gulf each year. Broad and squarish, the central structure resembles an oil refinery, with Erector-set skeletal girders. Three pipes come up beneath it, because it is the center of three radial wells. Its highest point is a long, cranelike tilted arm, whose upper end is abloom with orange flame. A safety device, it is known on the rig as "the flare." Signs wherever you look say "Danger Poison Gas $H_2S$." The tower at one end supports a three-story house, the crew's quarters. The tower at the other end accommodates a fourth well. Under the connecting footbridges are passages of open water, where boats can go through the platform. Eight boats are fishing here. A couple are tied to the structure. Most are trolling. Like shuttles going back and forth in a loom, ours and the other trolling boats woof the Triple Rig. The oil and gas platforms of the Gulf have the same effect as artificial reefs. In a soft-bottomed environment unappealing to invertebrates, they offer hard surfaces for the likes of barnacles and clams, which in turn attract reef fish and transient species. Out of sight of land, out in the marine wild, one of the best places to go fishing is under the Chevron flare.

One boat, surprisingly, is Play 'N' Hookie. Where we are fishing earnestly for prizewinning kings, Steve McConnell has stopped off to fish for shark bait. He is fishing for bonitas to take to deeper water and drag past the noses of hammerheads. The symbiosis between oil or gas platforms and recreational fishing is personified in Steve McConnell. Half his time, he lives on a rig. He is an operator of oil rigs. Every other week, he leaves his home, in Mobile, to spend seven nights headquartered on Eugene Island 42, about fifteen miles from land, south of Morgan City, Louisiana, at the Atchafalaya Basin Sea Buoy. Frequently, he fishes from the rig, catching king mackerel, red snapper, dolphin. Employed by Sonat—a company that sells its crude oil to Shell, Chevron, Mobil, and Exxon—he runs seven other rigs, too, across four hundred miles of the Gulf. Every day, he flies from rig to rig in a helicopter, and fishing rods are always aboard.

If you float a wooden plank, fish will be attracted to its shadow and shelter. You can fish productively near the plank. If you don't have a plank, try an oil rig. The public-relations benefits of rig fishing have not been lost on the energy companies. Chevron, in fact, has a "Rigs to Reefs" program, in which rigs that have ceased to produce oil or gas are disengaged from the seabed, toppled onto their sides, and, in many cases, dragged to appropriate fishing sites.

Albert Reynolds has three lines out, thirty-pound-test, with stainless-steel leaders, and fishes them close to the boat, scarcely ten yards back. He outlines the thought processes that go on in king mackerels' brains: "Near the boat, they think they've got to get it and run. Way back there, they look it over and think something's wrong and go away." As baitfish he is using blue runners—foot-long jacks locally known as hard tails. Gentle-mannered and quietly bemused, now in his upper sixties, Albert Reynolds has been fishing the rodeo forty-five years. He once took a second prize with a speckled trout but "can't remember when." His boat is Shazam and his wife calls him Captain Marvel. He has been successful enough as an investor for this to qualify as a reference to his work. "You catch the right fish, you can make a lot of money," he remarks about the rodeo. It may not be the All-American Futurity at Ruidoso Downs, and it's not the P.G.A. championship, but as fishing tournaments go it has attractive money. There's a prize worth thirty thousand dollars for most overall points, a five-thousand-dollar jackpot for the biggest king, and another hundred and twenty thousand dollars spread through the various categories. Rocky Marciano fished here.

Something hits a hard tail, and a reel zings. It is my turn to pick it up. The reel is rigged for right-handers, so I try turning it upside down, which makes Reynolds chuckle. It also doesn't work, and I fish right-handed. The thing on the line feels heavy. It is active in the water column. It is stronger than a bluefish. It feels like a big roe shad. As I hold up the rod tip toward the Chevron rig and the billowing flame, I pass the time, mentally, at an A.T.M. in New Jersey depositing the five thousand dollars. Nice fish. You can tell. You can feel it. Baby grand. And after eight or ten minutes it is out of the water and into Shazam. King mackerel. Forty-six inches long. Nineteen pounds, ten ounces.

I remember Willy Bemis saying about kings, "They're aggressive, torpedo-shape, fantastic animals. They're running very strong right now, fifty-pound size." I have at least caught dinner.

All afternoon at the judges' stand, fishermen arrive with long insulated white vinyl bags, like bulky ski bags zippered up for travel. These are king bags, so called, and the zippers open to reveal torpedo-shaped fantastic animals: a fifty-four-pound king, a sixty-one-pound king, a sixty-three-pound king. Robert Shipp, one of the judges, says, "The big kings are more than a hundred miles offshore. Fast boats go sixty miles an hour to get them. It is not uncommon for them to run a hundred and fifty miles to weigh 'em in."

Shipp, an ichthyologist at the University of South Alabama, is the author of "Dr. Bob Shipp's Guide to Fishes of the Gulf of Mexico." Long before he became an official of the tournament, he came to Dauphin Island every summer to teach his marine-vertebrate course at the academic sea lab. The immemorial judge of the tournament was Roy Martin, mayor of Panama City Beach, Florida. Over time, as prizes grew larger, and decisions with them, the mayoralty of Panama City Beach became an insufficient qualification for the rodeo bench. There came a great question: Is this a very small blue marlin or a very large white marlin? Roy Martin took the fifth. The tournament's underwriting bankers asked Bob Shipp if he would become assistant judge. Sure, he said. A student of the population biology of fishes, he was interested in the tournament for the fish. A question even more controversial soon arose as well: Is this a young king mackerel or a Spanish mackerel? Spanish mackerel have spots, and so do young kings, which resemble mature Spanish mackerel. This was all sort of academic until the jackpot prize for the biggest Spanish mackerel approached and then surpassed a couple of thousand dollars. Shipp—gray hair, equanimous mustache, handsome as a tenor—was addressed one day by a fisherman he describes as having "one or two teeth, breath of beer and garlic, and bloodshot eyes." The fisherman laid a fish before Shipp and said, "That beauty is a Spanish mackerel."

Shipp said, "I'm sorry. It's a small king."

The fisherman said, "I've got Dr. Bob Shipp's book in my boat. I'll get it and show you."

One of the rodeo's prize categories is Most Unusual. It illuminates the tournament, because a fish of any size can win it. A fish four inches long can be honored beside a tarpon. The winner is determined by what Shipp calls "unofficial subjective calibration." Shipp picks the winner.

The Most Unusual category was introduced in the nineteen-eighties. Tony Stuardi, a marlin fisherman, caught on early. He went so far out in the Gulf—at least a hundred miles—that he laid up overnight. Most Unusual, he thought as he lay there, rising on the swells, and he got up and baited two bream hooks—ordinary small hooks of the sort more accustomed to dangling in a pond—and dropped them on a long line over the side. He was dropping them into DeSoto Canyon—two thousand feet of water, off the edge of the continental shelf. He caught a six-inch fanged mackerelet. By anyone's calibration, it was a clear winner. The next year, Stuardi came in with something equally odd, and Shipp again awarded him the prize. Then he told Stuardi that in years to come Stuardi could show up with anything from an oilfish to a bearded puffer but he was not going to win.

The blacktail moray lives so obscurely in deep water that it was not even described taxonomically until 1980, when it was known from only twenty-five specimens found in the world. Since then, however, six blacktail morays have appeared in the Alabama Deep Sea Fishing Rodeo, three of them this year. Shipp no longer thinks them unusual. Subjectively, they haven't got a prayer. He looks for "something never entered before, and if it's a legitimate catch we'll move it up to the top of the list." Three-two-one on his present list are Wendy Kennedy's short-fin mako shark, Don Henderson's smooth dogfish, and David Simms's blunt-nose jack—a fish that Shipp has never seen anywhere.

The geographical boundaries of the tournament were established after a competitor fished off Costa Rica and flew to Dauphin Island with the catch. Money may not have been the whole motivation. It is not always simple to fathom what makes a fisherman cheat. Why did Marcus Antonius, the Triumvir, cause dead lunkers to be draped on his hook so he could lift them from the water in the presence of Cleopatra? For the prestige? Did he actually think so little of her? According to Plutarch, she sent a servant swimming under Antony's boat with a dried, salted fish from the Black Sea. The servant put it on Antony's hook. When Antony pulled up the fish, he was drenched by all present with derisive laughter. "Imperator," she said, "you had better give up your rod."

The late Roy Martin, when he was the rodeo's judge, opened the stomach of a fish scoring high on the tournament scale. A chunk of lead fell out. That was not an isolated moment. Over the years, enough lead has been discovered in rodeo stomachs to suggest a new link in the food chain.

There were fishermen who came in every year with entries of frozen red snappers. And a clergyman in the tournament brought to the scale an amberjack that weighed ninety pounds. It was full of frozen blue runners—stuffed with frozen bait. In recent times, the tournament has acquired a Torrymeter, a machine that tests flesh to see if it has been frozen. "Electrodes pass current through a fish," Shipp explains. "If cells have been ruptured by freezing or deterioration, the current is stronger. A computer chip translates it to a number." The tournament has also introduced a polygraph. Competitors agree to its use when they buy their tickets. When the polygraph was first contemplated, a mailer was sent out asking if the competitors would approve. Eighty-five per cent said yes. In the first polygraph year, a winner failed the test miserably and was disqualified. He sued the Alabama Deep Sea Fishing Rodeo, but soon withdrew the suit. In the summary words of Bob Shipp, "He was a lyin' sumbitch and they got him."

As a Confederate cannon ends the tournament, spectators are ten deep straining to look into the fish bin. A woman leaning over a vermilion snapper is wearing a green bikini. Jingling in her navel on an extremely short gold chain is a green pendant scarab. She is not alone in her choice of wardrobe. All the way down the back wall of the bin are women leaning forward in bikinis, resting on the cinder block their soft-rayed pectoral fins. We have come here for purposes of comparative anatomy, and we're getting what we came for. I mean this as a compliment: these women are almost as good-looking as the fish. Before them on the ice are whitebone porgies, whitespotted soapfish, wahoos, black drums, gags, and snake eels. Striped burrfish. Gray triggerfish. Violet gobies. Rainbow runners. Bearded brotulas. Sailfish. Tarpon. Horse-eyed jacks. Literally, it's a ton of fish, and only a small fraction of all the competing fish not retained in the bin by the judges.

The rodeo has been criticized for killing so many fish, which is, among other reasons, why Willy is particularly welcome here. The aura of research tends to mute criticism. One of my sons-in-law is the skipper of a trawler in the Bering Sea. He fishes for cod, for Alaska walleye pollock. Both in metric tons and in numbers of fish, he will often catch in a single pass, in five minutes, the equivalent of all the fish caught in the Alabama Deep Sea Fishing Rodeo.

Willy is now lecturing the crowd on pelvic and pectoral fins. He is actually in the bin himself, standing, in his sandals, among the fish on the ice, because he knows that spectators will soon be taking the fish, and he is keeping an eye on specimens he has chosen for the lab. Pectoral fins, which spread to either side just below and behind the head, are for steering and braking, he says. The pelvic fins are anti-roll devices. Anti-roll devices on ships include stabilizers and flume tanks. Commercial fishing boats will extend their booms to both sides and lower into the water delta-shaped weights known as flopper-stoppers. Their flop-stopping ability may be considerable but cannot approach the efficacity of a pair of pelvic fins. Dorsal fins, in erection, supply some power and are helpful with anti-roll and steering, but more often they are social: they attract or repel other fish. The caudal fin—the tail fin—is for power. Just as a tall, forked tail is for high speed, a squared tail is for easy going, moseying near the bottom.

A boy about four feet tall wants to know if he is as long as a king snake eel. Willy measures him with an eel. He is not.

A man in camouflage pants and a sleeveless red T-shirt reaches into the fish bin and picks up specimens one by one. He opens the mouth of each fish, looks down into it, and asks Willy what it is. "Almaco jack," Willy says. "*Seriola riviolana*. Pretty unusual." This one? "Cubbyu. *Equetus umbrosus*." This one? "Tilefish. *Caulolatilus chrysops*. See how the teeth are angled backward? If the guy bites into food, it's not going to come out." In the mouth of the short-fin mako shark are two sets of teeth. "They are made to cut and then slice," Willy says. "Which is really cool." The sailfish, with that long hard bill, stuns prey by hitting it as if with a ball bat. Like swordfish and all other billfish, it does so with a whip of the head. "Blacktail moray," Willy says, moving on. "*Gymnothorax kolpos.* 'Gymno' means naked. It hasn't got any scales. You can look at it and right away make a lot of predictions based on its anatomy. That eel-like body can live in cracks and crevices. Those tubular nostrils allow him to sample water farther away than would otherwise be the case. There are no paired fins. They don't need anti-roll devices."

Back in the lab by six P.M., Willy works through the evening without dinner, putting off until midnight the cooking of fillets of dolphin and sailfish. In three days, he has collected fifty-two species and a hundred and fifteen specimens. Fifty of the smaller fish are on the table now. Where to start?

He picks up a five-inch tattler bass. It was caught on squid bait three hundred feet down. Coming up so fast caused its air bladder to move into its mouth like a cherry. "These are serranids," he says. "This family has interesting reproductive biology. Females reverse to males, and vice versa. In the spawning rush, one tattler will release an egg, another milt. Next time, each does the opposite. Sex reversal is not uncommon. Some fish are born alive, but not these."

He fillets a one-pound leopard toadfish. There's not a lot to cut. The toadfish is seventy-five-per-cent head. It looks like a boulder with a tail. Its flesh is pure white. "Which is what you would expect in a fish that does almost nothing but sit and wait for something to go by." It is doing less than that when it pursues an oyster. That bouldery head, with its small molarlike teeth, is a shell crusher. Willy removes the jaw muscles. They are the size and shape of two golf balls. "Are those the coolest jaw muscles you ever saw, or what?" he says. "But here's what's even more cool about this fish." He removes a diaphanous spheroid that looks very much like a calf testicle—a mountain oyster. It is the leopard toadfish's swim bladder, wrapped in a veneer of sonic muscle, which the toadfish vibrates to make sound. "Some fish produce sound for social communication," Willy says. "Some species make sounds with their fins, with their teeth, with their gill arches. This one does it with the swim bladder."

After three days and nights, Willy's body is hurting; his hands are puffy and sore. What drives him on is that everywhere he looks he sees another golden chance. He has worked in the Tana River, in Kenya; in the Brisbane River, in Australia; in the Comoro Islands, off East Africa; in the ponds of the Osage Catfisheries Company, in Osage Beach, Missouri, which are full of paddlefish, sturgeons, and gars. "It's an unparalleled opportunity," he says, once more sharpening his knife. "I couldn't collect like this anywhere in the world."

# FIFTEEN

# INSIDE THE HEAD

When Willy was preparing for his orals, in the Ph.D. program in zoology at Berkeley, he would read a paragraph, tie a fly, read a paragraph, tie a fly, and so on through the night. Reading, say, Don E. Rosen, Peter L. Forey, Brian G. Gardiner, and Colin Patterson's "Lungfishes, Tetrapods, Paleontology, and Plesiomorphy," he tied royal coachmen and humpies.

"Humpies?"

"All-purpose terrestrials. They look kind of like a beetle."

Willy's older fly rods—some of which he uses to this day—were made from fiberglass blanks he bought in Walnut Creek when he was at Berkeley. He fished Hat Creek, above Lassen. Close to the Oregon border, he caught rainbows and brook trout in the Marble Mountain Wilderness, where falling snow is not unknown in any month of the year. He fished at Bearmouth, in Montana, at the mouth of Bear Gulch. He took charter boats from Berkeley to the Farallon Islands. He still wears, at times, a Bearmouth logging cap with a mosquito fly hooked in its fabric, rusting. He tied it.

Willy joined a rod-building group and took a fly-fishing class in Berkeley, developing a tight loop on the basketball floor, early in the morning. He says he could not have afforded a graphite rod even if he made it himself. The blanks were too expensive. Besides, he had an unimpeachable reason to be loyal to glass. His first fly rod had been given to him when he was six years old by his father's close friend and colleague Arthur M. Howald, inventor of the fiberglass fishing rod.

On the Maumee River near Toledo, they had a small company called Glaskyd, which made very tough fiberglass in short lengths. During the Second World War, Howald had been technical director of the Plaskon Division of the Libbey-Owens-Ford glass company. Fishing up in Michigan in 1944, he broke the tip of his bamboo fly rod. What to do? Ohio and Michigan were not well supplied at that time with Gulf of Tonkin bamboo. He tried fashioning a new tip with glass fiber and Plaskon resin. When he saw that it worked well, he tried making a whole rod in the same manner. He sought the advice of Henry Shakespeare, who made fishing equipment in Kalamazoo, and by 1946 Howald had a patent and Shakespeare was manufacturing the Howald Glastik Wonderod, the first of the kind that sent bamboo off to the velvet closet.

Henry Shakespeare's grandfather William had been a First Sergeant in the Second Michigan Infantry who was given a battlefield promotion to Brigadier General—at the age of nineteen, in 1863—when he was severely wounded and was expected to die before sunset. The sun set without taking him with it. He survived to become a rich Michigan lawyer. Eventually, he was president of the Central Bank of William Shakespeare. His son William Jr. founded the tackle company Shakespeare, a hallowed name in American fishing. William Shakespeare Jr. invented and patented the level-winding reel, which distributes incoming line evenly across its width. Sensing gains in venture capital, the Central Bank of William Shakespeare helped to underwrite production.

Arthur Howald and his family lived in Perrysburg, Ohio, not far from the Bemises, whose panoramic lawn descended to the Maumee River. The lawn had been a fairway, a major component of a three-hole golf course, the harebrained idea of a developer.

When Willy was twelve years old, and thereabout, he would water the lawn for three hours, causing nightcrawlers to come out of it like spaghetti. He put them in his wormerie, which was in his mother's garden, and fished with them in the Maumee, catching carp, bullheads, channel catfish, bluegills, pumpkinseeds, and crappies. In order to watch them feed and swim, he kept some of these specimens in an elliptical, bowl-shaped cement pond. He raised tropical fish indoors. He caught perch in Lake Erie on minnows. On family trips with the Howalds—to Montana, Missouri, northern Michigan—he learned fly fishing. Arthur Howald, who also developed plastic-coated fly line, showed Willy and his family through the Shakespeare factory in South Carolina on one of the Bemises' annual road trips to Florida. From age six, Willy fished with his brother Bobby on the bridge between the islands Sanibel and Captiva, catching weakfish, catfish, mangrove snappers, and a variety of jacks. In their early teens, they learned snorkeling on Lower Matecumbe Key, across Florida Bay from the Everglades. Willy built collecting boxes, filled them up, and, in his words, "became committed to studying marine animals." He went home and presented this news to Sam McCoy, his biology teacher at Maumee Valley Country Day, whose surprise meter stayed on zero. Willy entered Cornell University, Class of 1976, thinking that he would specialize in marine invertebrates. That plan vanished when he took a course called "The Vertebrates," which introduced him to comparative anatomy. Spiralling upward through the textbooks of his field, this future professor did not take long to find an enduring hero in David Starr Jordan (1851–1931), fountainhead of American ichthyology, first president of Stanford University, and author of the ultimate academic lament: "Every time I learn a student's name I forget a fish."

And now in the new spring of a new migration, in the lab at the University of Massachusetts, Willy picks up a fresh, whole, undissected buck shad, and with knife in hand remarks, "There are very few things as informative as a cross-section of a fish." The knife goes straight through the shad from top to belly, about halfway between the mouth and the tail. If this makes you squeamish, think what you do to a cantaloupe. A second cut follows, an inch back, and he lays on the table a perfect slice of *Alosa sapidissima*, not unlike a salmon steak, with the difference that the two sides, as in nature, tumble home and join at the bottom, and surround an interior neatly and thoroughly packed in French-curve geometries of advanced design. Willy addresses fiber-optic lighting to the section of shad. The spinal cord makes a white dot above the vertebral column. The dorsal aorta is a small open circle just below the vertebra. Just below the dorsal aorta is the kidney, slung above the peritoneal membrane, and then come the large veins that drain forward through the body. Below it is the air bladder, flanked by chalk-white ellipses of milt. As in a swordfish steak, the muscle above is divided into quadrants by a vertical septum, from the top of the fish to the vertebral column, and by a horizontal septum, reaching out from the center to the two sides. Sets of intermuscular bones reach horizontally from the shad's upper ribs to the skin, left and right. Above them, the other two sets of intermuscular bones rise in a V from the vertebral column.

The sectioned shad brings to Willy's mind the event that engaged his interest in sturgeons. He was scarcely thirty, and new in Amherst. Boyd Kynard took him down to Holyoke, where short-nose sturgeons were spawning below the dam. With a seine, five were trapped, and one unfortunately died when the net got caught in its gill covers. It was a big animal, four feet long. Willy took it back to the lab, where he removed the head and then sawed it in two from the nose backward with a band saw. "I wanted to see how they project their mouths to suck up food from the bottom," he explains. "They have no teeth. They have a projecting, suction-cup mouth, like an open-ended sock. They winnow edible things from the gravel. They can stick their lips out maybe two inches. It's amazing. It's so cool."

For traction, Willy pulls on a new set of cotton gloves, and with fine scissors begins to cut the left side of another whole shad, this one a female. Being careful barely to penetrate the body wall, he cuts an elongate oval, three by seven inches. After snipping resistant tissue, he lifts it, exhibiting in an oval window the undisturbed interior of the fish—stomach, pyloric caecae, air sac, and so forth, all tightly packed against but in no way interfering with a bright, ripe sac of roe. The roe sac is two-thirds of this elliptical cameo. It extends through the body cavity almost from one end to the other. From shad I've caught, I have removed roe sacs that weighed a third as much as the rest of the body, or something near it—for example, a pound of roe in a four-and-a-half-pound shad. When Alexander Wilson named this fish *sapidissima* in 1811, he was referring almost certainly to the nutty-buttery succulence of the main muscle, but the roe is the tongue of the buffalo, the tip of the asparagus, the cheek of the halibut, the marrow of the osso bucco.

And we are not the only creatures who think so. One May evening, fishing in waders far out in the river, I reeled in a roe shad. A stringer was dangling from a D-ring on my vest—a long set of sliding brass meat hooks designed, like oversized safety pins, to go in past the gills, come out through the mouth, and fasten. I put the shad on the stringer. It was a noisy, awkward, not to say absurd arrangement, but the current was heavy and I was too lazy to wade ashore. I caught another roe shad and hung her on the keeper, too. Now I had nearly ten pounds of living shad swimming in place right next to me while I kept on casting. I quit before long, and dragged the fish to the riverbank. As I routinely do, I hit them with a priest before opening them up. My priest is a Louisville Slugger fourteen inches long, a miniature baseball bat made by the Hil-

lerich & Bradsby company and player-personalized "Alosa sapidissima." Priests of various weights and configurations are sold in
sport shops that cater to meat fishermen. Sam Flick, a teacher of
fly casting and a sales representative in the headquarters store at
L. L. Bean, told me several years ago that he was one of a small
minority in the fishing department who thought that Bean's should
sell priests. Considering what else they sell, why not? On more recent visits I have noticed on the walls an arsenal of crankbaits,
each with two treble hooks, and among them a container for
worms.

I took a roe shad off the stringer, turned it onto its back, and
opened its cavity with the German scissors. Nothing was inside.
The fish had no intestines, no roe sacs. The inside of the cavity was
completely empty, the walls without blemish. For some moments I
thought I was dreaming. There were no ruptures of any kind in the
scales and sides. What had happened? I looked into the mouth.
The back of the throat was much torn up. Suddenly, a picture
formed, and as it did I think I might have cried out—a picture of
an eel going into the shad on the stringer. Had I looked down
while fishing, I would have seen at least two feet of the eel protruding from the mouth of the live fish while the eel's head was inside the cavity eating the roe and intestines and licking the plate
clean. I didn't see that happen. I probably would have slipped a
disk if I had. The roe in the other fish was o.k. I ate it under bacon
for dinner.

Two weeks later at five in the morning I was fishing from my
canoe in an enveloping mist. The stringer was over the side. I was
catching bucks and roes. Seven feet of water was below the hull.
Again, an eel went in through the mouth of a roe shad on the
keeper and ate her insides clean. Never again. I made two phone
calls. In Cabela's catalogue I found a wire basket that hangs in the
water like a birdcage, and I called 1-800. I also called the shad biologist Richard St. Pierre, of the U.S. Fish and Wildlife Service,

who told me that I was reporting something he had neither seen nor heard of. A few years later, when I asked Boyd Kynard about shads' interactions with other species in the rivers, he said, "The only relationship I've seen is when shad die eels are right in the body cavity. They feed on the carcasses a lot. We pull up gill nets and a dead shad is there, and—it's awesome—an eel is in the shad and comes crawling out."

Eels being catadromous, and shad anadromous, they share rivers, and both are exceptional very-long-distance swimmers. Willy reminds me that the shad's loose scales allow it to swim more like an eel than most other fish: "Shad scales are thin and deciduous because of the amount of lateral undulation. Shad have such a flexible body it needs a scale that will move with it, not armor plate. Eels and other eel-like fishes have independently lost their scales, or have reduced their scales a lot. In other words, eels have no scales and are correspondingly flexible." Willy thinks the deciduous scale has an evolutionary future about as promising as a saber tooth. "Deciduous scales—they're sort of on the way out."

An ocean sunfish has fifteen vertebrae and is stiffer than a clipboard. An eel has roughly a hundred and twenty vertebrae. "One way to get an idea about the body flexibility of a fish is to count the vertebrae," Willy continues. "A brook trout has about forty." Exposing the vertebrae of a shad in the lab, he counts fifty-five. "These are fish that have a lot of mobility, and when you catch one they don't just pull steadily. You feel 'em swimming."

I ask Willy, "How do you skin an eel?"

From a back room, Willy's colleague Al Richmond, a herpetologist, calls out, "Same way you skin a snake."

Willy goes on with his dissecting, adding nothing to Richmond's instructions, obviously considering them complete.

The adult eel has among its predators snapping turtles, otters, minks, and me. Actually, you don't have to know how to skin a snake if you want to eat an eel. You can cut it into three-inch seg-

ments and sauté them in butter. I baited a shad dart with a shad's
stomach one evening when some eels were hanging around while I
was processing fish. As I dangled the stomach in the shallow water,
an eel grabbed it, pulled it under a rock, and chewed through the
line. Next time, I used a wire leader and a plain hook. Eel is *sapidissima*—a firm, most savory fish. When the segments are sizzling in the hot butter, the skin turns blue.

A mature, green shad—a hard, female shad whose full sacs
have not yet ripened into spawning—may be carrying as many as
six hundred thousand eggs, but this would not impress an ocean
sunfish (*Mola mola*), whose sacs contain three hundred million
eggs. An Atlantic salmon might look twice. A hen salmon carries
about eight hundred eggs per pound of body weight. A roe shad,
per pound of body weight, is carrying at least sixty thousand. A
twelve-pound shad commercially caught in the Hudson River
some years ago had four and a half pounds of roe inside her. That
would approximate a million eggs.

Roe sacs are variegated—yellow, orange, speckled white-and-
red. Most are rich burgundy. Some commercial shad fishers cut
across the gill isthmus and bleed their fish, believing that this
might "improve" the roe sacs, toning them up from red toward a
more negotiable orange. If it comes out orange, though, it was
orange in the first place. The colors derive from the content of the
zooplankton the shad were eating in the ocean. Various carotenoids
produce the reds and the yellows.

Before shad roe achieved its belated status as a delicacy of the
table, it was used for little more than fish bait, a fact that raises an
obvious question: How could those myriad eggs cohere on a fishhook? "Frank Forester's Fish and Fishing of the United States
and British Provinces of North America" (1849) provides an answer in a discussion of "roe-bait for bass." You prepare it in the
same way that you would prepare salmon roe. "Paste composed of
roe . . . taken out when freshly killed, washed carefully, and

cleansed of all the impurities, the blood and filamentous matter, thoroughly dried in the air, salted with two ounces of rock-salt, and a quarter of an ounce of saltpetre to a pound of spawn, dried gently before a slow fire, or in an oven at a low heat, and then potted down and covered with melted lard or suet in earthen pots, is a most murderous bait . . . Within a few weeks old, it will cut out of the pots like stiff cheese, and will adhere readily to the hook." In "The American Angler's Book" (1864), Uncle Thad Norris describes what happens when "the Shad-roe Fisherman" baits a hook with shad roe and lowers it into a river. "Each ova as it is washed from the baited hook and floats off down the tide, is greedily swallowed by any fish . . . and he is toled along until he finds the 'placer,' when the 'nugget' is swallowed at a gulph." Among the numerous guesses in response to the mystery of why shad strike at anything, one involving roe was presented not long ago in *Fly Fishing Quarterly* by Robert Elman, who said that shad "will attack a fly—perhaps prompted by predatory instinct, but more likely in aggression toward any small fish or other creature that might be an egg-eater."

Under a microscope in the lab in Amherst, Willy looks at a roe sac, addresses it with running commentary, and steps aside once in a while so I can peer at what he is talking about. "Look at that amazing vasculature—a superb dendritic system, all those tributaries and rivers getting maximal blood to the eggs so they can develop. They're quite pretty as well. They come down from the dorsal aorta and through the mesenteries into the roe sac. The eggs have to contain everything that the creature is going to be, so they are accumulating proteins, they're accumulating nucleic acids—RNA transcripts of the DNA, so that when the embryo starts to develop it will be ready to start making new proteins for itself. They also accumulate fats, which are a good storage form of energy, and are one of the reasons they're such a rich and delicious food. As well, these egg cells are packed with the organelles—the individual structural components of the cell—which allow rapid cell division to occur, once the egg is fertilized. Each one of these cells has millions upon millions of components packaged together in a very highly structured way. One of the many functions of the liver—which is often referred to as a master organ, in terms of its ability to do all kinds of different functions—is to produce the yolk proteins that are going to wind up in the egg cells. They're synthesizing that material in the liver, and then it's being circulated by the circulatory system to the ovary, where it is released by the circulatory system and incorporated inside the egg cells. That process—putting yolk inside the individual egg cells—is called vitellogenesis. A tremendous amount of energy is involved."

Willy is married to Betty McGuire, who teaches introductory biology, human biology, and animal behavior eight miles away at Smith College. She wrote her doctoral dissertation on voles, and is an authority on their behavioral ecology. She has cross-fostered voles, causing one species to rear the pups of another species, later studying the manner in which the cross-fostered pups rear their own litters. Her insights have not been irrelevant to the rearing of human children, including Kate and Owen—her own and Willy's. Came a recent spring when Betty saved a rat from certain death in Northampton. It was a grade-school, schoolroom rat, and its summer vacation was about to be spent in a dumpster. Betty took the rat home to Kate, Owen, and Willy. After it had lived with them awhile, it developed an illness. She took the rat to a vet. The bill was seventy dollars. The rat had to return for a checkup. The family has five cats. The cats have had dental work. The cats have had tartar removed from their teeth. The cats have had teeth pulled. The cost of all this thins Willy.

Owen, Kate, Betty, and Willy have a twenty-foot forty-horse Godfrey Marine Sweetwater—a living room on pontoons—in which they cruise the Holyoke Pool. Now and again, Willy and I have used it as a fly-fishing platform, casting for bass and fallfish, he with his historic glass rod. Sometimes, he has a pole seine aboard, and a top-of-the-line Bausch & Lomb microscope, which he will use not only to examine small components of aquatic life but also to assist him in tying flies to his tippets, in the way that fishermen less richly equipped use magnifying lenses cantilevered from their hats. Fallfish rise in the evening and sip at the surface like trout. You follow the breaking circles, the successive rings of the rises, and try to lay your fly on the next one as it appears. Willy lands on the next one with a No. 14 Cahill. A fallfish is a minnow, not the sort of thing that galvanizes Trout Unlimited. Some minnows are larger than others, however. There are minnows four feet long. They live in Colorado, among other places, and are known as squawfish, but the American Fisheries Society calls them pikeminnows. They eat other fish and have teeth in their throats. The largest minnow Willy has ever seen is the fallfish—swirl, pow!—that hits his floating Cahill. He measures it in inches—11.5. *Semotilus corporalis*, it too is piscivorous. "There aren't too many minnows that specialize in eating other fish," he says. "Look at that terminal mouth, the long gape. It's a mouth set up for eating fish."

One morning, Willy skippered the pontoon boat into the Northampton oxbow, got out in shallow water, and opened the pole seine. It was something like a badminton net, a pole at each end. I moved one, he the other. Grad students in his field keep pole seines in or on their cars, and pull off the road wherever they see water. The Northampton oxbow is a cutoff meander in the Connecticut River that has been further occluded by Interstate 91, like a bar sinister traversing the letter C. The resulting lagoon is, in Willy's words, "a tremendous nursery ground for fish." Starting waist-deep, we hauled ashore twenty-five feet of net. It contained banded killifish, yellow perch, pumpkinseeds, bluegills, a two-ounce five-inch largemouth bass, an eleven-inch northern pike, and a gizzard shad that weighed two and a half pounds. "In order to study fish you have to have them right in front of you," Willy said. "It's not like watching birds in a tree."

Off New Island, in the main river, under the rising bulk of Mount Holyoke, we swept the seine through a stand of river-weed—"another real nursery area." The water was just deep enough to soak the big bass on Willy's T-shirt. In one haul, we brought in two hundred fish: tesselated darters, banded killifish, bluegills, pumpkinseeds, fallfish, yellow perch, rock bass, small-mouths. We picked up six brand-new golf balls. Onto the stage of the microscope Willy slid a banded killifish, less than two inches long. "*Fundulus diaphanus*," he said, "a topwater fish with a wide flat head like a pike. It's sometimes called a tooth carp. With those fins at the posterior of a long body, it can accelerate quickly, like a pickerel."

I remembered Willy picking up a shad, in the same boat in another season, and holding it level, as if it were swimming through the air. He spread a fin, exhibiting its fingerlike rays. "These fin rays are the basis of support for the fin web," he said. "The fin rays themselves are pretty cool. They are made of segments about half a millimetre long. The segments are known as lepidotrichia, and they surround a straight bundle. It's exactly analogous to a fishing rod. You've got a bundle of fibers that form the length of the thing, and then you wrap it—helically wrap it, whether you're building it out of carbon fiber or fiberglass. These little wrappings go around the length of the fin ray and give it great strength and flexibility. It's tapered like a fishing rod. It's exactly analogous to a pole. As you swish that thing through the water, you're getting a lot of stiffness at the base and a lot of flexibility at the tip. This fin is thus an extremely efficient structure in the water column. It's self-adjusting."

As one would expect in a world-class anatomist, Willy's tactile talents—his preparation of articulated skeletons, his tracings of nerves—appear to be exceptional. But they stop short of an ability to bone a shad. He once presented me with a whole adult-shad skeleton—easier to produce than a boned fillet. He gave me a block of acrylic containing the complete skeleton of a three-inch shadling. Like me, though, he lacks the dexterity of the fish-market boners of shad. These people, at one time or another, have all been chief residents in neurosurgery either at the University of Pittsburgh or the Mayo Clinic. Or so it seems. So wondrous is their skill, they have been covered in-depth in the *New York Times Magazine*. A shad-boning wizard in southern Connecticut gave up shad boning in order to teach foil fencing. I have stood for many hours beside such people—mainly at Jack Morrison's Nassau Street Seafood Company, in Princeton, New Jersey—intent on every move, only to be shown, again and again, that you don't learn magic by watching a magician. When you take a fillet off a shad, you are freeing it from the backbone. That far, I can go. The rib cage adheres to the fillet. You slice it away. I can do that, too. Now you have two series of fine, sharp, intermuscular bones to get rid of, some shaped like suture needles and others like wishbones. You can feel their severed tips with your fingers. From here on, you need to understand Braille. This is the point at which my dexterity founders. I will not even attempt to grade Willy's. Invisibly, the intermusculars curve away from those severed tips and toward the fish's skin. With a long and very sharp narrow-bladed flexible knife, the professional makes two curving cuts, parallel along the margins of one series of bones, and pulls them free in a strip of flesh. If you think that sounds easy, try it. Repeat with the second series—always taking care to cut to, but not through, the skin. You now have a boneless fillet that has four deep longitudinal slits, and has lost a fair amount of its original content of muscle. The percentage gone is the measure of the skill of the cutter. If more than fifty per cent of the original flesh remains, the cutter is above average. Boned shad fillets are tidied into resemblance of uncut flesh, and wrapped and sold in paper that holds them together.

The segments into which the muscles of fish are divided—the units that slide away from one another when you disturb them with a fork—are known as myomeres. In some fish, bones develop in the tissue that connects myomeres, "probably to allow a fish to focus where muscular attention is going to be applied," Willy says. "There are lots of different theories about why these bones form. Most of them have to do with locomotion. The idea is that they provide additional strength. When the muscles contract, they'll be able to apply their force to the vertebral column."

Which helps explain why a shad has so much more power than a rainbow.

In 1996, Sony Pictures Classics released a Robert M. Young film called "Caught," in which American shad are, to understate it, megametaphorical. Listed as "Consultant" in the rolling credits is Tony Olivera, a master shad boner at a Manhattan fish market. Under the title is an underwater shot of shad swimming near a commercial net among blue shafts of light. As the action begins, a fugitive drifter (Arie Verveen), running from police, takes cover in a small fish store owned by Joe (Edward James Olmos) and his wife, Betty (Maria Conchita Alonso). They protect him, take him home and feed him, give him a room to stay in and a job in the store. Joe, evidently a master pedagogue, teaches him how to bone shad. "There's no fish like it," Joe says. "A thousand bones like tiny needles . . . Any customer finds a bone, I give him his money back plus a quarter." In time, Betty and the young drifter are lovers, Joe asleep in the next room. They spawn in the kitchen. They spawn in a shower stall. They spawn in a closet, standing up like Warren Harding. She keeps opening and closing her mouth, like a fish. She closes it on various parts of him—his chin, for example. Mostly the symbolism—from teaser to credits—has to do with shad. After the closet scene comes a scene with the two men as boners. It is noted that Joe bones a shad in four minutes and fifteen seconds (two minutes faster than the best boner I have watched in real life).

Betty and Joe's son, Danny, moves back East from California, discovers his mother flagrante with fugitive. In visits that follow, Danny grows ever more hostile and crafty. After the drifter delivers fish to Danny's apartment and Danny, arriving, comes upon him there, Danny suspects him of boffing his wife, Amy, as well as his mother. The parameters are now set for a family picnic featuring freshly boned grilled shad. In a park, under tall trees, Danny sets up a shad-boning race between his father and the drifter. Danny by profession is a stand-up comedian, and he easily slips into the role of sportscaster doing the play-by-play while his father and his mother's lover bone two fillets of shad: "O.k., sports fans, our contestants are neck and neck and they're in the home stretch. We've got Shadrach and Meshad Abednago, the world's leading boners, in a shad fight to the death. Does the old guy still have it? Or the kid from nowhere, the young buck, our lucky leprechaun— will he take the day?"

Meshad Abednago is the cuckold. He is the first finished. But wait a moment, Danny says, "Which shad's got no bones left?"

Meshad Abednago: "You find a bone in that I'll give you a quarter."

The film has come to seem anchored in the thought that half the people in the human race, somewhere in their anatomy, have an expertly boned fillet of shad. Danny inspects his father's fillet for bones—gently, slowly running his third finger within a slit in the fillet. He says, "Clean as a whistle." Turning to the drifter, Danny says: "In this corner, the world champ's challenger . . ." and he inserts his third finger into a slit in the other fillet, moving it slowly along. He finds a bone in the younger man's shad, and waves the bone in his face. He takes hold of his father's arm, lifts it, and proclaims, "The winner and still champion! The fastest boner in the East!"

Danny tells his father, "It's not just fish he's been delivering, Dad. It's not just shad that he's been boning." Dad dies of heart attack in the raucousness of a confession scene with his wife and her lover. "Like shad, some of us get caught, some get away," Danny says, as he prepares to murder the drifter by slitting his throat with a boning knife. Under the closing credits, shad swim into a gill net.

Now alone by the Delaware in falling light, having removed the fillets from a roe shad and trimmed off the rib cage, I pick up the detached head, and turn it in my hand. I'm contemplating the complexities of it, and remembering what Willy said while he held an essentially identical shad's head in his hand in his lab. I look past the nostrils and the hard tongue far back through the wide mouth, where the several rows of very long gill rakers project like lashes from eyelids. Willy removed the gill arches, eight in all, and set them—with their long sweeping rakers, their harplike architecture—on a table. The gills, he reminded me, trap phytoplankton and simultaneously extract oxygen from water. Through the ventral aorta and branchial arteries the heart pumps blood forward into the gills. "In terms of an exchange surface," Willy said, "it's hard to imagine anything more wonderful than the gills of a fish."

Willy flipped out an eyeball and the lens stood alone on the table—spherical, a pure crystal pea. He remarked that a human lens is elliptical because of a change in refractive index between air and the watery cornea. Achieving focus, both the cornea and the lens bend incoming light. The fish lens must be spherical because there is no change in refractive index between water and cornea. The lens has to bend the incoming light by itself. The shad's retina has twin cones—an unusual type of visual cell found only in certain teleost fishes. Cones are associated with high visual acuity and color vision, and the exclusive presence of cone cells in the retinas of shad is additional evidence, Willy said, that shad are very visual animals. "The huge optic tectum, the big optic lobes, the big cerebellum, tell you that this fish uses vision and hearing and lateral-line sense as the primary sensory modalities. Olfaction is not its primary sensory modality. The brain is relatively large for a teleost fish. This fish takes in a lot of sensory information."

He exposed the brain, removed it, and addressed it with the nosepiece of a microscope. It was like white marble with narrow red streaks. He pointed out and described the "two fine, fine projections—maybe half a millimetre in diameter—that go from the air sac forward into the back of the skull through openings called foramina." There, in the head, is a wide space called the bulla, where a bit of air sac also expands. Anything that vibrates the main stretch of air sac in the body cavity causes vibration in the bulla as well—not only a passing train or a rock thrown into the water but also something as subtle as the pressure from a fish nearby. "This is the exquisitely sensitive hearing system that clupeids have," Willy said. "Clupeids can hear high-frequency sounds, and sounds at greater distances. They are particularly aurally sensitive."

I asked him to review the biological physics of a train going past a school of shad, an event that causes them to turn into seismometers, register 8.8 on the Richter scale, and ignore the presence of shad darts.

"The fish is detecting the train in three different ways," he said. "The pressure wave that comes through the water is sufficient to move the body of the fish relative to its otoliths, the stony structures that lie inside the vestibular system in the ear. Those things are denser than the body of the fish, they have more inertia than the fish, and they're just sitting there balanced on some little specialized hair cells—up on the tips of those hair cells. The body of the fish is hit by a pressure wave that moves the body of the fish, physically, while the otoliths stay in the same place, more or less. That's detected through the hair cells. The brain can process that information as an impinging pressure wave. There are two other methods. The pressure wave hits the side of the fish and presses water into the lateral-line canals differentially on one side versus the other. Water flowing into a canal passes hair cells that lie in the neuromast organs in the canal, and the brain can interpret that as a pressure wave on the fish. The third way is through the air sac. Whenever you have a pressure wave passing through water, it will pass through the body of the fish, and the air sac will decrease in volume. As the wave passes, the air sac will increase in volume. It will increase and decrease in volume at the frequency of the sound. If it's a thousand-hertz sound, the fish's swim bladder is going to vibrate at a thousand cycles per second. The pressure wave from the train has been transferred to the water from the ground. If you bang on the side of a sink, you can generate a pressure wave. You haven't touched the water. That's what the train is doing. It's banging on the side of the river."

The English anatomist Peter Forey, who works on fishes in the Department of Paleontology at the Museum of Natural History, in London, happened to be in the lab and watching while Willy dissected the head, and heard Willy remark that a shad's lateral-line system is not under the skin of the body but entirely in the head, a characteristic of herrings that is most unusual among fishes. Peter Forey asked if he could borrow the head for a bit. Willy handed it over. Peter injected the bright-silver cheek with black ink. It filled the canals that comprise the lateral line—the supraorbital canal, the infraorbital canal, the preopercular canal, the mandibular canal, the otic canal. Now sketched in the bright-silver face was a black dendritic pattern—intricate, feathery, like a very good drawing of nerves. "These are the canals that respond to pressure waves," Peter said. "The neuromasts in the canals are like the cells in our inner ear. They respond to sound and the vibration of other fishes. They are particularly important to schooling fishes, which have to keep contact with one another."

Finally, by the Delaware River, my fish "clean," I hold up the head, and turn it once more in my hand. I give it the long Yorick, then throw it far into fast water.

# SIXTEEN

# CATCH-AND-RELEASE

One hour without shad. Two hours. Fishing on the river, almost always alone, you have no difficulty finding enough time to talk to yourself. You cast, you think ahead, you cast, you remember, you cast, you argue. Under the metronomic motions, you argue with yourself, and with others, in dialogue that rises through the mind on contradictory vectors. You remember things you have read. You will look them up later.

On the Pennsylvania side, May 23rd, I bring in a fish—the largest so far this year. The big roe shad shines up my day, if not her own. Three hundred thousand eggs are out of the river. She has lived five years and was meant to end up spawning some reasonable percentage of three hundred thousand offspring; instead, she is on her way to a plastic bag, her eggs to a plastic tub.

> The roe that may go to the tickling of a single palate for one meal would be capable of development into thousands of lusty fishes that, even without a miracle, might feed the multitude.
>
> —DR. J. ERNEST SCOTT, *Bucks County Historical Society, 1908*

Has it ever occurred to you, sir, when you eat one of a pair of fried shad-roes for breakfast, how many shad you consume in embryo? If the roe is from a good-sized fish, cer-

tainly not less than twenty-five thousand. O thou piscivorous Leviathan! thou has devoured in germ, at a single
meal, and merely as a relish to thy coffee, a hundred thousand pounds of fish . . . But quiet thy conscience, gentle
monster, for with all the chances of hatching, and the dan-
gers to which the shadlings are exposed, it is doubtful if
the eggs thou hast swallowed would have produced more
than two or three four-pound shad at the end of three
years.

—THADDEUS NORRIS, *Lippincott's Magazine, 1869*

Keeping a single female may mean reducing the spawn by
a half-million eggs! Fried shad roe is delicious, but nothing tastes *that* good.

—ROBERT ELMAN, *Fly Fishing Quarterly, 1992*

I have a suggestion for Dr. Scott, Mr. Elman, and Uncle Thad.
Don't fry it. Place it on a bed of bacon in a cast-iron skillet. Cover.
Cook very low and very slow.

Cast. Remember. Cast. React. Why am I standing here doing
this? Robert Hughes has reminded us that fishing is a jerk on one
end of a line waiting for a jerk on the other. Thomas McGuane has
called it "an act of racial memory," evoking the atavistic mission of
the hunter-gatherer. Howell Raines has written that the ethos of
the hunter-gatherer does not always travel well, especially if it is
flying to Jackson Hole with a three-hundred-dollar rod. "In my
view, the people who fish do so because it seems like magic to
them," Raines says—magical enough to have inspired him to call
his book "Fly Fishing Through the Mid-Life Crisis." It is like
"pulling a rabbit out of a hat . . . Fish in the water represent pure
potential . . . To get them to bite something connected to a line
and pull them into our world is managing a birth that brings these
creatures from the realm of mystery into the world of reality. It's a

kind of creation." One might prefer the hunter-gatherer. In any case, Raines is crafting rationale, a challenging assignment for a catch-and-release fisherman. If you like to eat fresh fish, you might like to catch them yourself. That and the fact that fishing has the driving force of a treasure hunt is enough to put you in the stream. You don't need patience—the trait with which anglers are said to be most endowed. When I go fishing, I don't take patience with me, having none to take. My daughter Martha is without patience, too, yet she can write novels because her desire to complete the composition overrides her impatience. I can stand in the river three hours catching nothing. Anticipation keeps me there, never patience—anticipation, and the beauty of the scene. Raines ventures also into fishing as religion, the fish as the symbol of Christ, and he says, "I begin to wonder if having fish shapes around me is a way to stay in touch with the ideas of Jesus without having to go near the people who do business in his name."

Mainly, people seem to fish for the fight—shad fishermen manifestly included. In videos and in print, they mention primarily "the fighting ability of the American shad," carried out in "drag-defying escape attempts highlighted by aerial displays." Releasing a videoed shad, a fisherman says, "Go back and fight another day," and refers to it fondly as "the fightingest fish on the East Coast." From the *New York Times* to *New Jersey Outdoors*, shad writers across the seasons, in myriad publications, pile up the fight montage:

"Shad have seemingly limitless energy. They make screeching runs and spectacular jumps and dogged, throbbing dives into the depths of the river."

". . . a hard-fighting species available to all who can afford a freshwater fishing license."

"Hard-fighting game fish."

". . . when fighting a shad . . ."

"They make hard drag-sizzling runs, and perform aerial acrobatics similar to the prestigious salmon."

"The shad is a great rod-and-reel fish, a really strong fighter."

"Shad are hard and determined fighters that do not come easily to net."

"The sea-run spawner's fight was sparked with all the desperate, procreative amperage of springtime."

"She had put up a typically beautiful fight."

"They battle valiantly."

So far so true, if not correct. A shad, right enough, is a five-pound tarpon.

What all those writers were aiming to say has been put this way by Thomas McGuane: "The fish burned off fifty or sixty yards, sulked, let me get half of it back, then began to run again, not fast or hysterical, but with the solid, irresistible motion of a Euclid bulldozer easing itself into a phosphate mine." When McGuane, in "The Longest Silence," says of sea trout that "they bring an oceanic rapacity to the smaller world of the river," he could as well be describing shad.

"Fighting: This is the fun part," writes Peter Kaminsky in "Fishing for Dummies." "Having a fish on is the fun part of fishing. That tug. That pushing and head-shaking and throbbing. These are the prime thrills of fishing. It's you against the fish, and the fish is in his element . . . Win or lose, the fight is always a thrill. Learn to savor it."

In the Toronto *Daily Star*, on June 10, 1922, there was this from Ernest Hemingway: "If you are lucky, sooner or later there will be a swirl or a double swirl where the trout strikes and misses and strikes again, and then the old, deathless thrill of the plunge of the rod and the irregular plunging, circling, cutting up stream and shooting into the air fight the big trout puts up, no matter what country he may be in." In "Islands in the Stream" (1970), Hemingway described a hooked dolphin: "He saw it first when it jumped in the air, true gold in the last of the sun and bending and flapping wildly in the air. It jumped again and again in the acrobatics of its fear . . ."

The acrobatics of its fear.

Enter the People for the Ethical Treatment of Animals—the campaigners, protesters, and writers of Internet pages that say, among other things, "Scientific reports from around the world substantiate the fact that fish feel pain."

> Although they may not be able to scream out in pain, fish have the same capacity for suffering and the same right to our compassion as do dogs, cats, and other human beings.

> The poet Byron said it best: "[T]he art of angling [is] the cruelest, the coldest, and the stupidest of pretended sports."

Driving toward a river, you might pass a large billboard featuring a dog with a fishhook in its lip, and the message:

> IF YOU WOULDN'T DO THIS TO A DOG, WHY DO IT TO A FISH?
> FishingHurts.com

FishingHurts.com is a production of PETA.

Driving toward another river, you pass the six-foot block letters of another PETA billboard:

FISHING: THE CRUELEST FORM OF HUNTING

It has been asserted that PETA has been behind scuba-diving saboteurs who drive fish away from fishing tournaments, behind vigilantes who flail river pools with lengths of bamboo, behind strongarms who heave rocks to delete an angler's presentation. Bill

Hilts has written in *New York Sportsman*, "PETA has alleged ties with the Animal Liberation Front, a group that's being investigated."

PETA has campaigned against "the hidden cruelty behind Britain's traditional Fish and Chips."

Watching television news, I saw a PETA representative tell an interviewer that Fishkill, New York, 12524, should be required to change its name. There were scenes of central Fishkill. Incredulous barbers. But in every sense the campaign was deadly serious. The PETA person was young. She was slender to the point of endangerment. She had a firmly downturned mouth that may never have smiled. The interviewer said earnestly that Fishkill, on the Hudson, was a seventeenth-century Dutch settlement; in Dutch, the word "kill" means "channel," "creek," or "stream." On the young woman's face, there was no change of expression. Kill meant kill at PETA.

It could be said that the People for the Ethical Treatment of Animals are in flat-out disagreement with God, for did God not say "Be fruitful, and multiply, and replenish the earth, and subdue it: and have dominion over the fish of the sea"? That is what translators said, says PETA. When translators chose "dominion," the word they were seeking was "stewardship." PETA's home page includes the link Jesusveg.com and the headline JESUS WAS A VEGETARIAN. While PETA claims that "there is strong evidence suggesting that Jesus was a vegetarian," the loaves and fishes story might suggest otherwise. Before this thought can cross your mind, PETA moves in to say, "There is strong evidence that this story did not originally include fish." In Matthew 16:9–10, Mark 8:19–20, and John 6:26, Jesus refers only to bread. Jesus spoke in Aramaic. The Gospels were written generations later. The oldest that have come down to us are fourth-century versions in Greek, and the Greeks added the fish. Saith PETA.

"Get hooked on compassion" is PETA's advice. "Never buy or

eat fish, and, instead of fishing, try hiking, canoeing, or bird watching." A fish in your diet is about as good for you as a bull's pancreas. "Fish flesh contains excessive amounts of protein, fat, and cholesterol." A PETA release in the spring of 2001 was headlined PETA ASKS WARDEN TO MAKE MCVEIGH'S LAST MEAL MEATLESS. "Timothy McVeigh should not be allowed to take even one more life." PETA goes to battle in what appears to be a thousand-front war. It is undaunted by the odds. It has two hundred and fifty thousand members. Sixty million Americans go fishing with rod and reel.

> PETA opposes fishing because fish have neurochemical systems like humans, the brain capacity to experience fear and pain, and sensitive nerve endings in their lips and mouths. Fish begin to die slowly of suffocation the moment they are pulled out of the water.

PETA has a point.

When I asked Willy Bemis to describe the difference between fish and mammals with regard to pain, he said there was essentially no difference to describe—"vertebrate nervous systems are pretty similar."

And Boyd Kynard: "Their nervous system is like ours in its basic fundamentals. And they have the same stress hormones that we have."

"So when fish get a hook in the mouth, they feel it?"

"Oh, yes. There's no question that they feel it, and it's probably painful. It's probably not the same kind of pain that we feel, though. It's a really difficult area that people continue to debate. Because you can re-catch fish, I'm not sure how much they learn from that pain. Maybe not as much as we would learn."

"Learning is one thing, feeling is another."

"Whether there's any emotional feel—the way we attach emotion to pain—is very debatable."

"That has to do with conditioned response. What do they feel while it's going on—fish with hooks in their mouths?"

"There's no question they feel it. It's probably some pain. I'm not sure it's perfectly analogous for us to think about it, because our mouths are so sensitive and rich in nerves."

PETA:

Hooked fish struggle out of fear and physical pain.

PETA has larger concerns than the neurology of fish. In "Ethics in Action," the philosopher Peter Singer quotes an Associated Press story about an undercover PETA investigator who made a videotape "that showed technicians cutting monkeys while they were still alive, slamming them into cages and suspending them in air while pumping fluids through their noses." Stack that against a buck shad three feet off a river in leaping oscillation on a hook. Still, PETA has a point. As you stand alone in the river, such thoughts inevitably put a kind of wind knot in your cast. On the long spectrum between a mosquito and a fetus, where is a fish? When you read in *Sports Afield* that a shad is a "beefy silver fish, fresh from the sea, full of muscle, spirit, and flash," the spirit is a desire to remain alive. So why not let it remain alive? Release it. Catch it and release it.

PETA:

Fish who are released can suffer such severe stress from being "played" that they may die even though they manage to swim away.

PETA has a point. Anglers who release fish are not releasing the same fish they hooked. "Prolonged playing of fish, particularly when they are returned to the water subsequently, is to be deprecated," Gathorne Medway wrote in 1997, reporting to the Royal Society for the Prevention of Cruelty to Animals on the findings of a Panel of Enquiry into Shooting and Angling. "When teleost fish are severely stressed and exercised to exhaustion, they make extensive use of their 'white' muscle system," he said. "This differs from the red skeletal muscle of higher vertebrates, in that it is anaerobic and, although very efficient in the short term, when exhausted contains a great accumulation of lactic acid during the elimination of which the muscle system remains in prolonged fatigue. A completely exhausted fish will thus be almost unable to move for several hours after capture. During this time it will be at risk to attack by predators or injury from its inanimate environment." Gathorne Medway, Fifth Earl of Cranbrook, holds a doctorate in zoology.

So there is no free pass from PETA. The points it makes are at least as applicable to catch-and-release anglers as they are to fishermen who fill up their ice chests with meat. The philosophy of catch-and-release is variously expressed, each exposition differing somewhat from the one in the next pool; and while you lay out that long drapefold cast or spin a dart high across the river, they tend to echo through the mind—some with dissonance, some a little hollow, in the reach for rationale.

> Catch-and-release fishing is the most certain method yet conceived for ensuring that the same quality fish we catch today will be available tomorrow. It's also a wonderfully satisfying thing to do.
>
> —GEORGE REIGER, *Field & Stream*

> Game fish are too valuable to be caught only once.
>
> —LEE WULFF

> I think our own catch-and-release thing is a wonderful thing philosophically, because I think we put the emphasis on the experience, not the reward.
>
> —MEL KRIEGER, *in a video produced by Stephen Rider Haggard*

There is strong circumstantial evidence that "pain" in fishes is not comparable to that of higher vertebrates, nor is catching a fish a very traumatic experience for the fish (otherwise catch-and-release regulations wouldn't work).

—ROBERT BEHNKE,
*Professor of Fisheries Biology, Colorado State University*

The producers would like to point out that, although the Macleans kept their catch as was common earlier in this century, enlightened fishermen today endorse a "catch-and-release" policy to assure that this priceless resource swims free to fight another day.

—*Written message at the end of the film version of Norman Maclean's*
*"A River Runs Through It"*

Maybe catching them, even only hooking them, allows the angler to enter their pure state of being for a moment, the nonreflective alpha and omega of existence. It is what well-practiced hunting and fishing is all about—focusing one's attention until the awareness of intention disappears.

—TED KERASOTE, *in* Orion, *with head in stars*

Kerasote writes of "the beauty of catch-and-release fishing in an age that has grown dubious about causing harm to other life forms," and asserts in amplification: "When we consider that we're products of a century that has spawned many legal manifestations of justice to the unempowered—woman's suffrage, citizenship for Indians, civil rights legislation, the endangered species act, and global human rights—the act of releasing subdued fish resonates deeply in our psyches. Releasing what we have caught, we can indulge ourselves in all the uplifting emotions of the kind steward's noblesse oblige . . ."

We angle because we like the fight . . . The hook allows us to control and exert power over fish, over one of the most beautiful and seductive forms of nature, and then, because we're nice to the fish, releasing them "unharmed," we can receive both psychic dispensation and blessing. Needless to say, if you think about this relationship carefully, it's not a comforting one, for it is a game of dominance followed by cathartic pardons, which, as a non-fishing friend remarked, "is one of the hallmarks of an abusive relationship."

—TED KERASOTE, *in* Orion, *returning to earth*

Sanctimoniousness is where you find it. By the early years of the twenty-first century, plenty of it was wading in rivers.

Catch-and-release angling is becoming a religion. Although in some instances it is essential to the survival of the species sought, in others its major effect is to cloak its more evangelical practitioners in a mantle of righteousness.

—NELSON BRYANT, *New York Times*

To go a shade further than Bryant, catch-and-release fishing may be cruelty masquerading as political correctness. You can't help wondering what sorts of things people are doing today that seem clearly right and good, yet will one day seem wrong and bad. If I were strolling through the annals of incorrectness—up past the invertible heroism of General Custer and on through the safaris of Dennis Finch-Hatton—I would expect to discern, out in the future, catch-and-release fishing. At its best it is what Thomas McGuane calls "the thrill of the release, of a trout darting from your opening hands or resting its weight very slightly in your palms underwater, then easing off." At its worst it is dire—an unintended

failure. In the words of a shad biologist who works for a firm in
Pennsylvania called Ecology III Environmental Services, "A lot of
good Samaritans are killing fish." You watch a guy in Connecticut
catch a shad in a boat. He sticks a finger in past a gill cover and it
comes out the mouth. He lifts the shad to show its size and beauty,
then lowers the shad into the water and removes his finger. Rough-
ing gills is what biologists call "a pure death sign." Gill membranes
are sensitive, elaborate, and easily broken. When they are damaged, a fish loses its ability to extract oxygen from water. In a video
called "Fishing for the American Shad," instructor John Punola
reaches for a roe shad, saying, "Shad are very fragile. I can pick
him up easily by the gills." Even the most adroit underwater release can turn loose a fish sick with stress, destined not to recover.
And the more the catch-and-release angler fumbles—the more he
manhandles fish up in air, twisting and yanking to disgorge the
hook—the lower the chance of survival. Boyd Kynard: "That air-
handling time, it's the worst, it's the hardest thing on them."

According to New Jersey shad reports, anglers in the Delaware River release four out of five shad they catch—with overall
numbers in the many tens of thousands. The state has guessed that
one per cent of the released fish die. Biologists guess at least half
of them die. Some anglers use barbless hooks, which may reduce
damage in a fish's mouth but do not reduce stress. Some say that
when a fish hits a fly, that's it; that's what fishing is all about; the
rest is just housekeeping—an anticlimax. A few of them have used
hooks with neither barbs nor points—flies tied on hooks that have
eyes at both ends. Others have used bits of fur and hackle tied to
sawed-off toothpicks. This avenue leads back in history to a small
Chinese sage who played a lute and meditated while fishing with
utmost patience. Day after day, he caught nothing. Eventually,
someone asked him what he was using for bait. He lifted his line
out of the water. Nothing was on it, not even a hook.

I once had a waking dream in a large pavilion with open

sides—picnic tables, a smooth concrete floor—in a Forest Service campground in Arizona. No one else was there. I was thinking dark passing thoughts about playing fish: Never say playing. You are at best torturing and at worst killing a creature you may or may not eat. Playing at one end, dying at the other—if playing is what it is, it is sadism. A man with a fly rod, waders, and Polaroids steps into the pavilion. I mean, can you see this fisherman baiting a hook with a bit of Gruyère and casting the line toward a chipmunk? The fisherman pinches some cheese on his hook. He flips the cheese to the chipmunk. The adorable little creature—*Eutamias quadrivittatus*—swallows. The fisherman sets the hook. The chipmunk leaps high in a shocked and wild, terrified rage. It races up posts and across beams, and somersaults through the air. It leaves the pavilion and runs flat out toward a line of trees, the reel drag clicking. Steady and attentive, the fisherman plays the chipmunk, keeping tension on the line. What is the difference between a chipmunk and a fish? "Some neurologists regard the ratio of brain to spinal cord as a promising measure of mental advance," Stephen Jay Gould wrote. In a human being, the brain is fifty times heavier than the spinal cord. A cat? Four to one. A fish? "Fish generally dip below 1:1 (spinal cord heavier than brain)." So a fish is little more than a lively muscle, four times dumber than a cat, and the moral objection to catching one on a hook and line is pelletized anthropomorphism primed and shot from the pathetic fallacy.

Not so fast, Lefty. Are you really "playing" that shad on your line? The word is off-putting—you are attempting to end a creature's life. It was born here in the river, went to the Bay of Fundy, lived five years, and came back to the river to give birth to young, and now you have it on a hook at the end of a line and are moving its head from side to side as its body leaps and thrashes. Can you call that playing? Find a word for what you are doing that denigrates neither fish nor fisher. Meanwhile, Izaak W. Greenpeace, of the nail knot and the matched hatch, offers his quarry imitation food, then tortures the victim with a steel point in the mouth until the victim exhausts and flops to one side, whereupon Greenpeace, his pleasure complete, removes the point of steel and releases the battered victim. "Imagine reaching for an apple on a tree and having your hand suddenly impaled by a metal hook that drags you— the whole weight of your body pulling on that one hand—out of the air and into an atmosphere in which you cannot breathe," PETA suggests constructively. The chipmunk fisherman turns out to have company—enough bizarre comparisons to fill an anthology. Try "lassoing a white-tailed deer and hauling it in until it's exhausted."

In 1872, it was not infra dig to relish the joy of killing, and the standards of 1872, having withstood ever amplified assault, are not exactly absent now. In 1872, fourteen-year-old Teddy Roosevelt cruised up the Nile shooting birds by the dozen with his 12-gauge Lefaucheux, blasting away, in the words of his biographer David McCullough, "at anything in sight," and slaughtering ibises, pelicans, larks, doves, wagtails, warblers, chats, grosbeaks, plovers, cranes, pigeons, peewees, zick-zacks, and snipes. The mature T.R., defender of the environment, shot elks and grizzlies in Wyoming in such numbers that he wrote: "I have had good sport; and enough excitement and fatigue to prevent over much thought." After Elliott Roosevelt killed a tiger south of Hyderabad, he wrote to his brother Teddy: "Finished her . . . with a spare shot from the Bone Crusher—by George, what a hole that gun makes." And a stubborn elephant in Ceylon: "It was only after I had put sixteen bullets into him that his great, crushing weight fell down in the bamboos." Not long after Karen Blixen arrived in Kenya, in 1913, she went on a month-long safari in the Masai Reserve, near her farm. Known to friends as Tanne and to readers as Isak Dinesen, she is described here by her biographer Judith Thurman:

> This was to be Tanne's first prolonged experience of the wild and her initiation to the rigors of safari life. She had

never slept in a tent, sat up in a boma, handled a big gun, or taken a life, and before they left Bror gave her a rifle with a telescopic sight and some instruction. There is a photograph of her doing target practice outside the house, dressed in a very smart tweed suit, black pumps, and a felt hat. She was, in fact, quite unprepared for her own blood lust. A week into the safari, drunk with it, she offered her apologies to all hunters for any prior skepticism toward their "ecstasy."

From bases like these evolved not only Charlton Heston and the NRA but such branching antitheticals as PETA and catch-and-release fishing. In English fishing, according to Howell Raines, the Teddy Roosevelt branch consists of aristocrats and moral descendants of aristocrats, who kill fish and use the k-word to emphasize their approach to the sport. Great Britain's catch-and-release fishermen are largely underclass blokes, who stand shoulder to shoulder on the edges of canals and mutually enforce their beneficent code. In England, working-class fishermen are known as "coarse fishermen," Raines says. "They are the most militant catch-and-release fishermen in the world."

Looking back through history at such attitudes, pause in the days of Grover Cleveland. You find him lamenting not that people thought ill of him for killing fish but that fishermen in his time were looked upon as lazy, a viewpoint that did not exclude presidents. Cleveland fished all his life, and was the author of "Fishing and Shooting Sketches" (1906). It is fair to call him an aggressive live-bait angler. On Duncan Lake in New Hampshire, luckless, he noticed a kid in a boat catching bass. He rowed over, got into the kid's boat, baited his own hook with one of the kid's live crickets, and said, "Just call me Cleve." He started catching bass. In time, a carriage appeared on the shore of the lake and its driver called out, "Mr. President, it's time to leave." The kid grew up to be the

Chief Constable of Tamworth, New Hampshire, and told his story to Marjory Gane Harkness ("The Tamworth Narrative," Shiver Mountain Press, 1958).

In June, 1876, bivouacked on Goose Creek in northern Wyoming, General George Crook caught seventy trout in one afternoon. He and his thousand U.S. soldiers and more than two hundred and fifty native allies had been repulsed by Sioux warriors on Rosebud Creek in Montana and had withdrawn to Goose Creek to think it over. They camped there three weeks, during which the Seventh Cavalry, sixty miles northwest, was destroyed beside the Little Bighorn River and the troops on Goose Creek caught fifteen thousand trout.

"I frankly don't see much difference between the catch-and-release fish counters of today and General Crook's soldiers," I once remarked to Boyd Kynard. "These bean counters say to me that they're not happy to be standing in the river unless they get a certain level of pleasure out of it, whatever that pleasure is."

He said, "Entertainment."

I said, "I'm a different kind of fisherman. I like to eat the fish, and I don't catch nearly as many."

He said, "Most people don't eat the fish."

My desire to achieve a fifty-shad day having evaporated long ago, I said, "If I get two, I'm happy. If they get six, they're unhappy."

Some shad fishermen wear golfers' clickers on their vests—plastic wheels that count up to a hundred. They call out to each other, in competition for numbers. They won't go to lunch until they've caught a certain quota. Howell Raines' friend Dick Blalock says to him, "I'm very much opposed to any kind of competition in fishing. I think that fishing should not be a competitive sport . . . I'm not in competition with you—ever, ever, ever." By the third "ever," you are getting the idea that Blalock is in Counters Anonymous. A guy I know as Harrisburg tells me about shad fishing beside a guy we know as Scranton. When Harrisburg arrived in mid-afternoon, Scranton had caught forty-one shad. Harrisburg caught thirty-two thereafter. Neither Harrisburg nor Scranton ever keeps a fish. They talk about the number they have caught, and are obsessed with those numbers. Is this the nobility of catch-and-release? Certain catch-and-release types speak of "meat fishermen" in the same tone that fly fishermen generally use for people who fish with worms. I'm a meat fisherman. I think it's immoral not to eat a fish you jerk around the river with a steel barb through its mouth. I see no other justification for doing so. The whole panoply of barbless hooks and prestidigitational underwater releases leaves me ice cold. There's no such thing as humane torture, and striking steel into a fish and pulling it into submission is torture.

Yolanda Whitman appears to agree with me, but then fires a heavy shot across my bow. "Catch-and-release fishing is analogous in a general way to the form of 'humane' bullfighting that omits the kill," she says, and I nod in eye-to-eye agreement. She continues: "If you keep your fish, it's analogous to traditional bullfighting. The intention is to kill, and to extend the act of killing. Fishing is crueler than hunting, in that your goal is to have the fish fight for its life. That's the 'fun.' Hunting, you're trying to kill a creature outright; fishing, you want to 'play' with it."

"That is not a fair description of your husband."

"If you could just pull fish out of the water—boom—you wouldn't be a fisherman. Don't give me that, John."

If she thinks I'm so bad, she should read more Washington Irving. From "Tales of the Alhambra" (1832):

I had repeatedly observed a long lean fellow perched on the top of one of the towers, manoeuvring two or three fishing-rods, as though he were angling for the stars. I was for some time perplexed by the evolutions of this aerial fisherman, and my perplexity increased on observing others employed in like manner on different parts of the battlements and bastions; it was not until I consulted Mateo Ximenes that I solved the mystery. It seems that the pure and airy situation of this fortress has rendered it, like the castle of Macbeth, a prolific breeding-place for swallows and martlets, who sport about its towers in myriads, with the holiday glee of urchins just let loose from school. To entrap these birds in their giddy circlings, with hooks baited with flies, is one of the favourite amusements of the ragged "sons of the Alhambra," who, with the good-for-nothing ingenuity of arrant idlers, have thus invented the art of angling in the sky.

It would be nice to think that those idlers were fond of martlet breasts rubbed with garlic, dusted with flour, and sautéed in virgin olive oil. If you use a fishing rod, you are foraging, and a forager sees to it that what is collected is eaten. For me, nothing else is comfortable. I remember reading long ago that nothing else is comfortable to a German, either. When my friend Marc Fisher, who later wrote "After the Wall," was working in Germany as the *Washington Post*'s chief correspondent there, I wrote to him asking what he knew about German sport-fishing regulations and the attitudes that informed them. Was it true that Germans forbid the practice of catch-and-release? Marc's reply, with his unfailing humor, amounted to a guidebook to German angling (for Germans), here excerpted:

Germany's eternal quest to regulate virtually every aspect of life does not leave the weekend fisherman unscathed. You are correct: If you fish in Germany, you keep—and eat—what you catch, or you face painful fines. Each of Germany's sixteen states has its own fishing laws, but according to Uwe Schuller, managing director of the Association of German Sport Fishermen, all state laws have in common the following elements:

Before you head out for a morning of sport fishing in Germany, you must have passed a government fishing examination, which includes both written and practical sections. First, you must take a thirty-hour course prepared by the local fishing and water protection associations. The course includes sections on "general fish knowledge" and "specific fish knowledge," focusing on the individual species you hope to catch—and eat. There is a heavy emphasis in the course on environmental safeguards. After the course, you must pass the exam by answering at least forty-five of sixty questions correctly. Then, you must pass the practical. Your examiner might say to you, "Please build a rod fit for catching eel." You must then do this. The ordeal ends with the awarding of a fishing license (*Fischereiprüfung*).

Do not go fishing at this point. You still need a fishing permit (*Fischereierlaubnisschein*). This document allows you to fish in a particular body of water for a particular period of time. Permits are granted only if you prove that you have a "sensible reason" to fish. For most types of fish, the only permissible reason is *"menschliche Ernährung"*— human nutrition. You fish to eat. If you attempt to fish without a permit, a friendly neighbor will be sure to follow the German tradition of filing a complaint against you, an experience you will not find pleasant.

With a permit, you may now go fishing. But Herr Schuller wants you to be very careful: "You are never, ever to throw a fish back. We have none of this American style catch-and-release. That is verboten. That is a violation of the animal protection law and can be severely punished."

The animal protection law considers it an offense to injure fish for no good reason, and sport fishing in itself is no good reason.

Nelson Bryant, in the *New York Times*, has expressed a certain weariness with published pictures of anglers cradling fish to be released after the picture is taken. In Bryant's view, "it would be pleasing to see a photograph of an angler with a nice fish, legal to keep, under which the caption informs the reader that on the same day the angler filleted it, brushed it with a butter-herb sauce and broiled it over a hardwood fire." I fish for American shad because they are schooling fish that come into the rivers wild. They are not an endangered species. They are not raised in hatcheries and brought as adults to the river in trucks. And above all, as a most savory food, they merit their taxonomic description. I catch to eat, and with that purpose am not troubled by the killing. As Jennifer Price observed in her book "Flight Maps," "most of us do not personally snap the heads off the poultry we eat." If you're going to be a fisherman, you have to be prepared to kill fish, because you will kill them if you catch and release them, you will kill them with barbless hooks. You won't kill everything, but you'll kill. They are going to die after you release them, and they are going to die if you keep them to eat. You don't need to develop a protective theology, as Ted Kerasote does: "We're making choices—more spiritual than economic—about grounding our souls in landscape through participation, about becoming participatory citizens of a homeplace through the eating of what the landscape produces." All you need is a stove. In the words of George Reiger: "The reason our fly-fishing forebears developed this technique was to catch trout so they could eat them. To characterize such sensible behavior as unenlightened is not only snobbish, it provides fuel for those who insist that the only purpose of angling is to torture fish."

In this at times acrimonious and always three-pronged debate—catch-and-release, catch to eat, don't molest fish—it is not impossible to empathize with the widely varying points of view of a pair of brilliant Australians, each of whom acquired strong early attitudes in large part derived from their fathers. Peter Singer, who has been called "the ideological father of the modern movement for animal rights," used to take long walks with his seriously asthmatic father along Australian riverbanks past fishermen with newly caught fish beside them, gasping pathetically. "He used to say how cruel that was," Peter Singer told the writer Sylvia Nasar. "He didn't understand how people could think it was fun." Robert Hughes, who grew up fishing and hunting in and near Sydney, was instructed by his father: "Never shoot anything alive unless you mean to eat it."

Of course, as is quite well established, there is nothing like a rod, a reel, a stream, and the privacy of nature to make a liar out of anybody. Not to mention hypocrite. I release shad sometimes, I confess. I prefer females to males. But, soon after recording my German attitudes toward catch-and-release, I went to the river and caught and released three roe shad as large as any I had seen all year. It was a test. Could I do it? Would I do it? I'm here to tell you, it was not easy. I returned to the river, in those living fish, about a million eggs. Or did I? That noble move was tempered by the odds-on possibility that the fish would die—as a result of my interference—before they had a chance to spawn.

Two of the two things I have in common with Cotton Mather are that he fished in canoes and that he evidently fished to eat. If he was not the first American to tell exaggerative and mendacious fish stories, he missed the honor by a narrow margin. In 1712, Mather wrote "The Fisher-mans Calling. A Brief ESSAY to Serve the Great Interests of RELIGION among our Fisher-men; and set before them the Calls of their SAVIOUR, whereof they should be Sensible, in the Employments of their Fishery." He told of thirty ocean fishermen who, after being frustrated by foul weather, went fishing on a day that they had previously reserved for the "Exercises of Religion." Five other fishermen did not join them but "tarried" to worship Jesus Christ. "The Thirty which went away from the Meeting, with all their Craft could Catch but four Fishes; The Five which tarried, went forth afterwards; and they took five Hundred." On Wednesday, August 15, 1716, near Cambridge, Massachusetts, Cotton Mather fell out of a canoe while fishing on Spy Pond. After emerging soaked, perplexed, fishless, he said, "My God, help me to understand the meaning of it!" Before long, he was chastising his fellow clerics for wasting God's time in recreational fishing.

Not a lot of warmth there. Better to turn to the clergyman Fluviatulis Piscator, known to his family as Joseph Seccombe, who was twenty-one years old when Cotton Mather died. Beside the Merrimack River, in 1739, Piscator delivered a sermon that was later published as "A Discourse utter'd in Part at Ammauskeeg-Falls, in the Fishing-Season." There are nine copies in existence. One was sold at auction in 1986 for fourteen thousand dollars. The one I saw was at the Library Company of Philadelphia. Inserted in it was a book dealer's description that said, "First American book on angling; first American publication on sports of field and stream. Seccombe's defense of fishing is remarkable for coming so early, in a time when fishing for fun needed defending." Fishing for fun and food reached a high level at Ammauskeeg Falls, where Manchester, New Hampshire, is now. It was a rite of the spring migration, of the arrival of American shad, with Indians and colonists dancing, writing treaties, feasting, fishing. When Fluviatulis Piscator came into this scene, he was famous for his work as a missionary in Maine, an assignment that could only have advanced his development as a sport fisherman. He reminded the Ammauskeeg festival that the apostles were not only fishers of men but fishers in the first place, and they fished not only on business but also at times for diversion, and that the "Lord not only appoints the Leisure, but supports them in it, by giving them a lucky Draught of Fishes." He further said, "Fishing is innocent as Business or Diversion . . . Diversion is the turning aside from Business, in some proper Period, to refresh ourselves, and fit us for a more chearful and lively Discharge of Duty." Shifting his address to people concerned for the ethical treatment of animals, he said,

> Some among ourselves fear whether we ought to take away the Lives of Creatures for our own Support; and are positive that we should not for Diversion. Many have a great Aversion to those whose Trade it is to take away the Lives of the lower Species of Creatures. A Butcher is (in their Apprehension) a mere Monster, and a Fisherman, a filthy Wretch . . . He that takes Pleasure in the Pains and dying Agonies of any lower Species of Creatures, is either a stupid sordid Soul, or a Murderer in Heart. He that delighteth to see a Brute die, would soon take as great Pleasure in the Death of a Man. But here, in Fishing, we are so far from delighting to see our Fellow-Creature die, that we hardly think whether they live. We have no more of a murderous Tho't in taking them, than in cutting up a Mess of Herbage. We are taking something, which God, the Creator and Proprietor of all, has given us to use for Food, as freely as the green Herb. Gen. IX. 2, 3. He allows the eating them, therefore the mere catching them is no Barbarity. Besides God seems to have cary'd out the Globe on purpose for a universal supply . . . and he has implanted in several sorts of Fish, a strong Instinct [or Inclination] to swim up these Rivers a vast Distance from the sea. And is it not remarkable, that Rivers most incumbred with Falls, are ever more full of Fish than others? Why are they directed here? Why retarded by these difficult Passages? But to supply the . . .

Thoreau went through an arc with respect to treatment of fish. In 1839, in the notes that would evolve into "A Week on the Concord and Merrimack Rivers," he mentioned "the Common Eel . . . still squirming . . . in the frying pan." And "the Horned Pout, Pimelodus nebulosus, sometimes called Minister, from the peculiar squeaking noise it makes when drawn out of the water, is a dull and blundering fellow, and like the eel vespertinal in his habits, and fond of the mud. It bites deliberately as if about its business. They are taken at night with a mass of worms strung on a thread, which catches in their teeth, sometimes three or four, with an eel, at one pull. They are extremely tenacious of life, opening and shutting their mouths for half an hour after their heads have been cut off."

By 1854, in Walden, he was saying, "I cannot fish without falling a little in self-respect . . . Always when I have done it I feel it would have been better had I not fished . . . With every year I am less a fisherman . . . At present I am no fisherman at all."

If you were growing up in Philadelphia in the eighteen-fifties, odds are that you were under the influence of a children's book called "City Characters; Or, Familiar Scenes in Town." It said: "You may take your hook and line some summer afternoon, and sit by a stream in the country under some shady tree, catching sunnies, perch, roach, and other little fish. Do not do so, however, merely to throw them away again; for that is wasteful and cruel. If you take them home, they will be cooked, and make a nice supper for you."

In early-colonial and pre-colonial time, certain bands of the Lenape fished at the mouth of Brandywine Creek during the spring migration. Upstream a few miles, on more agreeable ground, they set up camp. Brandywine Creek is the next downstream tributary after the Schuylkill on the right bank of the Delaware River. The site of the ancient fish camp is in the heart of downtown Wilmington. According to A. R. Dunlap and C. A. Weslager's "Contributions to the Ethno-History of the Delaware Indians in the Brandywine," an article in *Pennsylvania Archaeologist* (1960), the Indians planted corn in fields to the west and then came down the creek to "fish and turtle" at the river's mouth. When the braves returned to camp with shad and turtles, a fire of deep coals was waiting. They grilled the shad. They turned the live turtles upside down and set them on the red-hot coals. A while after the turtles stopped struggling, the Indians removed them from the fire and ate them from their bowl-like shells, a procedure you will understand if you like lobster.

And still another season nears an end as the shad swim into June, the spawning month of exhaustion. This will be my last day, my last afternoon, a set piece of two hours in fairly high water. I'm in my canoe. I just want one fish. I'm fishing for my dinner. The first cast, well into the retrieve, is hit hard. But there's no follow-up. No fish. I reel in the dart. It has impaled a shad scale. Deciding that the shad are close to the canoe, I pick up my fly rod and get one no-fault AWOL, but no other strikes. Back to the spinning rod.

An hour and a half has gone by. If I don't catch a fish, I'll be boiling pasta.

Five minutes to go. No strikes. I'm getting ready to quit, when a shad hits.

She is on the line fifteen minutes before she is anywhere near the boat, but she is nearing it now. I reach for and lift the long-handled net. A snake is in the net. Pinhead. No rattle. Nonetheless a snake. In my left hand is a fishing rod with my dinner on the line. In my right hand is a boat net with a snake in it. The handle of the long-handled net is two feet long. The snake is longer. I lack the sense of companionship that some people seem to have with snakes. This snake has obviously been in my canoe with me for two hours, and I'm just now detecting its presence. If a snake is in my canoe, I feel crowded. When snakes come into Yolanda Whitman's greenhouse, she picks them up and carries them outside, even if they are longer than she is tall. I may be married to her, but not to those snakes. Or this one. It has woven itself into the mesh of the net. Over the left side of the canoe, I try to keep the shad on a taut line. Over the right side of the canoe, I shake the net hard, trying to force the snake to drop into the water. The snake is having none of it. The snake stays in the net as if it were sewed there. The shad takes off on a run against the drag. My arms are beginning to weaken. Leaning right, I plunge the net straight into the river. The snake receives the message and is cured of indecision. Away from the canoe, across the water's surface, it races like a snake. I swing the net around and land my dinner.

# APPENDIX

# COOKING SHAD

All you need is a stove, yes, but it helps to have a cast-iron skillet with a tight-fitting glass lid, if you like shad roe. Before going into this appendix, I should declare that it is not intended as a survey of shad cookery or extensive collection of shad recipes. First, I want to describe how I cook shad roe, then milt, then fillets unboned and boned, then whole shad. I will put all the personal experience up front and then gradually work in some things I don't often do— or, more likely, know how to do—that others do and have done. My way of cooking roe I learned from another fisherman many years ago, and I promptly stopped sautéing it in the conventional manner.

## SHAD ROE

Cover the bottom of the cast-iron skillet with bacon, thick-sliced if you want to go sooner. Snip the bacon to fit. One contiguous layer will do. There's no need to separate the sacs at this point; they look nice in their bilateral symmetry. Place them vein-side up or vein-side down—cosmetically and otherwise, it doesn't matter. You can cook two or more sets of roe sacs side by side if your skillet is large enough. The ones I use are nine inches across the top and seven inches across the base, with glass lids. Salt and pepper the roe sacs. Cover the pan. Put it on the burner at medium heat, and do not go away. Do not answer the telephone. Exile wives, children, and even grandchildren—out!—for a couple of minutes while you listen. After the bacon begins to sizzle, turn down the heat to the lowest level you are able to achieve without turning the burner off. Shad roe can explode if steam inside it builds up too rapidly. What you want to hear is a low, regular, consistent sizzle—not the sound of bacon rapidly crisping. If your lowest heat level is too vigorous, slip a wire spacer or heat diffuser under the pan, or some other device to hobble the burner.

Now set your timer for thirty-five minutes. Relax your injunctions on your family. Don't stray too far, though. Go back every five minutes to listen—to be sure that the sizzling is neither too active nor extinct. The checkup is entirely aural. You'll see almost nothing through the lid but dense fog. This method is an attenuated hybrid of sautéing and steaming. The bacon becomes watery and the roe gradually tightens up in steam. Cook it until it is quite firm. Thirty-five minutes should do it, less if the roe sacs are small. The ideal result, in cross-section, is wet in the middle with an aureole of dryer eggs. With a couple of minutes to go, put on your oven mitts, take hold of the lid handle and the pan handle, and pour off the accumulated water and bacon melt into the kitchen garbage wadded with paper towels. Employ the lid to prevent the roe from falling out of the skillet. Put the pan back on the stove, uncovered, and turn the heat back up to medium, so the bacon can brown. Just pray there's no explosion. If one occurs at this point, though, it will probably be a small one, and the damage will be minor.

At the end of the thirty-five minutes, gingerly feel around with a small spatula and free up any bacon that is sticking to the pan. Jiggle things a little and make sure that the roe-and-bacon will slide, but don't attempt with the spatula to turn anything over. Cover the skillet with an upside-down serving plate. With one hand on the pan handle and the other spread flat on the bottom of the plate, flip the skillet. Set the skillet aside. On the serving plate the finished roe is concealed beneath a thatch of bacon, beautifully hued by carbon fixing, its circular dimensions framed by the edge of the plate.

The bacon may be undercooked. Sometimes it isn't. Sometimes it is. I have no idea why. This is not a perfect world. If the bacon is undercooked—or, more likely, undercooked here and there—remove the offending strips, finish them off in the skillet (or the microwave), and repair the thatch. Seen out in the light, the cooked roe is cosmetically disadvantaged, in that the veins are evident and there has been no browning. In my view, it is a mistake to try to brown the roe purely for aesthetic reasons. The dish is quite attractive with its roof of bacon.

Chop the ends off a lemon, render it hexapartite, and sit down. That's all the sauce you need, and—in my house—is all you are going to get. You have your shad roe. You . . . are . . . in . . . business!

## MILT

In "The Market Assistant, Containing a Brief Description of Every Article of Human Food Sold in the Public Markets of the Cities of New York, Boston, Philadelphia, and Brooklyn" (1867), Thomas De Voe reported that not a few people prefer shad milt to shad roe. On some days, I'm one of those people. The milt of the buck shad—in its firm, pink pods—sketches the same bilateral outline as shad roe, but is thin and lies flat. The milt within has the consistency of heavy cream and is as white as the whitest quartz. The matrix is water. The sperm cells are white and opaque. But all that is invisible, being well sealed in its encasing membrane. In euphemious England, milt is called soft roe. The French call it *laitances*. Salt and pepper the pods. Shake flour over them, lightly. Sauté them in butter and oil. Pan-fry them as if they were eggs. Place them on soft variable toast—white, whole wheat, sourdough, Russian rye. This dish bestows status on the buck shad. It is reminiscent of the marrow in osso bucco. The word for it is not semen but savory. In England, herring milt on toast is served at the end of dinner as a savoury. American shad semen, after all, is herring milt. On toast, with squeezed lemon, it is melting with freshness. If you had your choice between shad semen and a pink-iced Pop-Tart, which would be more acceptable? Which would you take between a shad's semen, a calf's brain, a chicken's liver, and the inside of an ox femur? You just can't sit there eating Ferdinand's tongue and talk that way about shad milt, so cut it out.

### UNBONED FILLETS

Lay out the fillet, slice away the ribs, sprinkle with lemon pepper (Lawry's, if you can find it), and broil, about nine inches below the heat. As noted in Chapter 12, if shad fillets are put in a broiler very soon after swimming, they will rise like bread as they brown. As shad muscle broils, it will soften before it sets. After eleven or twelve minutes, it will almost be soup. At fifteen and a half minutes, it is firm and just done. Past sixteen, it is overdone. The window is that narrow. Moreover, the window moves around from stove to stove, because stoves are idiosyncratic. So if fifteen and a half minutes is not your windowsill, better luck next time. Add or subtract thirty seconds until you find it.

The meat itself is easily on a par with pompano. It's moist and succulent; very pale, almost white after cooking. The

meat is so exquisitely delicate you must force yourself not
to overcook it.

—RUSSELL CHATHAM, *Fly Fisherman*, 1979

When the fillet is on a plate and you have lots of fresh lemon
to squeeze on it, sit down under a bright light. Slide a fork into the
meat, and lift. In many places, you can raise a boneless forkful.
When intermuscular bones come up with the flesh, they protrude
glistening, and—pinched between thumb and forefinger—will
easily slip away. Don't try to be thorough. Take what you can con-
veniently get. You will not be lonely, even if you are alone. Eating
unboned shad requires so much concentration it's as if you were
eating with someone else. And you can do it with great pleasure.
Never mind the nineteenth-century Pennsylvania doctor mentioned in Richard Gerstell's "American Shad in the Susquehanna
River Basin" who "recommended against eating shad because of
the difficulty of removing their bones from children's throats." He
may have been a lazy doctor.

A shad-bone anthology would fill a thick volume. "The champion place for getting up an appetite for shad is at a Brooklyn
boarding-house," said the anonymous nineteenth-century author
of "A Dissertation on Shad" (Chapter 12). A boarder, having been
told that dinner will be shad, arrives at table wearing "the poorest
shirt he has," and carrying a magnifying glass, a bone basket, a
toothpick, and tweezers. "He will get so full of the bony parts that
he will sigh for a little more Bourbon. When he swallows a bone,
all he has to do is to take his tweezers and pull it out . . ."

"The shad-bone season for thumping people on the back is almost here," said the Columbia, Pennsylvania, *Columbia Spy* in the
spring of 1880. (Dr. Heimlich may have had shad in mind when
he invented his maneuver.) In "The Historie of Travaile into Virginia Brittania" (1612), William Strachey, First Secretary of the
Jamestown colony, wrote that the rivers of Virginia Brittania ("a

country in America") had "no meane commoditie of fish," including "shaddes, great store, of a yard long, and for sweetnes and
fatnes a reasonable good fish, he is only full of small bones, like our
barbells in England." Nearly four centuries later, Ruth Spear, writing in the *New York Post*, described American shad as "gastronom-
ically the finest of all white fish but with a maddening number of
bones." So there is a certain consistency in writers' reports on this
aspect of this fish, but for me the broiled unboned fillet remains
the most appealing way to present a plate of shad. If you think you
are eating a Norway spruce, pay closer attention. Avoid conversation. Are we eating or talking?

## BONED FILLETS

Broil as above, and consume them with an arsenal of freshly
wedged lemons. A shad has plenty of adipose tissue. It comes with
its own nutty butter—the fat it is living on while eating nothing on
the spawning run. That's why it is *sapidissima*. To a large extent it
is self-seasoned. And it will baste itself. Amazingly, for such a fish,
it can be successfully frozen, retaining most of its flavor. But eat it
all up before Christmas. For variety, I sometimes spoon over the
fillets a two-to-one mixture of soy sauce and sesame oil full of
chopped scallions. I put it on before broiling and add a little toward the end. Sometimes I include lemon juice, and incorporate
bits of fresh ginger instead of the scallions. You can decide
whether the sesame-soy concoction deepens the taste or disguises
it. It's good, surely, but the shad doesn't need it.

## WHOLE BAKED SHAD

Ever since I learned how they cook whole shad in the Maritime Provinces of Canada (Chapter 6), I have seldom done it another way. You make turkey stuffing, stuff the fish, bake it for thirty-five minutes at three hundred and fifty degrees, and eat it. Canadians told me to bake the shad with the scales on, but if I did that it would superalienate the person with whom I share the kitchen. If there is one thing in this world she detests, it's a shad scale. No one knows why. As far as I can make out, she finds it inconvenient that they are nearly invisible and—in drains and drainpipes—can laminate themselves in a manner that could bankrupt Roto-Rooter. I therefore suggest that you remove the scales, and with them the head, tail, and fins. Salt and pepper the skin and the empty cavity. Pack it up with turkey stuffing until the filled gap between the belly flaps is something like two inches. During the thirty-five baking minutes, you don't need to roll the fish over. On a serving platter, cant it upward, more or less on its back, and open it as you would a trout. Choose your own instruments. I use two fish servers—or two small spatulas. At any rate, you cause the shad to split open, and the sides to lie down symmetrically on the platter. Then you lift away the backbone and ribs. The white muscle shines like polished marble and is very moist and tender. A man in Doaktown told me not to eat it with a knife and fork, calling it "finger food." Suit yourself. I eat it with a fork in one hand and a wedge of lemon in the other. The stuffing, meanwhile, has been enhanced by the nutty essence of American shad.

So much for my predilections. For at least two hundred years people have stuffed shad with oysters and baked them in parchment, but I haven't tried that. I also haven't tried this way of cooking shad, which was taught by the Lenape to white settlers on the Delaware River, according to Mrs. J. Ernest Scott's "Cooking Shad by the Open Fire," a paper read before the Bucks County Historical Society in 1912:

> We gathered some reference of this method of cooking shad in the early days. It was not likely it was ever used in the home, but was probably sometimes used in the open and in the fishing camps along the river where no suitable cooking utensils were at hand. A freshly caught shad was rubbed against the scales and gills with soft mud from the river bank. When this had set a little the whole fish was rolled in a thick blanket of clay. It was then allowed to dry in the heat before the fire for some fifteen minutes, then it was buried in the hot coals and ashes till the clay was baked hard and the fish was thought to be well done. It was then raked out of the fire and cracked open. The fish readily split open, the head was removed, the insides, shrunk to a little ball, were scraped off and the scales adhered to the clay. A little salt was dusted over it. A dish thus prepared was fit for a king.

On the Susquehanna, early European settlers called shad May Fish—in German, *Maifisch*, in dialect *Moifisch*. William Woys Weaver preserves this baked-shad recipe, from about 1900, in his "Pennsylvania Dutch Country Cooking" (Abbeville Press, 1993). I have shortened it slightly by deleting gram equivalents. The recipe calls for a buck shad, because it was thought that males were lighter, juicier, and more flavorful than females, a prejudice that is lost on me. I can't agree.

## G'BACKENER MOIFISCH
## MIT GRAUT UN TOMATTS

3 tablespoons unsalted butter

1 cup plain breadcrumbs

1½ tablespoons minced fresh parsley

2 tablespoons minced fresh chives

1 teaspoon minced fresh winter savory or
   ½ teaspoon dried savory

1 three-to-four-pound buck shad, gutted and cleaned but
   with head and tail left on

6 cups finely shredded cabbage, resembling angel hair
   noodles

1 cup shredded sorrel

1 cup chopped onion

1 cup peeled, seeded, and chopped fresh tomatoes

⅔ cup dry white wine

4 slices country smoked slab bacon

Preheat the oven to 350 F. Melt the butter in a skillet and fry the breadcrumbs until straw colored, stirring constantly to prevent scorching (3 to 4 minutes). Add the parsley, chives, and savory, and remove from the heat.

Open the shad and cut the cavity from the head toward the tail with a sharp knife so that the fish opens out flat when lying on its back. To accomplish this, press down with the point of the knife under the neck and follow the backbone so that all the "rib" bones are cut at their bases. Fill the cavity with the browned breadcrumb mixture, then sew it up with trussing thread.

Poach the cabbage in salted water for 3 to 4 minutes to tenderize it, then drain and combine with the sorrel, onion, and tomatoes. Cover the bottom of a shallow roasting pan with the cabbage mixture, then lay the stuffed shad on top of it. Pour the wine on top, then drape the bacon slices diagonally at even intervals over the fish. Bake for approximately 40 minutes, depending on the size of the fish. Baste from time to time with liquid from the pan. When the fish tests done, serve immediately.

After Charles Dickens travelled by canal boat between Harrisburg and Pittsburgh in late March, 1842, he wrote in his "American Notes" that he was served "salmon, shad, liver, steaks, potatoes, pickles, ham, chops, black-puddings and sausages" for breakfast, and "salmon, shad, liver, steaks, potatoes, pickles, ham, chops, black-puddings and sausages" for dinner, and "salmon, shad, liver, steaks, potatoes, pickles, ham, chops, black-puddings and sausages" for supper. Had he lived until Chapter 2, he would have been at home with Boyd Kynard on the Danube.

In the nineteenth century, more so than now, people boiled whole shad, as in these 1849 instructions from "Frank Forester's Fish and Fishing of the United States and British Provinces of North America": "Scale, open, clean, and wash your fish; boil him quickly, wrapped in a napkin, in boiling water; serve upon a napkin, garnished with fried parsley; eat with caper sauce."

My friend Lynne Fagles bakes whole shad at three hundred degrees for an hour and a quarter. In and around the fish, she includes flat-leaf parsley, chopped onions and scallions, celery, wine, oil, and lemon juice.

Ed Cervone's wife, Marian, bakes a layered assemblage—shad fillets under and over shad roe. First, she picks the bones out of the fillets one by one by hand. I have from time to time asked myself, What did he do to deserve it? The lower fillet is flesh side up, the upper fillet is flesh side down. Several strips of bacon go on top. She pours in at least half a cup of white wine, lays a sheet of foil above the whole edifice, bakes it for an hour at three-fifty, and serves it with fresh lemon.

When Pierre Franey was chef *poissonnier* at the Pavillon, in New York, half a century ago, he improvised *Alose farcie*, stuffing it largely with roe: "I boned the shad and filleted it. Then I spread the shad with a mousse of sole, with bread crumbs, hard-cooked eggs, shallots, salt, pepper, parsley, and cream. I put the roe over one fillet, covered it with the other fillet, topped it with sliced mushrooms, then tied it and baked it with shallots, thyme, and bay leaf. I served the shad with a sauce made of the fish juices, white wine, cream, and beurre manié."

A related method is suggested by my friend Alan Lieb, who is in the river with his face mask and fins even more than he is on it with his rods and reels. On the bottom of the much-canoed Delaware, he picks up spinning rods, cell phones, car keys, Cannon towels, Swiss Army knives, and shad darts. With the rods and the darts he later catches shad that he cooks in various ways, including this way, which he wrote out for me a few years ago:

Make a stuffing of fresh sausage (made with pork that is not too lean, and with Morton's Sausage Seasoning), cooked apples (peeled and cut into quarters), and fresh soft breadcrumbs. Lay a boned fillet on an oblong platter (buttered), dust with flour, and cover with stuffing. Cover with the other boned fillet. Pipe rosettes of potatoes duchesse around the shad and bake for 45–60 minutes at 350–400. Duchesse potatoes are made like mashed except they are dryer and are stiffened with a couple of eggs and flour. You'll want a good strong sauce made with a fumet of shad perfumed with celery, onion, carrot, bay leaves, and peppercorns, and moistened with cider, not water. Strain this. Thicken with beurre manié (butter whipped into a little flour). Adjust taste, add some diced cooked apples, and you should be able to serve 5 or 6 very decently. It's the kind of dish A. J. Liebling might have eaten in Normandy.

In "Philadelphia on the River," a 1986 publication of the Philadelphia Maritime Museum, Philip Chadwick Foster Smith presents a baked-shad recipe in which roe is mixed into a stuffing:

### BAKED SHAD WITH ROE

*2 pounds shad*
*1 pair roe*
*1 tbs. chopped parsley*
*Pepper, salt (if desired)*
*1 tbs. butter*
*Soft bread crumbs*
*Clarified butter*
*½ cup sauterne*
*1½ cups chopped mushrooms*
*1 tsp. paprika*

Split and bone the shad. Scald the roe, split them, and scrape out the eggs, to which add the parsley, desired seasoning, butter, and a few soft bread crumbs. Stuff the shad with this mixture and secure with string. Place in baking dish and brush on clarified butter. Cook in slow (300 F) oven for 35 to 40 minutes, taking care to baste frequently with the cooking juices. Sauté the mushrooms in some of these juices, add wine, heat, and pour over the shad. Garnish with lemon wedges dipped in paprika.

When I asked James Webb—in Upper Economy, Nova Scotia, on the Bay of Fundy—if his family likes to eat the shad he traps in his brush weir, he said, "There's a lot of shad ate around here. They're very bony, but boy they're some sweet fish." The Webbs fry, bake, and barbecue shad. He said they bake whole shad thirty minutes at three hundred with a stuffing of potato, onion, and summer savory. "Eat them with pepper, salt, and vinegar. Fried: cut them in one-inch steaks, but first wipe the fish dry. There should be no fresh water on fish. It takes the taste away. Roll the steaks in cornmeal or flour. Fry them in some oil—not too much. Barbecue: wrap them in tinfoil with thin-sliced onion on it. Jab holes in the tinfoil to let the fat run out. Cook for roughly twenty minutes on a grate over hot coals."

Following a recipe in A. J. McClane's "The Encyclopedia of Fish Cookery," I once steamed a buck shad—the whole fish minus scales, head, fins, and tail—for five hours on the elevated rack of a fish poacher. Although I am not much tempted to do it again, the method worked. The flesh remained firm and flavorsome, although scarcely with the taste of a fresh broiled shad. The backbone was slightly crunchy but edible. The small intermuscular bones melted in the mouth. The recipe described a caper sauce. It was too rich. Try another sauce.

The purpose of long cooking is to defeat the bones without ripping up the fish to get them out. Defeat equals dissolve. The large bones soften to the point of edibility, and the myriad small bones simply disappear. Marilyn Yates, whom I've known since high school, bakes whole shad at two hundred and fifty degrees for seven hours, as her mother did. Marilyn has never cooked shad another way. She begins with a spotlessly cleaned fish—unsplit, and without scales, head, or fins. She continues: "Season it with salt and pepper, lay three or four strips of bacon on it, place it in one cup of water, and surround it with sliced onion and sliced lemon.

Cover it tightly with foil or the top of the pan. Check every two and a half hours to see if the water level is o.k. If not, add a little more. Good eating!"

Tom Horton, in "Bay Country," mentions a long-bake method for Alose, the French first cousin of American shad. The result is called *Alose sans os*. As noted in Chapter 3, members of the shad-minded Pamunkey tribe, with their shad hatchery on the Pamunkey River in tidewater Virginia, tightly wrap whole shad in two sheets of aluminum foil and give it six hours at two hundred and fifty. Described as "baked," the shad is baked in the same sense that a restaurant potato in foil is "baked." It is steamed in its own fluids. I have known people whose strategy in the bone war is to leave shad in a refrigerator for two days, and then—like Willy Bemis preparing fish skeletons—scrape the flesh from the bones with a spoon. They make shadcakes. Sooner or later, almost anybody will, at least once, try the bone war's ultimate weapon. You can nuke a shad with a pressure cooker. I did it for the first time a decade ago, and plan to do it a second time some year soon. I put inch-thick slices in the pressure cooker with onions and celery, and timed the hiss (at fifteen pounds) for one half hour. After the fish cooled, I peeled off the skin, removed the backbone, and refrigerated the rest. It was served cold under a mayonnaise thinned with lemon juice and thickened with chopped fresh dill. The intermuscular bones and even the ribs had disappeared.

As an alternative to the dill mayonnaise, Alan Lieb suggested gooseberries cooked the same way you cook rhubarb—in a small amount of water with sugar. "In June, when gooseberries are available, you could make a puree and freeze it," he said. "It's a wonderful counterpoint to the richness of the fish." Also he mentioned a green-peppercorn sauce—"crushed peppercorns in a meat glaze, with a little vinegar in it to bring it all to life."

Armand Charest, the master dartmaker of the Connecticut River, has an alternative to the gooseberries and the green peppercorns. Armand Charest: "You take a shad. You put it in a pressure cooker with a brick. You cook it for eight hours. Then you throw away the shad and eat the brick."

Baking any fish on an oak plank is said to improve your chances of enjoying its natural flavors, and the custom of propping up the plank before a bed of hot coals is, as noted in Chapter 8, the memorial fate of the American shad. Dr. Samuel L. Howell, in 1837, wrote of "nailing the fish to a clean oaken plank, previously heated, and setting it before a brisk fire. By this method the juices of the fish are all preserved."

In 1849, "Frank Forester's Fish and Fishing of the United States and British Provinces of North America" included a "Sea-Shore Receipt for Roasted Shad":

> Split your fish down the back after he is cleaned and washed, nail the halves on shingles or short board; stick them erect in the sand round a large fire; as soon as they are well browned, serve on whatever you have got; eat with cold butter, black pepper, salt, and a good appetite. This is a delicious way of cooking this fine fish.

In 1855, Hannah Bouvier Peterson gave a detailed description of planking in "The National Cook Book." Find an oak board three inches thick and two feet square, she wrote. Stand it before a fire "until it gets good and hot." Nail to the board a salted, split shad. Stand it before the fire head down. When juices begin to run, invert it. Do that frequently. When done, butter it, serve it on the board.

Mrs. Scott's "Cooking Shad by the Open Fire" (1912) reviewed shad cooking in colonial America, culminating in planked shad. Colonists generally cooked shad on the gridiron—a rectangular iron frame with bars set maybe three-quarters of an inch apart. Hickory coals were "raked out on the hearth." The gridiron, standing on legs, was placed over them. Shad were also cooked in long-handled frying pans. Elevated on hickory sticks, they were cooked in covered baking pans set in glowing coals. They were also cooked in rectangular boxes known as roasting kitchens. And they were planked:

> A slab of hickory or oak was used. This was split, cut and hewed down to two or three inches thick, a little wider than the opened fish, and about two feet long. This was propped up before a bed of coals till it was sizzling hot. The fish was split down the back, wiped dry and then fastened skin side down to the hot plank. The plank was then propped up at an angle of about 60 degrees before the fire. The shad was constantly basted with a piece of fat pork on a switch held above it. The ends of the plank were reversed from time to time, so that the shad would be uniformly done. When the flesh was flaky when pierced with a fork, it was done. The shad was then served on the hot plank and was said to be a dish of rare gastronomic excellence.

Charles Hardy III, historian of Delaware shad, describes an "advertising war" among hotels on both sides of the river which "brought planked shad to national prominence" at the time of the national centennial, in 1876. "The craze for fresh planked shad continued to spread in the eighteen-eighties." People came "from as far away as Pittsburgh to eat planked shad."

According to an endnote by William Woys Weaver, "most American cookbooks before 1850 do not even mention shad roe, and there are still quite a number of people today who consider roe-eating a repulsive refinement." Weaver's article, "When Shad Came In: Shad Cooking in Old Philadelphia," was published in 1982 in the thrice-annual *Petits Propos Culinaires*. In eighteenth-century America, he says, shad roe was "thrown away, fed to pigs, or given to the poor." At the turn of the twenty-first century, you could order Shad Roe with Bacon and Lemon Chive Butter from the luncheon menu in the Four Seasons on Park Avenue in New York for thirty-six dollars à la carte.

A "Joy of Cooking" recipe for broiled shad roe calls for "1 cup canned shad roe," but don't go away. "The Joy of Cooking" knows from roe. Or knew from roe. The edition in which I found that recipe appeared in 1972. In all, it had eight shad-roe recipes. Seven mentioned fresh roe. The recipes for fresh whole roe sacs were two-stage procedures: first you parboiled them, then you broiled, baked, sautéed, or creamed them. "Use only white pepper," the "Joy" recommended. It also said, "Hard roe, to be cooked and served alone, should be pricked with a needle to prevent the membrane from bursting and splattering the little eggs"—a precaution I have not found to be a hundred per cent effective.

Canned shad roe, in the twenty-first century, is a small industry concentrated almost exclusively on Columbia River shad. Nelson Crab, in Tokeland, Washington, cans shad roe, smoked shad, and smoked shad pâté. Bell Buoy, in Seaside, Oregon, folds broken roe sacs into small cylindrical cans. Steve Fick's Fishhawk Fisheries, in Astoria, Oregon, fills an elegant oval tin with integral sacs.

We have two other editions of "The Joy of Cooking," and they suggest a dimming of shad roe in the American consciousness and a trend ominous to Cannery Row. By 1975, "Joy" was down to five shad-roe recipes, three of which specified canned roe. A fourth was AC-DC—your choice, fresh or vacuum-packed. The "Madrilene Ring with Shad Roe Cockaigne" was built on "chilled canned shad roe," as was "Creamed Shad Roe," whose fundaments included curry powder, paprika, melted butter, and three-quarters of a cup of heavy cream. I have been there and may not be returning soon, in hopes of seeing a little more of my grandchildren. You will look in vain for any such recipe in "The All New All Purpose Joy of Cooking" (1997). At eleven hundred and thirty-six pages, it is twenty-five per cent larger and even more encyclopedic than its predecessors, yet it contains only one brief and simple recipe for shad roe, tersely telling you to sauté it fresh.

Steven Raichlen, in his 1988 cookbook, "A Celebration of the Seasons," pays passing homage to corporeal shad ("an epicure's morsel: rich as herring, buttery as swordfish, delicate as pike") on his way to saying

> For many people, the fish is of small consequence—the mere packaging for another springtime delicacy, shad roe. Raw shad roe is not for the squeamish: two soft, squishy banana-shaped egg sacs, containing 300,000 eggs, connected by a veined, often bloody membrane. But cooked it's the sort of fare one should savor, kneeling with one's head bared. The taste of shad roe is ineffable, but to get an idea, imagine the richness of sweetbreads, the subtle liver flavor of foie gras and the sensuous crunch of the finest caviar. If I've failed to convince you, please pass your plate to me!

"They are sometimes treated like hams," Dr. Howell wrote in 1837, "viz. by rubbing them with fine salt, salt-petre, and molasses, and smoked for a few days, and in this way are very superior to those cured with salt alone." In Columbia County, New York, in the twenty-first century, people smoke shad over apple wood, put signs in their yards, and sell it. The *New York Times* has described smoked shad as a "real working-class delicacy." The fillets are soaked in brine with black pepper, lemon juice, molasses, and brown sugar, and smoked for as little as two and as much as twelve hours over low heat. Oak, ash, or maple will do if you don't have an orchard. Patroons can seek admission to the working class.

If you ask Boyd Kynard what he does with his shad, he says, "Smoke 'em—smoking is the best thing to do with any bony fish." As in kippered herring. A shad, after all, is a herring. Boyd cuts his shad into one-inch steaks, soaks them in brine and sugar, then hot-smokes them. "The flesh dries. You can see the bones." He may be the Bernini of the shad smoker. He says to make your shad smoker a foot and a half square and two feet high. A pine frame is o.k., covered with quarter-inch hardware cloth. The smoker should have a door at ground level, and inside you want three racks, four to five inches apart, all in the upper half. They, too, can be made of pine. On a hot plate on the floor is a small cast-iron skillet with wood chips in it and a lid or a piece of sheet metal that restricts oxygen so the wood won't flare up. The lid's diameter should be slightly smaller than the pan's. In the door, for the intake of air, make three one-inch holes at the level of the hot plate. To vent the smoker, make four one-inch holes at the top of the back. A candy thermometer can rest in one of those upper holes, monitoring temperature from the start.

Philip Reed, of Friendship, Maine, "smokes shad elegantly," says his friend Sam Chapman (the aquaculturist of Chapter 5). Reed shuffles his feet. He is in his eighties and modest, a retired herring fisherman. "It isn't how much brine you use, it's how long you soak the fish," he says. And that is all he says. His shad are split down the back, and left intact at the belly. He leaves the scales on.

Sam Chapman, who has never had shad another way, says, "Nothing makes beer taste better than smoked shad."

At the beginning of June, some years ago, I stopped in at Alan Lieb's house in Wayne County, Pennsylvania, and had a delicious lunch of fresh saltless bread and pickled shad. It had been pickled in apple-cider vinegar with brown sugar in a quart jar. "You use about a cup of sugar and a cup and a half of cider vinegar," he said. "Two teaspoons of allspice, two teaspoons of ground cloves, and a little water to soften the vinegar." He filled a Mason jar with those ingredients, and gave it to me so that I could practice boning shad and then pickle my mistakes.

This was sort of an echo of eighteenth-century Philadelphia's teatime pickled shad (Chapter 8). In 1857, Elizabeth Nicholson echoed it, too, in "The Economical Cook and House-Book" (Willis P. Hazard, Philadelphia). She said to use salt, pepper, allspice, cloves, and mace. Put seasoned pieces of shad in an earthen or stone vessel and fill it with vinegar. "Then tightly close the jar with dough, put it in the oven of a baker after the bread has come out." Let it stand ten hours.

Skip Trimble, of Allentown, Pennsylvania, makes shad quenelles with sorrel pesto and cheese. "It's fish dumplings in a cheese sauce," he told a reporter. "It's pastry, like cream puffs, that's mixed with ground fish, and when you cook it, it blows up like a balloon, the size of a fist."

For dinner one evening after fishing, Alan Lieb fed me and George Hackl shad with whisky sauce. We had actually caught the fish the previous day, and he had corned the fillets. They had stood for twenty-four hours in a gallon of water in which three-quarters of a cup of sugar and three-quarters of a cup of salt had been dissolved. He grilled them over a smoky fire on a grill he had found on the bottom of the river. The sauce was cream, butter, a bit of flour, and a shot of The Glenlivet. Alan said there was a fisherman on the river who was known as the Marquis de Shad. I believe that was actually Alan Lieb.

We also had shad sausages. Alan had put some unboned shad into a hand meat grinder, which kept the bones and expressed the meat. He mixed it with salt, pepper, thyme, sage, mace, marjoram, some egg white, some stale crustless bread crumbs, and grated lemon rind. He had bought sausage casings, which he limbered with water, and filled with the shad mixture, using a sausage nozzle. The sausages were dense, moist, excellent. But they tasted just like pork sausages.

Thinking aloud, he said, "You could try taking some shad bones with meat attached and pressure-cook them with a little white wine. Pour them into a Teflon pan and continue to cook them with a quarter-pound of butter and three fillets of anchovies and a quarter of a cup of capers. Then run it all through a food mill, a blender, or a processor. Put it in a jam jar, cool it, cap it, and refrigerate it. I'll bet it would be a wonderful spread, a cross between gentleman's relish and tapenade. Then you'd be able to truthfully say, 'The bones are also delicious.' "

I will save that one for my old age.

Universally, asparagus is served with shad, all the better if the asparagus is also wild.

In Maritime Canada, the rites of spring incorporate shad with fiddleheads.

My late friend Grete Fvide Bang, a Norwegian, salted and peppered whole shad, stuffed the cavity with fresh dill, oiled the pan, poured in some wine, and—after fifteen minutes at three-fifty—poured in a little more wine. After thirty minutes, she peeled off the skin and straightforwardly went at the shad. To a fish-eating Norwegian, bones are beneath conversation.

The French serve their shad with fresh-sorrel sauce—*Alose à l'oseille.* In Craig Claiborne and Pierre Franey's "Classic French Cooking," Claiborne described shad and sorrel as "a liaison fit for the gods." In America, you can buy the imported sauce. If you make your own with fresh sorrel, don't be shy. *Larousse Gastronomique* will tell you to use two kilos of fresh sorrel.

Worldwide, there are thirty-some species of shads, of which the American shad is the largest. Asians generally serve them steamed. In India, they are steamed with banana leaves. I have no idea what Africans do with the denticle herring of Cameroon. I'd kipper it.